Tanya Pursglove

Innocence Lost

STRENGTH FOUND

TANYA PURSGLOVE

All the names in this book, with the exception of Tanya and Neil
have been changed. The location has been anonymised.

This book is dedicated to all those who have carried me through the first 30 years of my life, without whose unwavering support wouldn't have seen me flourish.

Special thanks go to my parents, who have only ever tried to do the best for me. To my husband who has mopped my tears more times than can be counted. To my children, whose relentless love has brought incredible joy, even in the darkest of hours.

To my friends, who have provided me with hours of shoulder bearing, bitching, and wine.

To *my* DC, Jason, who believed me and worked compassionately to bring me justice.

To Kate for the years of therapy that has finally brought me to a place of peace.

To Tanya Pursglove, the girl that was. This is your story. You're going to be OK.

The list of people in my life who have helped me through these years is endless, and I feel guilty for not mentioning all of you, but if you think this final sentence is about you, you're right!

And finally, to all the other victims of grooming, sexual abuse and sexual violence. You are heard. You are believed. Your feelings are valid.

Tanya Pursglove

Prologue

The court bailiff opens the door where Neil sits and waves him through. Just like that, he is free. He is the first to be discharged from the courtroom, whilst I sit there in the spectator gallery between him and the exit. I feel his eyes on me as he shuffles a handful of paces in my direction. I can't look at him. But, when he stops just a few inches from me, I can't resist staring at his hand as he supports himself on the bench in front. His tired, old hand grips tightly on the highly polished oak. It isn't the hand I remembered from those early years. That hand was huge and masculine. This one is thin, and the veins protrude through his silver papery skin and leave trails of blue that disappear under his sleeves. I trace the imaginary course of those veins up his arm, but as I reach his shoulder, I catch a glimpse of his face. His pursed mouth opens, and I hold my breath in anticipation of what I am about to hear. I never get the chance, as his barrister all but shoves him out the door.

Surely, he isn't about to try and talk to me in front of the judge and the CPS? I look to Katelyn, my victim support worker, for reassurance. Part of me is disappointed that I never heard what he had wanted to say.

Tanya Pursglove

CHAPTER 1

The funny thing is, I don't *actually* remember the first time I saw Neil. I don't remember our first conversation; I don't even remember where we met. The events of those early few weeks seemed so inconsequential that they hold no memory, even now. I was somewhere close to my 14th birthday, whether it was just before, or just after, I can only take an approximation by what I was doing around the time.

In the early months after my 13th birthday, my aunty purchased an ex-racehorse that we renamed CJ. I'd been a horse fanatic since I could talk, so I'm told, but my parent's finances would never have stretched so far. Luckily for me, my aunt, Marilyn, had been an avid equestrian from a young age, and since her husband's death, she'd adopted a "you only live once" philosophy to life. We were close as I grew up, but when I hit my teens, we morphed into best friends, so when she bought CJ, she did so on the proviso that it would be a joint venture.

We didn't have the space or facilities to have CJ on our own land, so we did what thousands of other equestrians do- we scoped out a few local livery farms to find CJ a place to call home. After visiting a couple of farms, we stumbled across the most perfect, idyllic, and welcoming livery, in the form of River Farm. It was situated about three or four miles from home in the suburb of a small non-descript, working-class town in the middle of England.

But, before we get down to the nitty-gritty, and the crux of this story, I think it's probably important that you know a little bit about my early years on the planet.

In a nutshell, I had a fairly average upbringing- if there is such a thing. I lived at home with my two parents and younger brother in a 3-bedroom semi-detached house on the edge of a small town. We came from a long line of working-class families of Anglo-Irish ancestry. We were clothed, and fed, and we had a roof over our heads, but aside from an annual holiday, there weren't many additional luxuries in our household. Both my parents had multiple jobs to make ends meet, but we didn't live in squalor- we had the same things as most of our peers at the time. Nothing from our household really set us apart from other people in our working-class community.

I was fortunate in that I was naturally bright, so I quickly became a favourite of my teachers in both primary and secondary school, but this didn't stop me from making friends. There was a group of us who would hang out on a regular basis, and our parents all knew each other well. We were all well-mannered, intelligent kids who had the ability to flit amongst the social groups. So, I'm not sure what group within the school social hierarchy we could be classed as; we weren't 'popular', but we weren't 'unpopular' either- just your average kids.

From an early age, I remember having set my heart on becoming a doctor. I had grown up, immersed in Holby City and Casualty and I remember my favourite book being a Complete Family Health Guide. Some of my earliest memories are of me flicking through that book and completely burying my face in the pictures of a caesarean section and a dog bite. Upon reflection, this was probably the only thing that ever set me apart from my closest friends- my love of science and the human body.

So, fast forward to my early teens. Marilyn and I had just bought CJ and we had arrived on River Farm, where my 'family' grew overnight.

The farm itself stood back from the road. A long, rubbly dirt track formed a narrow and bumpy driveway from the country lane to the front of the old white farmhouse. An overgrown hawthorn hedge lined the right-hand side of the driveway as you turned towards the farm, whilst on the left, a post and rail fence encircled a small field that was speckled with yellow buttercups throughout the summer months. To the side of the farmhouse, a green six-bar gate sat across the bridge that straddled a stream that ran through the farm ground. Hence, its name.

My first Summer on the farm was delightful, and it fills me with so much nostalgia when I reflect on my time down there. Shortly after my arrival, two new liveries also arrived on the farm, and by way of chance, they were people I knew from school. Cleo and I went to the same secondary school, whilst Rebekah had been at the same primary school as the both of us but had gone to a different secondary school. So, the Summer of 2003- my 13th year of existence- was spent hanging around the farm with my friends. Unfortunately, it was also when I started smoking- my only form of rebellion as a young teen. We used to sneak off the farm onto a neighbouring dirt track and smoke for hours on end, feeling the constant rush of nicotine flood our young brains as we chain-smoked through packet after packet of cigarettes. We spent most of the day together, from dawn to dusk, and our friendships grew tight. Between the hours galivanting with Cleo and Rebekah, I also enjoyed the time building a relationship with CJ.

As a retired ex-racehorse, CJ was far from the ideal type of horse that we should have looked for as first-time owners, but Marilyn and I had fallen in love with him. He defied his breeding and behaved more like a lazy old dog than the racing machine his pedigree suggested. He loved nothing more than resting his head on me as he fell to sleep in his stable or whickering over the door when he heard us calling him from up the driveway.

Towards the end of that Summer, we attempted our first show, and although we both were clueless about what to expect, we had enjoyed it regardless. In all fairness, it was an absolute abysmal attempt. CJ felt my nerves travelling down the reins to his mouth, and we just couldn't get ourselves together. I couldn't even get him over a single jump and I left the arena red-faced. However, despite all that, this is where 'showing bug' bit me, and unsurprisingly, showing horses played to my natural tendency for showing off and being the centre of attention.

As the Summer stretched out, I became more acquainted with the other liveries as our paths crossed more regularly. Rebekah, Cleo, and I were the only children on the farm, and although the adults seemed friendly, they were an old-fashioned bunch and didn't care much for us kids. They all had their own little cliques, but despite that, everyone got on well. As there were in excess of 30 adults down at River Farm, I won't bore you with the names, occupations, and personalities of every member, but just those that will form a key part of this story. Firstly, there was Geraldine. Geraldine owned the farm and is the primary reason why we ended up calling it our new home. She was a woman of formidable presence; loud, camp, and personable. She loved, though, would ever admit it, to gossip. She oozed the knowledge of a horse woman, although didn't ride, but she had been through the circuit for many years with her daughter. Samantha was a young stable girl. She was just a couple of years older than me and had newly been taken on to work full time. Cerys was about 20 years old and had taken on the official role of head girl, but when there were only 2 full time members of staff down there, with hindsight, it seems like a fairly redundant title, but obviously, at the time, I was super impressed. Finally, we have Anne. Anne worked there on a Saturday. She was a livery with a full-time weekday job, but in order to reduce livery costs, she worked there on the Saturday to free up Samantha and Cerys. By which, I of course mean, that she ensured the legal working requirements of providing 'rest days' were met.

As Winter approached, I started to grow up. I began to understand that I would have to tone down my childish ways to be taken seriously. I would chip in on the weekends to ease the burden from Anne and Samantha by helping with the yard duties, and in doing so, I found I was being treated as one of the team. My enthusiasm for helping saw my popularity rise and soon the adults started to rely on me. I felt as though I had found my place, and I enjoyed being accepted by the people I admired.

As the first Winter passed, I started receiving invitations to travel to the winter show jumping to support Kelsey, Geraldine's daughter, whilst she competed. It drove my ambition; I wanted to be just like Kelsey. So, when I started having lessons with Kelsey, I gave it my all.

*

In a buzz of excitement, my 14th birthday arrived, and I became a proper teenager. Not just a little bit of a teenager, not just an introductory teenager, but an established one. I had looked forward to that day for months, telling anyone and everyone I encountered that it would be my birthday soon. My actual birthday fell on a school day, but despite this, I was able to spend the day celebrating. I carted gift bags throughout the school, filled to the brim with bath products and makeup from the body shop, and costume jewellery from Claire's Accessories.

We weren't much of a family for throwing birthday parties, so at the weekend we celebrated my birthday by going to the cinema to watch Stitch the Movie, followed by a Deep Pan Pizza. It was the way we liked to celebrate birthdays. The birthday person would pick the film and the meal, and the rest of the family would have to go along with it. We never got to spend much time together as a family, because my parents worked long hours and I enjoyed spending so much time with CJ, that I rarely wanted to be off the farm.

*

By February 2004, I had put in a year of work with CJ, my friendships on the farm had blossomed, and I was ready for some experience at the summer shows. The 'show season' typically ran from March to September, but with the shadow of the previous attempt hanging over my head, I was eager to get more experience before reintroducing CJ into the mix. This is where I developed a friendship with Julie and Liam.

Julie and Liam were masters at their craft, and every show season, they would travel to shows with their Hunter, Gethro. At the beginning of March 2004, Julie and Liam asked me if I wanted to go to some shows with them. In return for my help with Gethro, they spilled the tricks of the trade and took me under their wing.

I got on well with Julie and Liam. They were both in their late thirties, down to earth, and swore like sailors. Julie had fiery red, shoulder-length hair and she was the type of person that could hold themselves in a confrontation. She was quick-witted with an extensive vocabulary of slurs, which I soon adopted when out of earshot of my parents. Liam was entirely the opposite of Julie. His floppy salt and pepper hair was voluminous and bounced like spaniel ears, perfectly matching his spaniel-type personality. He also had a colourful language, but he was far more laid back and easygoing than Julie.

They had been married for about ten years when I met them, and they seemed made for each other. They were not remotely affectionate to each other in public, but it was clear that they were a solid unit. They had a great sense of humour, often griping and bickering like schoolchildren. Those two became my people. They didn't treat me like a child. I spent more and more time with them as the weeks passed and would rush to complete my jobs in the evening so that I could help them.

I liked that they could rely on me. I enjoyed pleasing them and I found it even more flattering that they had taken a shine to me because they had been clear about their dislike of Cleo and Rebekah. My friendship with Julie and Liam grew, and I became more distant from the other girls at the farm. They were fun, and they were adults, and most importantly, they treated me like the person I wanted to be; a grown-up.

Anne lived a couple of doors down from Julie and Liam, and they had been friends for years before I arrived at the farm. Although Anne and I had shared the odd conversation and exchanged pleasantries, it wasn't until I became friendly with Julie and Liam that she started to treat me like a friend too. She would regularly attend shows to support them, accompanied by her partner, Neil, who would tag along for the day out.

I can't remember if I met Neil at a show, or if it was down at the farm after a show. I can't remember if we ever introduced ourselves to each other. One minute he wasn't there, the next minute he was, but how that instantaneous bridge was formed, escapes my memory. The only thing I do remember about my first impressions of Neil was that he smoked like a chimney.

CHAPTER 2

The farm had a strict no-smoking policy, and the only place that was an exception to the rule was next to the school. However, as I was underage and Marilyn had lost her husband to lung cancer, I had never dared to smoke on the farm. I had only smoked with Rebekah and Cleo secretly down the neighbouring dirt track for fear that Marilyn would have killed me if she had caught me.

One of the first conversations I remember having with Neil took place on the farm after coming back from a show with Julie and Liam. Julie and Liam unloaded the horse, and Neil and I sat on a lorry ramp in the middle of the farm whilst everybody else pottered about their jobs. As he pulled a cigarette from his 24-pack of Royals, he waved the packet in my direction and offered me one. I was taken aback and felt my face flush.

"Oh, no, I don't smoke!" I blurted as I swatted my hand to encourage him to get rid of them, afraid that someone would see.

Neil let out a wily snort that suggested he knew otherwise and for some reason, I no longer felt panicked. I felt as though my secret would be safe with him. I flashed a cheeky grin.

As I mentioned, I don't remember the first time our paths crossed. I don't remember if he'd ever introduced himself, nor if Julie or Liam had introduced him. He had completely slipped in under the radar- an inconsequential presence in my environment. One minute he wasn't there, the next he was- but there wasn't a *tadaa* moment. This conversation is the only *tadaa* moment I recall, but I know this wasn't the first time I had met him, or even spoken to him, but it was the point where I can trace back to where it all started.

From that point, Neil frequented the farm more and more often. He hadn't been present at the farm during the weekday evenings, but he started coming to the farm after Anne had finished work. He didn't help her with her horse. He didn't seem to have any interest in horses- he was quite wary of them; giving them an excessively wide berth as they walked through the farm. It was quite funny to watch, especially as Anne was so comfortable around them, that they were almost like a second skin to her. Neil would float around the yard, chatting with the other liveries, and frequently disappearing to the school for 'cigarette breaks'- as he called them. As I had got into the habit of flying through my jobs in the evenings, I often found myself at a loose end before everyone else had finished for the night. I would sit beside the sand school with Liam and Neil watching Julie and Anne ride. I'd be hovering around the school most of the evenings, so I'd find myself with Neil more and more often.

At 14 years old, I was *reasonably attractive*- well, I wasn't unattractive, of that, I am certain. People my own age didn't pay me much attention as I didn't fit into the 'popular crowd' aesthetic. I wasn't super slim and athletic like the girls in school. I didn't have the same interests as most of them. Although I enjoyed things like makeup, I didn't wear it all that often as it wasn't novel for me by this point. I had spent so many years being covered in it for Ballroom Dancing.

I was mature for my age, and my interests didn't align well with my peers- despite being a close group. I had always been ambitious and competitive. I was also probably a bit self-indulgent for most people my age. I was always overconfident, and my tendency to show off had made me naturally flirty. I wasn't outrageous and certainly no worse than my friends and people would now consider it as 'flirty banter', although that phrase wasn't around at the time. I was eager to please and enjoyed the feeling of being appreciated. I had a habit of trying to induce happiness in other people, although probably not from genuine altruism, but rather because I relished feeling liked.

Over the following days and weeks, I found myself talking to Neil more and more. He had a dry and wicked sense of humour that would have me doubled over in belly-cramping giggles. His comic timing was pure genius, and his humour was different from what I had previously experienced. He was crude, but it always seemed appropriate within a joke and never had me cringing or feeling awkward. I think the outrageousness of his jokes was what had me hooked from the start. He reminded me of John Cleese. He was *so* funny. He would have me howling with laughter with tears streaming down my face as I begged him to stop. He enjoyed taking the mickey out of people, so as I cracked up at the side of him, it would give him further ammunition to continue in the ridiculousness of it all.

One evening, I was sitting at the side of the school before the evening liveries arrived. I'd finished all my jobs and the jobs I would do for Julie and Liam. I passed the quiet time by stewing over my day, listening to music on my CD player. A sucker for classic soul resulted in the battered CD featuring regularly on my Sony. It featured all the greats- Marvin Gaye, Dionne Warwick, and Stevie Wonder to name a few. All the music that my peers would take playful jibes at me for, as they preferred the modern hits of our time. I had it on full blast, and I was lost in a train of thought when someone whipped an earbud from my ear. I looked up startled. It took me a few seconds for my eyes to adjust in the bright late-spring sunshine, but as my vision cleared from the glare, the tall slim silhouette morphed into Neil.

As Neil was a fan of a mickey-take, I felt as though he was going to rip me a good one about listening to 'shite'- as my school friends did- so I tensed in preparation for having my backside handed to me on a plate. Neil offered the earbud to his ear and his face turned from one of amusement to quiet contemplation. He listened carefully and pulled a look of surprise before he complimented me on my taste in music. I felt a pang of surprise that someone had *actually complimented* me on my taste. I breathed a sigh of relief and made space for him to sit at the side of me so he could continue to listen to my CD player. We spent the rest of the evening flicking through my CDs and secretly sharing his cigarettes when nobody was watching; each of us sat side by side, putting the world to rights with the likes of Aretha Franklin filling in the pauses.

Over the following few evenings, we talked for hours at the farm. The conversation came quick and easy, and it didn't feel as though I had to filter what came into my head before I said it aloud. This was something I had always had to do when talking to my friends. I was constantly weighing up the social implications of any opinion I had about stuff. The conversations would often start with the music that played in our ears, but we would eventually find ourselves talking about other topics such as films or books. Over a few days, the conversations not only varied in breadth, but we also found ourselves talking in depth. It felt strange that I could talk so freely to Neil, and despite us having only known each other for a few weeks, something between us felt familiar, as though we had known each other forever.

Neil was fifty-five and had been retired for a considerable time before I met him- he had joked about having had a couple of heart attacks that had nearly 'finished him off'. He told me about his experiences after surgery, how the morphine had given him terrible and very real nightmares. It was so alien to be able to hear someone's unfiltered thoughts- I had always been so heavily protected at home. Never completely shielded from reality and in no way was I wrapped with cotton wool, but we never really disclosed things like inner thoughts or nightmares. Neil came across as intelligent- not necessarily from formal education, but from worldly experiences. His eyes seemed open to the things around him, and the extent of his observational skills, ironically, hadn't gone unnoticed by me.

He told me that he used to be a lorry driver, collecting milk from farms in the moors, and he spoke about it with such a sweet, nerdy enthusiasm that I regularly found myself gripped by his stories. He'd recite the names of tiny villages in the Peaks, and I could see the road map play out in his head as he talked about a few near misses that he'd had in the lorries. His general knowledge was astounding, and I'd often sit there wide-eyed and open-mouthed at the facts he would recall. He'd have made a worthy addition to any pub quiz team, particularly if the specialist questions were about music. As the CD player flicked through the songs, the Beatles began to play in our ears.

Neil went quiet and closed his eyes to the sounds of Paul McCartney and John Lennon. There was a flash of anguish in his face- his eyes contorted revealing the creases in the corners. His furrowed brow grew heavy, and he held his breath as he closed his eyes. I wanted to reach out and put a hand on his arm to comfort him. He looked like he needed to be brought back to earth. I didn't. I returned my hovering hand back to the arm of the chair and averted my gaze to the muckheap, aware that I had been watching him for too long. It was clear that he had a strong emotional attachment to the song, and I felt powerless to help.

"My head's a mess," Neil broke the silence. "I've always been like this. Found myself in the looney bin a few times over the years."

I nodded sympathetically, making eye contact. I saw his vulnerability, and my heart shredded like a piece of newspaper as the words continued to fall from his mouth.

"They thought it was schizophrenia for a while, but it's bipolar. I'm up and down like a pair of tart's knickers," he smiled, almost apologetically for oversharing, but he didn't stop. "When I go down, I just crash."

He lifted and dropped his hand, slapping his thigh, the thud reverberated around in the still air.

"I'm alright most of the time. The pills, you know... but every now and again, it just creeps up and takes me out by the knees."

He looked so sad, so broken. I didn't know what to say- there were no words of comfort that I could offer him.

"When *he* was shot," he pointed to the earbud as the Beatles played, "just knocked me for six. Ended up in the funny farm. It completely wrecked me. Music has always been a comfort. It's always seen me through the worst. It's all I could do in there. I was too drugged up to do anything but lie there, listening to music. It still helps. Keeps me grounded, mostly. Every once in a while, though, it reminds me of how shit it was. How close to death I was."

A light bulb flickered in my head. It explained why the music I listened to had created so many vibrant conversations between us- it was the music of his era.

For the first time, Neil seemed vulnerable, fragile and fractured. He had never come across that way before. He had always been the one to lighten the mood with his quick one-liners and jokey demeanour. I never felt awkward about the intimacy of this conversation. I felt like a connection had been formed. I couldn't understand why Neil was able to tell me something so raw, so personal, but he had, and I was deeply touched that he felt able to share it with me.

Neil had lived such an interesting life, and although some parts of it were clearly traumatic, I felt privileged to hear about it. He trusted me, and I was flattered that he could talk to me about something so personal. It was the first time that he allowed me to see behind his curtain. All his bravado and humour were just a mask, and behind it lay a man with deep-rooted issues. Issues that ran so deep that they wrapped themselves around his organs, compressing him from the inside. It made sense why he had lived his life like a caricature covering his vulnerability and fragile personality. Although he never told me not to talk about it with others, I knew I couldn't. I couldn't have betrayed his trust. I hadn't seen him talk to others about it. I hadn't ever seen him so close to tears or even remotely distressed. Instead, he kept up his mask, his jokes, and his deflections. Not once had I seen Neil having a heart-to-heart with anyone else down on the farm, not even Julie and Liam, despite their friendship having gone back years.

I could talk more freely with Neil than anyone else I had ever met. Although my life had been relatively uneventful compared to Neil's, I was able to contribute to the conversation, and he seemed interested in everything I had to say. He sat there listening intently whilst I spoke about school and my dancing. He never took his eyes off me. Even when I looked away because his gaze made me blush, I could still feel his eyes scanning my face. He complimented me on my walk. He noticed that I had a distinctive walk, a long stride, and he liked how my hands never hung down. Years of dancing had conditioned me to always be expressive with my hands, but nobody outside my dancing circle had made this observation about me before. I was impressed and touched that he had noticed it. I had to fight back the flush I felt rising in my cheeks. It was the first time I had felt noticed by anyone. Really noticed. Noticed for being me, not for what I could be for someone else. Although I had become friends with Julie and Liam, and they appreciated the things I did for them, they had never mentioned anything about what set me apart from others. We didn't have the same connection that Neil and I had formed.

*

"Neil's been looking for you," Teri called from the barn as I dropped my bag outside CJ's stable shortly after arrival from school.

"Oh, I've only just got here," I shouted back as I looked up in her direction. "Where is he?"

As I glanced around, I needn't have asked as Neil had stood up from the side of the school and made his way over. I could see Anne circling the school on Apollo behind him. I turned to open CJ's stable door and opened the packet of Polos that I'd concealed in my pocket. CJ started to nuzzle at my hands, trying to speed up the process.

"One minute, you greedy bugger." I gently pushed his nose away so I could peel the foil paper from the roll. I teased a mint from the packet and offered it under his nose and the pleasant sound of crunching filled my ears.

"Cigarette break?" Neil asked.

"OK," I smiled.

Neil paid me so much attention and he gravitated towards me as soon as I stepped foot on the farm. His focus was completely on me when I spoke, so much so that someone would have to shout his name a couple of times to get his attention. He would pierce me with his blue eyes. They felt as though they were penetrating me. Initially, I struggled to make eye contact with him and found myself looking off into the mid-distance when we spoke or trying to pick out another facial feature to glance at, so to avoid appearing rude. When I knew I would have to make eye contact, so that I could show I was engaged in our conversation, his gaze would throw me off my stride and make me catch my breath. He didn't just look at me, he looked inside me. It felt too intimate. I liked it too much and I feared that he would be able to tell. Throughout our conversations, he would shower me with compliments.

"It's so easy to talk to you," he said and I smiled, uncomfortably, but equally flattered. "You are not like anyone your age."

"I've had a hard life," I laughed dismissively, unable to accept the compliment, but thrilled to have been given one.

"I mean it, you're so insightful. You have such an intelligence and depth of thought that it doesn't compare."

I secretly loved it. It never felt forced or uncomfortable- despite my blushes. I yearned for his attention and my blood would rush through my body whenever I sensed a compliment was coming. Neil would sit smoking whilst we spoke, and when nobody was near, he'd pass me his cigarette discretely to have a drag or two before I handed it back to him. Occasionally, his fingers would brush mine as we passed the cigarette to and fro and my arm would shoot the electricity throughout my body. I felt awakened, I felt alive. I felt seen. We didn't even have to discuss the secrecy of it. I didn't have to ask or signal for a drag; he instinctively knew when I wanted one, and only passed it to me when nobody was around. He could read my mind.

A pang of sadness hit the centre of my chest each evening when he went home. I missed his company and felt lonely on the farm when he wasn't there. I *used* to enjoy the quiet time on the farm in the evenings after everybody had left. It was nice to sit at the side of the school or outside CJ's stable with the crisp evening air wrapping itself around me. I *used* to find contentment in the quiet tugging of the horses' hay nets followed by their rhythmic munching. Instead, that changed, and I would sit alone at the side of the school where Neil had left me until my dad arrived to take me home. Instead of listening to the sounds of horses eating, I sat and thought about Neil and what we had discussed each evening. I got butterflies when I remembered the compliments that he had paid me, or whenever I recalled how he brushed my hand with his. A deep flutter in my belly rose and sent pleasant shudders up my back, that left goosebumps on the back of my neck.

I played the conversations on repeat in my head; the more I thought about it, the more I became convinced that he fancied me. The compliments came thick and fast, and it filled me with equal parts of schoolgirl excitement and trepidation. I never thought anything would ever come from it, but I bathed in the attention he paid me. I would go home and think about him. I liked the way he made me feel; he made me feel confident and good about myself. I craved the way he made my pulse quicken, like when he noticed things about me, even when I hadn't clocked him looking at me. He highlighted those small details, like the way I walked or how blue my eyes were. My waist-length dark ringlets had long been a joke with my peers. They would call me a mini-Diana Ross, and it wasn't designed to be a compliment. The early 2000s was the era of the sleek, over-ironed hair phase, but my hair never pulled off the straight look, so I gave up and defied convention. Neil was the first man outside my family to compliment me on it. He liked the way it bounced and swished from side to side when I walked. He liked how I would throw my hair forward to ruffle it loose from its tangles or the odd piece of hay. I was sure that Neil fancied me, but I never thought anything would happen between us; he was forty-two years older than me.

One weekend, after having been at a show with Julie, Liam, Anne and Neil, we arrived back at the farm to unload and digest the day's events. Neil and I sat side by side on the mounting block outside the Barn with the sun beating down on us, whilst Julie, Liam and Anne unpacked the horse and paraphernalia. The mounting block was a stack of breezeblocks plonked on top of each other, bottom-heavy and narrow at the top, but Neil and I had squeezed ourselves together to sit on it. Neil sat, leaning back against the external wall of the barn, his feet dangling a few inches from the floor. I sat to his left, one cheek of my buttock clinging to the space at the side of him. I had turned myself slightly, so I didn't slip off and graze my bum on the edge of the blocks. The atmosphere between us was electric. He shifted around on the makeshift seat and leaned forward onto his elbows. His thigh brushed mine. *Did he mean to do that?* But he didn't move it. His thigh remained pressed against my thigh, increasing in intensity as the weight of this upper body pressed further through his arms into his knees. I shivered as I came to the realisation that it was intentional.

We had been casually flirting and joking for most of the day, but I still hadn't established whether he fancied me or whether it was a figment of my imagination. Although I was burning to know, I was never going to ask him. But I relished in the attention he paid me. The flirting between us had been undeniable. I laughed outrageously at his jokes. It seemed as though he had taken it up a gear in response to my amusement. We sat there for a short while, brushing legs. The air was palpable, and I realised that my dry mouth needed lubrication. I offered to go into the tack room and make drinks for us all. The tack room, within the shipping container, had an electric kettle so there was no need for liveries to go in the house anymore. As I stood up and asked the other four what they wanted to drink, I heard Neil from a few paces behind me, loudly stating that he'd give me a hand.

The tack room was doubly enclosed. Its big metal double doors offered security when locked at night. Those doors were open in the day, but an additional half-glass inner door and a wall with a small window stood behind the external doors. The inner door offered a barrier from invading rodents, and so we kept closed all day. The tack room was a tight squeeze. It wasn't wide when empty but was made even narrower by Ikea-style shelving units that lined both long walls. Horse rugs and grooming equipment filled the shelves to bursting point, producing a 3-foot-wide pathway down the middle of the tack room. It was cramped but fully serviceable. With that said, we could barely carry a saddle from the back wall to the exit without knocking something from the shelves. As soon as I opened the door, a plume of stagnant air, smelling like old leather and sweaty horses escaped through the narrow gap and filled my lungs. Despite the tack room having an overhead light, it was dark and shadowy inside. The natural light barely penetrated the small window, and the overcrowded shelves prevented the florescent strip light from reflecting off the walls. The dark leather and canvas rugs absorbed most of the spectrum which resulted in a low-lit warm glow.

I stepped up into the tack room and I flicked the kettle on at the wall, rustling the plastic sleeve of the disposable cups as I placed them in a line next to the illuminated kettle. I wiped the dust and horsehair off the tray under the cups leaving a block of the bright floral pattern peeking through the murk of the muted tray. I dusted my hand on my trousers, then pinged the material to disperse a grey cloud in the air. This was immediately illuminated by a stream of light that invaded the room as Neil opened the door. He squeezed his way behind me and stood in the narrow path between the shelves. His 6-foot-2 frame filled the entire space. I didn't say anything. I'm not sure my voice would have travelled through the vacuum we had created. The atmosphere encased me like a weighted blanket. I don't know why I felt that way because when we were in the middle of the farm I felt as light as a bubble. Once we were alone and out of sight, the atmosphere felt oppressive. I felt like something was going to happen, but I couldn't put my finger on it. The air was static, both of us silent and confined in a small space. I couldn't breathe. Something felt 'off'. My giddiness had gone and been replaced by a shadow. I had stood or sat next to Neil a hundred times before but this felt claustrophobic. It felt too intimate. I couldn't face him, our bodies were too close, so instead, I stood with my back to him, leaning my elbows on the narrow ledge as I tried to peer through the murky window to the outside world. We didn't utter a word whilst we were in there. I couldn't think of anything to say as my brain had completely left me. There was a moment of slight relief as the kettle started to rumble, that indicated that my time in the oppressive cubicle would soon be over. As I turned my head to face the kettle, I felt Neil's hand slide gently onto my right hip, and his middle finger traced the line down my groin. I felt my body tense and stiffen unable to respond in any meaningful way. He pressed his pelvis into my bottom and I could feel his erection between my buttocks. My mind was pulled back toward his hand as he slowly moved it from my hip toward my right breast. I was frozen to the spot. I didn't want to move. I didn't know what to do. My heart pounded against my ribcage ready for me to take off in flight, but there was nowhere to go. I was trapped by Neil's body and the front wall of the tack room, his hand and arm between me and the door. The sudden click of the kettle snapped me out of it, brought my body back to me, and gave me my excuse to move.

"Oh! Nearly there," he jokingly groaned, as I quickly pulled away to finish the drinks.

I tried to hide how I felt. I didn't know how I felt. My head had been nuked and the dust cloud wouldn't dissipate. There was no clarity. No understanding of the situation I had found myself in. I flashed through my mind and tried to make sense of it, but all I could see was a plume of debris where my thoughts used to be. It was a moment that lasted 2 to 3 seconds, but it felt as though time had stood still. As the ash cloud began to settle, I was left with the realisation that he wanted me. Neil wanted me. This older, funny, worldly man wanted *me*. He saw me as a woman. I was buzzing and terrified in equal measure.

I tried to make out that what had happened wasn't a big deal; like this sort of thing happens all the time. I told myself to play it cool, so as not to invite any more touching, but not to come across as startled and out of my depth. I didn't want a repeat performance, but I also didn't want it to become awkward between us. I didn't want to put him off or invite him in for more. My threshold had been reached. I had got my confirmation and that was enough. I feigned casual, albeit rather clumsily, finished pouring the boiling water into the cups, and pulled the tray off the shelf as I walked out of the door. My chest pounded and I couldn't fill up my lungs, even as the air hit my face. I fought the urge to hyperventilate, whilst I trembled with the drinks in my hand. I watched the coffee splash around the rim of the cups and I watched as the escaped drops scald the back of my hand. I felt his eyes on me as I walked away. I felt them boring into my waist and bum. I knew Neil was aroused as I had felt his excitement when he pressed against me. He had wound himself up into a frenzy and I knew he was frustrated, teased even. I fizzed inside, bubbled up like a shaken bottle of pop, and tried not to explode from the mix of thrill and confusion. We didn't talk about the moment that we almost shared, but it was clear to each of us that we were playing it on a loop for the rest of the afternoon.

That evening I disappeared up to my bedroom, still having palpitations from the adrenalin. Although my confusion hadn't left me, my brain had returned and brought a huge number of thoughts about the tack room incident with it. Nothing made sense. I felt my eyes dart about my head, looking for answers, trying to understand what had happened. *Did it happen? Of course it happened, but what did it mean? Did it mean anything? Was it one of Neil's jokes that just went a bit too far? Does he want me, or am I reading too much into it? These things happen all the time, don't they? Perhaps he was trying to push by me and I completely blocked his way out. No, it wasn't that, he definitely pushed his pelvis into my bottom. His hand placement was too intimate. He held me in place as he pushed towards me. That isn't something you do when squeezing past someone.* I stood with my back against my closed bedroom door and traced my hand over the route Neil had taken a few hours earlier. Every time I did, I trembled. I couldn't get it out of my head. I couldn't get *him* out of my head. He had confirmed my thoughts; he wanted me. I wanted him. I felt out of my depth, like I was running out of air, but I couldn't shake off the exhilaration of his touch. Half of me wished that I hadn't pulled away so suddenly because I was curious what would have happened if I hadn't moved. I also felt overwhelmed. He filled my head constantly. I thought about him incessantly. Every time I thought about him, I shivered, and my teeth chattered so violently that I could hear them clink together. He was exciting. It was exciting.

*

Neil plagued my mind, and I felt lost without him. I was empty. I would wish the school day away so I could rush straight down to the farm. I sought memories of our previous conversations to fill in the void I was experiencing. I'd sit there daydreaming about him during my lessons. My teachers would try to catch me out, but I was too quick for them. Thankfully I seemed to develop extra senses, where I could be aware of my periphery, whilst still being completely submerged in my own world too. As the school day continued, my brain exhausted quickly and I couldn't keep up with the demand of Neil in one hemisphere, and the demand of school in the other. By the time I got on the school bus, I could feel myself wilting like a neglected houseplant. The bus home took about an hour, which meant there was plenty of time to switch off my academic brain and recharge my batteries for the evening. I couldn't wait to see Neil, I knew he would inject some life into me once we were sat side by side at the farm.

I'd had altered my routine in the evenings, so I could be at the farm sooner. Instead of catching the school bus home to wait for my dad's workday to finish, I started to stay on the bus longer and take my 'horse clothes' to school in a bag. I got off the school bus about a mile away from the farm and finished the last stretch of the journey on foot. It meant that I arrived at the farm about an hour earlier than my previous routine. Unfortunately, it meant that I didn't have time to grab a bite to eat as I ran out of the door but food could wait, Neil couldn't.

Conveniently, Neil lived on the route to the farm, so I had to walk past his house on the way. I hoped that he would see me walking down, but I avoided looking at his house in case I looked desperate. We never walked down together. He would arrive either just before or just after I had got there, even if Anne wasn't expected for a while. I would get butterflies as I turned the corner to walk down the farm's driveway. I would feel the anticipation in my chest, the quickening of my heartbeat, and the heaviness of my breathing. If he'd got there before me, he would be waiting on the box outside of my stable. I had to suppress the glee from my face as I looked down the yard and saw him sitting there waiting for me. My stable gave him a good vantage point, as it was a clear line of sight to the gate. There were other suitable places to sit that provided equal visuals, but he always sat outside my stable, waiting patiently. If I had got down there before him, I would change from my uniform into my horse clothes in CJ's stable, where I would listen out for the familiar clatter of the gate opening and closing.

In the same way that I could tell which one of my parents was walking down the stairs, I could tell if Neil had opened and closed the gate. I didn't even have to pop my head out of the stable door to know. I could feel his presence, his timing and rhythm had been etched into my brain. It had become so routine. Once I had identified the 'right clang' of the sliding bar on the gate, I'd get flutters up my back and I felt a pleasant tingling of anticipation as I wondered what that evening would bring.

A couple of days after the tack room incident, I sat at the side of the school with Neil, secretly sharing a cigarette and talking. It was late in the evening and the cool spring air had descended in the valley the farm inhabited. I knew we were about to part ways as felt the mood between us drop as the light began to fall. Anne had left thirty minutes before, but we were still talking as she left, so Neil hadn't attempted to move. He had begun to stay down at the farm most days and hovered around long after Anne had left. We would be the last two people down there, sitting alone by the school and talking for some time after everyone else had gone. I loved that time of night. The conversation flowed and we were so connected, as though we were bound by invisible webs. We never had to pause to think, the conversation was easy, thoughtful, and deep. Our discussions were intricate and natural, and I would feel his eyes gazing intently at me when I spoke. We'd sit with the arms of the chairs touching, but it never felt claustrophobic, never oppressive, just comfortable, like we'd been doing it forever. We'd split the earphones, so we had one free ear, whilst the other played the music we enjoyed. The wire connecting our minds, giving Neil access to my innermost thoughts. We could have easily stayed there all night, talking from the moment the sun slept, until she reappeared at dawn. That evening Neil looked more pensive than usual, and although I couldn't work out why initially, it soon became evident when he opened his mouth.

"I have developed feelings for you", he blurted. "I don't know how it happened, and I know I shouldn't, but I can't help how I feel".

I didn't know what to say. I was stunned, dumbfounded, and yet equally overjoyed. I tried to keep my face neutral as I stared off towards the sand in the middle of the school. I couldn't look at him as I was sure my eyes would have revealed my inner truth. I couldn't make eye contact. I wasn't embarrassed, but I couldn't think fast enough when I knew he was staring at me. I knew he could see right into my mind, and it made me vulnerable. My mind flitted through a state of panic as I flashed between images of him, Anne, my family, and the countless people who would be devastated to hear what he had just said. The guilt weighed down on me and I couldn't turn it off, but I also couldn't deny having fantasised about that moment. I didn't know what I was supposed to do with his declaration. Although the flirting had become a frequent thing, and Neil had touched me intimately, I was unprepared for him to come out and say it, I was genuinely shocked.

As a teenager, telling someone how you felt was alien. We hadn't once discussed the tack room incident. Although I'd picked up on vibes, I felt as though the Tack room incident should have been brushed off as a joke that had gone too far. Either that or Neil had instantly regretted it and didn't want to embarrass either one of us by bringing it up. However, that confession had left me in a state of turmoil. He filled me with excitement but also with anxiety. I wanted him. He had spent all his time stuck in my mind for weeks. He seemed to understand me more than anyone else. I can't begin to explain how well he knew me; he knew exactly what I was thinking all the time. He studied me so intently that he could see my soul. I had nowhere to hide and although it was terrifying, it was equally liberating. He saw all my strengths and all my weaknesses. I had never felt a connection to anyone like the one I felt with Neil.

I didn't know what to do, what to say. My voice had surrendered to my brain's incapacity. What could I say? A vice-like grip enveloped my ribcage and I couldn't breathe. I wanted to say it back to him. I desperately wanted to cut him off his monologue, but I didn't have any words. I felt trapped and freed all at once, like the captive animals that see grass for the first time, I was hesitant to leave my confinement but captivated with the curiosity that my environment offered. I sat and listened, but my stomach churned. The whole contents of my abdomen twisted with such ferocity that I thought I might vomit. Flashing glimpses of Anne only exacerbated the nausea, but then as my eyes moved towards Neil's bouncing knee, she vanished from view. I wanted him so badly. I felt torn in half. I felt so guilty.

"I'm going to go and let you think on that," he ended abruptly and jumped up from the chair.

He pressed his palms into the back of his chair and paused for a second, causing me to wonder what else he had to say. He took a deep breath and turned on his heels setting off for home before I'd even had the time to form a sentence in my mind.

Knotted strings replaced my thought process and as I tried to unpick one thought, I'd find a hundred more strings wound tightly around it, pulling me down a rabbit hole, where there were more questions than answers. I felt engulfed by his confession, and my thoughts flashed through my mind like strobe lighting in a nightclub. My world felt surreal. I sat where he left me, but my surroundings were ethereal, and I was afraid of moving in case the world fractured around me. I wasn't in my body, but I watched myself from an apparition. As I saw myself slowly blink, my senses returned to me, and my eyes felt dry and gritty from the dust of the school. I think that was the first time I had blinked in 10 minutes. I swallowed a lump from my throat as I replayed his words. I knew I felt the same, but I didn't know how to say it or whether I should say it. I wanted to say that the feelings were mutual, but where would things go from there? Would things become awkward at the farm if I cooled things off? I depended so heavily on his friendship that I could no longer imagine him not being there constantly. I didn't want the friendship to end. I wanted more but I couldn't silence the voices in my head. I chased around and around, trying to catch my thoughts as they whizzed throughout my mind, but I couldn't make sense of them.

I had been sitting there, alone, for about half an hour when the familiar sound of my dad's car on the rubbly driveway snapped me from my trance. I collected my things from my stable and made my way to the car. I tried to look as normal as possible, and I silently prayed that my dad wouldn't be able to tell.

Tanya Pursglove

CHAPTER 3

I couldn't think clearly. I couldn't sleep. Every time I closed my eyes I'd see Neil's face gazing at me, followed by Anne smiling warmly at me, haunting me. My guts would twist and gnarl as I became submerged by guilt. I would lay there fighting to breathe. I was drowning in my own shame. I wanted him so badly, but he wasn't mine to have. Shame swelled inside me as I thought about how much of a bitch I was. *He isn't mine. He isn't mine. He belongs to Anne. Tanya, what are you doing? She's your friend. I shouldn't have flirted; he is not mine to take. But I need him. I need him more than I need oxygen. I can't love him. I have no right to love him. So why, why can I not switch it off?*

Neil had flooded my entire brain. I had broken up for the half-term holiday, so I didn't have the distraction of school to keep me preoccupied, not that I think it would have made a difference. I had started to sink into my world where all I could picture was Neil, and all other thoughts were blocked by an impenetrable barrier in the shape of this 6ft older man. He had completely taken over my mind. As much as the shame of my feelings towards him felt like smog wrapping around me, I welcomed his presence in my brain. It was such a contradiction. I felt awful when I thought about the repercussions of admitting how I felt, but when I thought how he made me feel when we were together I would bury the guilt and succumb to the euphoria. I loved thinking about him. My whole body tingled and my mind would race, my heart beating out of my chest as though I had consumed too much caffeine. It felt as though my vision had transformed from black and white into colour when he came into my life. Once he penetrated my core, my sight transformed from grainy, static-y, monochrome, to crisp vibrant colour. I appeared distracted to the people around me, but the truth is, I had never felt more focused. My new ultra-high-definition, 4K vision failed to provide me with any true clarity, though. I still hadn't worked out what I would do about Neil's revelation.

I felt a mixture of trepidation and nausea as I tried to work through my thoughts. Had he not confessed his adoration, I would have never brought it up. My friendship circle never discussed our feelings about boys. It wasn't the 'done thing', and never, ever would they have told the boy they liked, that they liked them! If they weren't being outright mean to their crushes, there would only be lots of silly giggling, and hair flicking. If someone ever confronted us about it- *deny, deny, deny!* Denial was the default setting at 14-years-old, even if we had been secretly practising our future marital signature. I was a confident girl, but I was never confident enough to make a move, and my instincts screamed at me to remain in my default position and run a mile. Still, there was something about Neil that I just couldn't ignore.

I wanted to tell him that the feelings were mutual; that I thought about him all the time, but I couldn't ignore the voice in my head. Although he wasn't technically married to Anne, they had been together for almost 20 years and she was my friend. I liked and admired her. So, when the circumstances around his relationship flashed into my mind, the guilt felt like sludge running through my veins, poisoning my organs, and bringing about a nausea so intense that I couldn't breathe. I had never experienced such deep-seated guilt before, but, as the darkness descended on me, I'd force myself to ignore it, reverting back to my 4K images instead.

Although there was an obvious issue because our age gap, my mind chose to eradicate this from my decision-making. It certainly wasn't at the forefront of my mind, and I quickly convinced myself the age-old saying 'age is just a number'. Neil spoke to me in a way that made me feel on a level with him. I felt his equal, and it certainly didn't feel as though there were almost 42 years between us. We had clicked straight away, and we shared the same interests and opinions. I was mature for my age, so it made sense that I could deal with it like an adult. He put me on a pedestal with his constant compliments and flattery, so clearly, he must have viewed me as a woman too.

As it was the school holidays, I spent the following day down at the farm. I moved through my jobs slowly, killing time. I wasn't bored, far from it. I had so much to think about that I couldn't possibly be bored. The monotony of my jobs gave my body something to do whilst my mind disappeared down the worm hole of thoughts. I was eager for something to play a slight distraction and release my mind from the wandering roads it had chosen to take. Cerys and Samantha weren't helpful at providing adequate distraction. I wasn't close to either of them, so I was never tempted to tell them my secret, but I desperately wanted to tell someone, anyone. I needed to get back to reality. There was nothing worse than sitting around, stressing about every tiny detail. I knew Neil wouldn't come down in the daytime because it would have looked suspicious. Even I could see that- I wasn't stupid, and I knew the others wouldn't understand. I could see that even our friendship wasn't the most conventional, particularly with how much time we spent together. So, rather than flying through my job list and then sitting around for hours as the rising panic set in, I faffed around the stable, perfecting every tiny detail.

I rode CJ and tidied his stable at a snail's pace; two or three times throughout the day! Virtually, as soon as he had started to poo, I fetched the wheelbarrow and shaving's fork. I even went to the lengths of bathing him, as I knew it would take me a couple of hours. I asked Cerys and Samantha what I could do to help. My own jobs were not fulfilling my needs. They gave me the laborious job of sweeping the yard. *Perfect*. My body could keep moving, whilst my brain processed the things Neil had said to me. It subsided the panic for a short while and had the added benefit of reaffirming my 'helpfulness'; I had neglected the worker relationships for a few weeks. I watched the clock move so slowly that I was convinced time had stopped. I walked up the hill to the shop to buy cigarettes and ambled back down an alternative scenic way, chain-smoking. I couldn't bring myself to walk past his house. I used the nicotine as a brief relief. There was no rush, and I used the time to work out what I would say to him. *Should I bring it up, or should I wait for him to bring it up?* I had decided to tell him how I felt if he asked, but I wouldn't volunteer the information, he'd have to ask me. I was walking a tightrope. There was so much room for error- so many possible complications. If I told him how I felt, what would happen? I didn't want to have an affair with him, but I didn't NOT want to have an affair with him either. Everything about that whole thing was a contradiction. I wanted his friendship- but I wanted more than his friendship. I wanted him to touch me again- but I didn't want him to touch me again. I wanted him to make me feel like that all the time- but, also it felt terrifying. I couldn't make sense of it. I did have feelings for him. I was in love with him.

I started my last round of jobs at about 4 p.m. If I started them at that time, it meant I would be ready for when Neil arrived. I knew he could turn up at any point as that was the 'safe period', which meant it wouldn't raise too many eyebrows from the other liveries. We had discussed this a few times, as we knew how our friendship looked to the outside world. Sure, as clockwork, as I had just finished CJ's hay net, I heard the clang of the gate as the bar slid open.... I paused to listen out for the perfectly timed second clang. That rhythm was unique to one person on the farm, and my stomach started doing flips that rivalled an Olympic gymnast. My chest felt as though someone was sitting on it. My anxiety peaked as I heard the familiar gait trudging down the farmyard. I step out of the stable, the lack of strength in my legs apparent as the toe of my boot grazed the threshold of the door. As I began to cross the yard and head for the side of the school, I glanced up and saw Neil, hunched shoulders, his hands in his bomber pockets, looking up at me. He tipped his head subtly, alluding to *our* space, and I walked as casually as I could manage to take a seat next to the school.

He seemed agitated too. His knee bounced as he repositioned himself numerous times in the heavy wooden chair. Normally, he'd have pulled the chair right next to mine, so the arms of the chairs touched. But he didn't that time. He left a couple of feet between us. I was equally grateful and annoyed about the distance. I think he wanted me to have an escape route- either that or he wanted an escape route. I couldn't work out which one was truer. Maybe they were both true. He tried to instigate a conversation with small talk. Naturally, the weather came first on the list, in true Brit fashion. I responded with a non-committal "mmm" when he said how nice it had been. His words seemed to pour out of his mouth without much coherence. I knew he was brewing up to ask me what I thought about his declaration. I knew he wanted to know if I felt the same. I wanted him to ask as the small talk was hard, but I also hoped that we could just forget and pretend that it never happened.

"Have you had a chance to think on it?" He asked. *'It'*, so sharp out of his mouth, stung like a dagger. Like he wanted to label 'it' something else but couldn't think of anything else to call *'it'*.

I paused for a couple of seconds.

"I feel the same way too," I responded.

I felt partly relieved that I heard the words come from my mouth. It felt like a release from the chains that I had been wrapped up in all day. Yet, as I heard the words fall out of my mouth, I screamed internally *SHUT UP TANYA. STOP!* But it was too late. I'd already said it. I had already put it out there in the stratosphere. There was no undoing what I had done. There was nothing that could remove the shame of telling a 'married' man that I felt the same way. I had cemented my position in the universe as a whore.

The anguish left Neil's face. His eyes widened and the cheeky sparkle returned. He looked elated, almost childlike. It was clear that he'd been thinking about our conversation all day, too, stressing over how I would deal with the affirmation of his feelings. *I passed the test*, I told myself. There was a feeling of triumph; my natural need to succeed had been rewarded. However, I wasn't sure that this test was one that I wanted to pass. Despite feeling the relief of meeting the expectations set for me, there was a nagging doubt in my head that I had done the wrong thing, and made the wrong choice. It was too late; I'd said it and there was no undoing what I had done.

It felt safer to tell Neil that I felt the same way, rather than elaborating on every single emotion I had felt over the past few weeks. We talked about it for a while, and he told me that he was relieved that the feelings were mutual. We never discussed where things would go from there. There wasn't any sordid planning or looking to the future in any way. We were just concentrating on the there and then. We both confessed to the relief that it was out in the open, though I'm not sure it was relief that I felt. I never offered much to the conversations about how I felt about Neil, but I did say that I wasn't sure whether I should have told him. I didn't know what that meant for me- whether I was a homewrecker or not. It felt weird to discuss our mutual feelings so openly. It's not something I had ever done before, with anyone, but he made me feel at ease and the conversation came easy, even if a little one-sided on his part.

It was during that conversation that I gave him my mobile number. I knew that I had to do it discreetly, so I gave it to him on a small torn piece of paper. It felt as though we had reached a point where talking at the farm might become problematic. He looked at it and smiled, his eyes widening with glee as though all his Christmases had come at once. I suspected that he had wanted my number as he had said several times over the course of those few hours that he wished it was easier to get privacy. I briefly made my excuses to walk off for a few minutes. I remember wanting to give him time to think about what we had discussed. In all fairness, I did it for dramatic effect, to imitate what he had done the night before. I wasn't experienced enough to develop my own ideas, so I had to copy his.

The rest of the evening panned out predictably. We sat and talked about anything and everything. Although we frequently came back to discussing our attraction, we would talk about music a lot of the time too. I enjoyed music, but I was not on the same level as Neil; he could talk about it for hours. I liked listening to him talk with such enthusiasm. He was interested in what music I enjoyed and would compliment me on my 'excellent, eclectic taste'. We enjoyed the same music from The Eagles to Queen, Aretha Franklin to AC/DC, and everything in between. We seemed to have a lot in common, especially about music, but he was far more knowledgeable about it than I was, and he revelled in educating and moulding my enthusiasm. It felt like he was trying to impress me. It worked, of course.

I spent the following day at the farm, and once again, I was wholly immersed in my thoughts when Neil arrived. He'd come earlier than expected, so I was still finishing my jobs when he appeared at my stable and suggested a 'cigarette break'.

I strolled to the seats at the side of the school, a couple of paces behind Neil. He grabbed the back of one of the heavy chairs and scraped it along the ground to meet with another chair, lightly tapping the arm to indicate my seat. He lit up a cigarette and the first couple of puffs of smoke filled the air and were welcomed into my lungs. It had been hours since I last had one. I'd been too distracted to walk off the farm, and hadn't noticed just how much I craved nicotine. He passed it low down to my hand, pausing for a split moment longer than necessary and brushed my fingers.

"I've disposed of your number," he said.

My heart plummeted to my feet. *Oh no! Was I too eager? Was it too much? Now I look stupid, desperate. He's come to his senses and now he's going to give me a wide berth. Things are going to get awkward.* My face must have displayed my disappointment.

"0754..........." He continued after a few seconds.

He hadn't disposed of my number, he'd disposed of the paper with my number on it. He'd spent the night memorising my number. My heart reinflated.

I became aware that I was smiling from ear to ear. I felt reassured. I was impressed and touched that he had memorised it so quickly. It made me realise that he thought about me as often as I thought about him. I was still on his mind after he had gone home. I was overjoyed. My heart fluttering within my chest, goosebumps appearing on my arms. *He really did want me. He thought about me all the time too!* It reinforced the conversation that we'd had the night before, that he couldn't stop thinking about me either.

We got onto the subject of meeting up away from the farm so that we could talk a little more freely. So frequently, over the course of the evening, we would find ourselves having to change the topic of conversation quickly or drop our voices if someone entered our periphery, even before our confession. Once everyone had left the farm for the night, it wasn't such a problem, but time was of the essence once we were alone because people had already passed comments about us having spent so much time together. Neil said he would ring me when he could, and we would arrange to go somewhere out of the prying eyes of the gossipers. I tried to be casual, but I was nervous. Nervous and excited. The thought of being alone with Neil made me nervous, mostly because he was not shy about touching me, as I had deduced from the tack room incident. I was sexually inexperienced, and though we had broached the topic briefly, I had exaggerated my experience to him. I didn't want him to think I had no idea about sex, as I was worried that it would have made me seem childlike. I wanted him to visualise me as a woman. It was bad enough that he'd seen me in my school uniform and knew exactly how old I was, without coming across as a completely inexperienced little girl. I wasn't concerned about my safety; not once had it crossed my mind that he could hurt me. He made me feel safe. He made me feel loved and cared for, so I wasn't afraid of being harmed. I was worried that he would want to have sex with me if we were on our own, and I wasn't ready for that. I wasn't ready for him to see me naked, but I didn't know how to say no without offending him or embarrassing myself.

He rang me the following morning. My heart leapt into my mouth when an un-stored number popped up on my screen. I answered it, hesitantly, concerned that it was Anne rather than him, and for a moment, the guilt rose inside me like bile. When Neil's voice said hello the guilt washed away as quickly as it had arrived. He told me to walk up the hill towards the cigarette shop after lunch and he would pick me up in his car. Anne would come home for lunch, so he couldn't arrange to meet me before as he was worried it would raise suspicion if he had gone out unexpectedly. The morning flew by, and I put that down to feeling more anxious than excited. I felt the twisting hunger pains in my stomach, but the idea of lunch repulsed me.

I waited for the workers to go in the house before closing CJ's door and making my way up the driveway. I felt as though they knew where I was going, and who I was going to meet. I imagined their conversations in my head as my feet struggled to navigate over the driveway.

"Did you see Tanya and Neil last night?" Cerys would say. "They were all over each other, sat there, rubbing it in Anne's face."

"I know, they are always like it," Samantha would add. "He held her hand the other day whilst he passed her his cigarette. It's so obvious that she fancies him, she can't leave him alone."

"No, he didn't! Did he really?" Kelsey would chime in, feigning shock laughing like she'd just heard something unbelievable from a soap opera. "I bet she loved that, didn't she?"

The imagined conversations played over and over in my mind like a flowchart. I could hear all the things they were saying about me- calling me a slag for chasing after a married man four times my age. I'd mentally argue back.

But I'm not chasing after him, I'm responding to him. I'm not the one that invited his touch, that invited his declaration of love. He did that, I just didn't stop him. My knees and ankles were like jelly. I felt them rolling over the rubbly terrain as I left the driveway onto the main road. It felt as though I was in one of those dreams. A dream where you are trying to run away, but it doesn't matter how much effort you put into a sprint, your legs barely propel you. Like trying to run on air. There was no strength, no stability in my limbs. They didn't belong to me anymore.

My thoughts darted between the people at the farm and Neil. My mind was a whole mess of confusion. I wasn't even sure if I wanted to go and meet Neil. I didn't want the people at the farm to think less of me, I didn't want Neil to try any funny business. *What if he thinks I'm meeting him for sex? I don't want to have sex with him. I don't want him to touch me. Is he expecting this rendezvous to be something more, something he wouldn't get away with on the farm?* I felt sick. My heartbeat pulsated in my ears. Air wouldn't fill my lungs. I couldn't breathe. There was a tight band around my chest, winding tighter and tighter every time I got a few paces closer to the pick-up point.

It will be fine, I told myself. I couldn't understand why I felt so panicked. Why I couldn't breathe. I had walked that hill so many times and I had never struggled with it. I looked around to see if anyone could hear my struggles; hear my roaring chest. The road was clear. Parked cars lined the side street, but nobody would hear me gasping for air. I let myself gasp freely, giving in to my body's need for oxygen.

As we had agreed on the phone, I continued to walk past his house, and I crossed over to the right-hand side pavement. His car wasn't on the drive when I walked past, so I had wondered if he'd changed his mind as I had envisaged that he would see me walk past before pulling off this drive. I worried that something had come up at the last minute and glanced down at my phone. *No missed call. Has he changed his mind?* I walked for another few minutes and tried to take control of my breath but failed miserably. I glanced around one last time to make sure that I hadn't been followed, giving in to my paranoia, and felt relief as the street remained motionless.

As I reached the halfway point of the hill, Neil's car appeared over the brow and started to manoeuvre around the parked cars. I didn't want to appear breathless and flustered, so as I reached the passenger door of his large 4x4, and clutched the handle, I forced myself into a normal rhythm. He ushered me into the car with a sense of urgency, and I barely had time to close the door before he drove off.

"Just slide down," he said as we approached the farm.

Dutifully, I did.

As we drove past the farm, Neil looked down the driveway but didn't say anything. I sat back up and turned my body to the door, looking out of the passenger window at the hedges that lined the country road. I didn't want to look at him. I felt shy and uncomfortable. Despite feeling safe in his company whilst we sat outside the school at the farm, I felt unsettled being alone in the car with Neil. I didn't know if going somewhere to 'talk' *actually* meant to talk or something else, something darker. I had tried to think of a way of creating a distraction if he had tried to initiate sexual activity, but in all the scenarios I had played out in my head, I came out looking like a frigid little girl. I wanted to play it cool with him like it wasn't a big deal, but I most definitely didn't want to have sex. I didn't feel remotely ready for that, and the vomit would rise inside of me every time I thought that it could have been a possibility.

As we continued the journey, the roads became less and less familiar. In the five minutes that we had been in the car together, we had only spoken a few short sentences, and even small talk was hard. I concluded that Neil was just as anxious as I was, which did nothing to calm my rising panic- *why is he nervous, what does he know that I don't?* I tried to force conversation, but it was like trying to get blood out of a stone. I don't think he was being difficult intentionally, but it was clear that his mind was firing on all cylinders. After a few minutes of trying to converse, I decided to sit quietly and wait and see what unfolded. At least whilst the car was moving, he wouldn't be able to instigate sex.

After ten long minutes of sitting in awkward silence, we got to a place I now know to be Falmer's Woods. As he pulled down the long narrow country road, I was disappointed to see that the place looked almost deserted. In the distance, the sun reflected off the roofs of a couple of cars, but they were so far away that the light looked like a diamond sparkle. My apprehension of the deserted road only intensified when Neil turned off the main stretch of the road onto an abandoned side track. *He's pulled down here because it's empty- he wants to have sex with me! There is no other reason to be so secluded, it's not like we couldn't have explained being seen together- we are always together.*

As soon as the car climbed up onto the verge and the engine stopped, I unbuckled my seatbelt and lunged towards the door handle.

"Let's go for a walk; get some fresh air," I said as the door clicked off the catch.

I thought getting out of the car and into the woods would be the easiest way of making it clear that I had no intention of having sex. He nodded in agreement. Relief poured over me as the whoosh of the air hit my face and my chest expanded to drink it in. I walked past the rear of his 4x4 and climbed down off the verge, slightly misjudging the height of the ground and catching the toe of my boot on the long grass. I felt my face flush but brushed off my embarrassment when I realised that Neil hadn't seen it. I walked in front, back in the direction of the main track and could hear the scuffing of his shoes on the ground behind me. Despite having told myself that it didn't matter if anyone saw us, I felt like a sitting duck on the exposed road and wanted to be under the cover of the woods, away from prying eyes.

As I stepped off the tarmac onto the spongy ground of the wood floor, I eased off and allowed Neil to catch up with me. He casually pulled out his packet of cigarettes from his leather coat, opened the lid and extended one out, offering it in my direction. I reached forwards to pull the cigarette with my first two fingers and offer it towards my mouth. The smell of petrol shot up my nostrils, as he rolled the wheel of the Zippo under my nose to ignite the wick. The first drag filled my whole chest with warmth. Comforting and all encasing as the nicotine entered my bloodstream and filled me with relief. I held it in for as long as I could, until I started to feel the head spin, then I slowly controlled the exhale and watched the smoke as it left my mouth and disappear into the atmosphere. As I looked around, having succumbed to the calming effects of the cigarette, I drank in my surroundings.

The warm damp air clung to me, as the smell of pine and fern wafted under my nose. The debris left the ground spongy and cushioned my footfall. It was silent, peaceful. The tall trees stretched out in front of me, with rays of the sun penetrating the spaces of the canvass, illuminating the floor. Pockets of light lit up circles of foliage and the neon green fern that cradled the bottom of the trees. I propped one leg on to a fallen log and turned to face Neil, looking at him for the first time since he picked me up. He looked more relaxed too, his face tender and body having lost all tension. I realised that sitting in the car had created a charged atmosphere that was no good for either of us.

We discussed how nice it was to be away from the farm, and acknowledged that it was the first time we could talk without having to fight the urge to look over our shoulders. He opened his arms, gesturing for me to move towards him. I had long wanted to get close enough to hug him. I wanted to feel safe in his arms, unlike the last time. Last time, I felt trapped, but this invitation didn't feel like that, it felt inviting. I put my arms around him, and my hands met at the middle of his back, just below his shoulder blades. I leaned forwards and felt his cotton t-shirt gently brush my cheek as my head rested on his chest. He was warm and comfortable. It felt just like I imagined. It felt like I was home.

It was the first time I had really noticed the height difference between us, the top of my head barely reaching the height of his breastbone. I felt dwarfed by his body. I felt protected by his arms. I felt safe and secure wrapped up inside of him. His heartbeat rhythmically drumming in my ear through his t-shirt, periodically being drowned out by the sound of his creaking leather jacket has he offered his hand to his mouth for another drag of his cigarette. The air rustled in his chest as his lungs inflated with smoke. I sank deeper and deeper into his arms, closing my eyes to shut off the outside world. Despite the difference in height, he felt comfortable, and I found myself not wanting to let go when he pulled back.

"We better think about getting you back, before they notice," he said, referring to the girls at the farm.

I was disappointed, I had only just calmed down and I didn't want the feeling of euphoria to disappear. I didn't want to come back to earth, but Neil's statement had reignited the feeling of guilt that I'd been carrying around with me for weeks. Whilst wrapped in his arms, the world had disappeared from view. It was just him and me. The guilt, the shame, the dread had all been eradicated whilst wrapped in his cocoon, but in the instant that his arms released me, it came rushing back.

As we had reached the main stretch of road, side by side, I stopped and drew the last breath from the cigarette, and noticed that the filter had got painfully hot between my fingers. I squatted down to stub it on the tarmac and a flash of light hit my eye as my knees lowered me. My eyes focused as I reached forwards to pick up a ten pence piece glistening on the ground. As I stood to turn and put my stub in the bin, the rhyme concluded; *find a penny pick it up and all day long you'll have good luck.* I rolled the coin in my hands as I jogged a couple of steps to catch up with Neil; he hadn't noticed that I had stopped. As I caught up with him, I turned my head to look at him, and a wry smile flashed upon his face.

"Am I going to get a kiss then today, or what?" He asked.

Am I going to kiss him? Shit, no. What if it doesn't stop at a kiss? I've thought about kissing him, but did I actually want to do it? No, I didn't. But he wants to, he's just asked me. What do I say? I broke eye contact immediately and looked at the floor.

"Yes, but I'm not fucking you."

I shocked myself at the speed at which it had flown out of my mouth, and immediately felt my face flush with embarrassment. *Oh god, did I really just say that?* He laughed, but I didn't feel relieved. I felt flustered that I had retorted it so rapidly. I didn't want him to think that I'd been worried about it all day. Thankfully, he seemed to find it humorous. I flashed a brief smile, so I didn't look too defensive. *That's it, Tanya, play it off as a joke. I think you've got away with it.*

I was wearing a pale yellow broad strapped vest top. I was large-chested for a teenager, and although I never had a nice tight abdomen, I was shapely and curvy in all the right places. Of course, I had my body hang-ups like most teenagers; I didn't like my arms, so, I wore that vest top underneath a black buttoned shirt. The devastatingly difficult climb up the road of the farm had caused me to remove the shirt and tie it around my waist. It sat brushing the top of the waistband of my clingy jeans and revealed a painfully white inch of my abdomen if I raised my arms. My jeans weren't skinny jeans per se, those weren't really a thing at the time, but their snugness around my developing curves and the way I folded them inside my long boots gave them the appearance of being so. I knew what I was doing when I got dressed that morning; dressing to flatter my developing body, without dressing like I had tried too hard.

We continued to the car and my unease had returned, causing my pulse to throb inside my neck. *He asked me to kiss him, and I agreed to it.* I tried to convince myself that it would be fine. *I'll give him a quick peck before we get to the farm, that way it won't go any further.* As I approached the passenger door of his car, I fidgeted as he patted his pockets in search of the key. I pulled on the door after the click click of the unlocking mechanism indicated entry. I struggled to lift my leg into the footwell of the car and realised that I had left my strength in our 'pre-kiss conversation'. Once again, my toe clipped the edge of the doorframe. I pointed my body to the window, and overdramatically turned my back to at Neil, hoping he'd get the hint, as I reached across to haul the heavy door shut with a thwack. *Shit! Bit more forceful than I thought. Calm down Tanya. Don't be an idiot.* I reached over with my right hand, still twisted towards the door and pulled my seatbelt from behind me and across my chest, sitting back in the chair and looking down for the buckle. *Click.*

I had no sooner clicked it into the buckle and looked up when Neil's face appeared directly in front of me with his mouth pushed against mine. *WOAH!* He made me jump. My eyes clamped shut as the shock set in. *Oh my god! Oh my God! Neil is kissing me. Neil is kissing me. There is no going back from this. There is no going back.* His mouth moved on mine and forced my lips open as he pushed his tongue in, invading my mouth. His mouth was wet and warm. His tongue moving frantically inside my mouth, his face pressed hard against mine. I couldn't open my eyes; I couldn't do anything. My body had left me once again. It didn't belong to me. I sat there as a passive receptacle whilst he kissed me with such urgency and longing. All I could do was to try and get my body to behave like my body and not like a ragdoll. *I should do something back. I can't sit here doing nothing. He needs to know I'm engaged in this.*

I tried to reach up with my right arm, but it was trapped between the seatbelt buckle and the full weight of his body. *Just kiss him back*, I told myself. I forced my jaw to relax into him and moved my tongue around his. *Is this right? Is this how it's supposed to feel?* I tried to put my left hand on his chest, but that wouldn't move either. I wasn't even sure that the message from my brain was reaching my hand. There was no communication between my head and the rest of the body. All I could do was wait for the rest of me to catch up. Wait for it to stop. I felt awkward. Tense. *Why is my body not listening to me?* The only communication between my arms and my brain was the awareness of the ten pence piece, that I was now clutching tight in my hand. It felt heavy, alien. I clutched that coin like my life depended on it. I was paralysed.

I had imagined kissing him before, but it had never played out like that in all my fantasies. I had thought it would feel magical and romantic but all I felt was panic. The world had stopped, time had stopped. I felt self-conscious about my lack of involvement, but I couldn't do anything about it. *Has he noticed?* I asked myself. He came at me so quickly I hadn't had the time to process what was happening. I'm sure I'd have let out a gasp of surprise if he hadn't already clamped onto my mouth before I had the opportunity. *What's he doing? Oh no!*

I felt Neil slide his right hand up the left-hand side of my body and stop as he reached my breast. He cupped it, gently squeezing it, then pulled back and his hand left my breast and his tongue left my mouth. The kiss had lasted no longer than 30 seconds, but so much seemed to have happened. My body returned to me as he sat back in his chair and reached around for his seatbelt. After a couple of churns of the starter motor, the engine fired up.

"I should get you back," he said as he knocked the car into gear and pulled off the verge; the rocking motion of the wheels as they rolled off the grass brought me back to earth.

I was relieved it was over, that it hadn't gone any further, but I could not silence the notion that it had left me panicked. I hadn't expected a choir of angels to descend on us if we ever kissed, but I thought I should have felt more than terror I experienced. I never expected to freeze. I did want it, sort of anyway. I had thought about kissing him, and I had 'consented' to it. I could have said no when he asked me, but I didn't. *I chose to be the slag, I chose to say yes, and this is what I get. It serves you right that you didn't like it. You brought it on yourself.* I felt a little shell shocked, a little self-loathing, a little euphoric, a little confused. I didn't feel any single overwhelming emotion, just a combination of every overwhelming emotion available.

We drove back a direct route, and despite taking the same amount of time, it seemed much quicker than the journey to Falmer's Woods. We sat in silence for most of the way back, apart from discussing the logistics of where he could drop me off so that I wouldn't be seen. We agreed that he would drop me off at the top of the road, and I could walk back down as though I had been to the shop. It meant that it would be unlikely anyone from the farm would have seen me in his car, and I could say that I had been delayed at the shop if they asked. Not that I'd thought they'd dare to; it was easier to pretend they didn't know.

As we approached where he had planned to drop me off, we said our goodbyes, and he winked at me as I turned to close the door. He swiftly pulled away whilst I adjusted my clothing before beginning the walk down the hill. Once out of the car and on my descent to the farm, I felt on cloud nine. Neil had kissed me. I played it over and over again in my head as I walked the mile to the farm, and each time I revisited it, I got a fiery flutter deep in my belly. I knew that I could never tell anyone what had happened, but I felt sure they would have known. Of course, I wasn't troubled by that, as I would have denied it if they'd have asked. But I shone like a beam, had a spring in my step, and I had disappeared from the farm for an hour. *Surely, someone is bound to have noticed?*

When I arrived back at the farm, I made a beeline for CJ's stable. I had stopped at the shop on the way down, so I plonked the carrier bag containing a sandwich outside his stable and I squeezed my way in, closing the door behind me. I was desperate for a wee but didn't want to go in the house for fear of an inquisition, so I pushed CJ over to the edge of his box, lowered my trousers, and squatted. As relief overcame me, I looked down to notice a slightly dirty smudge on my left breast. It wasn't a noticeable handprint, but it was enough to give me the smug satisfaction that I was harbouring a massive secret right under everybody's nose.

A few hours later, after I had spent the entire afternoon thinking about him, Neil arrived at the farm at the same time as I had grown accustomed to expecting. As we always did, we sat by the school and he asked me if anyone had said anything. I put his mind at ease and told him that my absence from the farm had gone unnoticed. He was relieved and blew out a controlled sigh. We continued the evening as always, but this time, both of us with a glint in our eye.

Tanya Pursglove

CHAPTER 4

I lived off our first kiss for days, for the rest of the holiday, and once I returned to school. I started to kid myself, telling myself that it was incredible, and the only reason that I didn't like it at the time was because I was unprepared. Goosebumps appeared when I recalled his hand on my breast, his gentle squeeze. My face flushed and I felt people looking at me, trying to see what was behind my mind. I couldn't tell them. I desperately wanted to tell someone, but I knew they wouldn't have understood. Nobody would have understood why there was an attraction- I was a little girl and he was an old man. *What possibly could they see in each other?* My inner voice would mimic. They were right to some degree. I didn't fancy Neil, not in the traditional sense. I didn't find him physically attractive. I found him captivating and enchanting; charming, even, but it wasn't his physical looks that drew me in. I liked the way he made me feel. I liked the way he could see inside my mind. I was addicted to the compliments, the flattery, the longing he had for me…. but I didn't *fancy* him.

Whilst at school, I became increasingly solitary. I had a great circle of friends, and we always had a laugh and gossiped about the drama but was all starting to become rather menial. *Who cares if Chris from year 10 got caught smoking on the school field? or if Shannon and Ian had broken up for the 5000ᵗʰ time?* My secret was far bigger, far more important, and everything that took place in that pitiful place was insignificant compared with the drama unfolding in my own life.

Although I hung out with my friendship group regularly, my mind was never there. Sara and Cleo would be talking about the latest music or who had been given detention, but my mind would be off down the rabbit hole, wondering what I was doing there when I could be out with Neil somewhere. I'd drift in and out of the conversations, thinking about my own problems and it wasn't just my friendships that suffered, but schoolwork too.

I just about kept on top of my schoolwork, but it had lost its joy and become a chore. I had little desire for anything except Neil. My concentration dwindled, my heart wasn't in it. I sat and thought about Neil all day and regularly disappeared into my own world, where Neil and I featured as the main characters. I thought about his kiss and his touch all the time. My heart flitted between crazy excitement and an ache so hollow I thought my rib cage would collapse in on itself. I was continuously preoccupied. At half-past three, the tannoy would sound to mark the end of the day, and I'd make my way to the bus stop. I found myself sitting alone on the bus instead of with my friends. I'd plug my headphones in my ears and gaze out of the window whilst I listened to the music that Neil and I enjoyed. Neil had a hold over me, a constant and relentless pull on my soul. I couldn't explain *why* I felt that way. I couldn't explain why or how it started, but although I felt as though it was snowballing out of control, I didn't want it to stop.

The days became routine. I spent all day on autopilot, wishing the time away until I could be with Neil, then I'd race down to the farm at breakneck speed. I'd get to the farm to try and complete most of my jobs before he got down there, so we could maximise our time together. If he had beaten me to the farm in an evening, he would sit on the box outside of CJ's stable, waiting for me like a loyal Labrador. I'd go inside the stable and get changed out of my uniform with the door closed whilst he sat there talking to me the whole time. He never peeked, that I noticed, not at that point anyway, but I could tell that he enjoyed the mystery of my undressing.

I was running late one day. There had been an accident on the motorway and consequently, the town had been backlogged with traffic. The 12-mile journey was spent nose to tail, never getting to more than 40 miles per hour for more than 1 or 2 minutes at I time. I bubbled with rage. The universe conspired against us. I just wanted to be at the farm. By the time I arrived, I was well over an hour later than expected. *Neil will be worried about me. What if he's already gone home because he got pissed off waiting for me?* I almost sprinted down the road from the bus stop. It was about a mile away from the farm, and by the time I turned to walk down the drive, I was flustered and sweaty. *Anne's car is still here, maybe he'll still be here.* I prayed as I slowed myself down, trying to compose myself before getting within eyesight of the yard area.

Yes, he's still here. I noticed, as I caught his eye as I reached the gate. The gate clanked and it brought me out of my head, and my frustration left me. A wash of relief rushed up from my feet, my body relaxed, and the feelings of want took over me. As I made my way through the farm gate, I caught his eye as I turned to close the gate shut. Excitement had replaced my irritation at running late, and the rising shivers ran up my back as I held his eye contact whilst walking towards him through the farm.

"Hey, you," he silently mouthed as I approached the front of my stable.

I couldn't hold my smile back as I dropped my leather rucksack in front of his feet, keeping hold of the tote that contained my farm clothes. He kept his eyes locked on me as I reached passed his head for the catch on CJ's stable door. The air was charged, and I could feel him burning with desire, fighting the urge to reach forward and touch me as I squeezed passed him to get in the stable. I pulled the door shut behind me and Neil turned slightly to put the bolt on the door. He asked me why I was running late, so I explained that the bus had got stuck. As I did, I slipped my navy blazer off my arms and placed it over the door at the side of his head.

"What have you been up to?" He asked, "You been busy?" his voice quickened and became breathy. I carefully lay my tie and white shirt over the top of my blazer.

"Not really, just the usual," I replied nonchalantly, despite having become aware that he was getting aroused.

I knew he was curious, and his curiosity in me felt empowering. I bent down to remove my navy box pleated skirt and added it to the pile over the door. The conversation paused for a few seconds, and I could tell that he was too side-tracked to think clearly. I loved having that effect on him. I loved it when I distracted him to the point where he couldn't formulate a sentence.

As I reached to pull my jodhpurs and boots out of the bag, I heard him say that he loved my uniform. I could hear the smile in his voice when he said it, and I felt my face beam with flattery. I didn't respond as I was trying to play it cool. Thankfully, he couldn't see my smile as I had been bent over, pulling my jodhpurs over my knees and inserting my feet into my boots. I prized my purple striped rugby shirt from the bag as I stood upright and pulled it over my head. I opened the door as I made the final adjustments to my shirt, straightening it down around the hem, and freeing my hair from the collar. He looked up at me as I stepped out to scoop my uniform from the door. I passed him the tote and indicated for him to hold it open as I plucked a carrier bag from within it and placed my ballet pumps into it. I lowered the carrier bag into the tote that Neil was holding and carefully rolled the rest of my uniform inside, ensuring that my blazer pockets didn't empty their contents all over the floor.

"You smell nice," he whispered as I took the tote from his hand and placed it at the side of my rucksack.

"Thank you," I mouthed and smiled, as I stepped back and began to scoop my long dark ringlets into a high ponytail, securing it with an elastic from my wrist.

He stood and asked me if I wanted to go for a cigarette break, inviting me to walk ahead. As we walked between the back of the house and the barn, I felt a tickle in my hair, and as I ran my hand over the top of my head and ponytail, I felt the gentle tug of Neil removing a piece of hay that had become entangled as I got dressed. We made eye contact as I flashed a flirty smile of gratitude and sat at the school to share a cigarette.

On the occasions where I had managed to complete my jobs before he arrived, he would signal, with a quick nod, as he walked through the farm. It was my cue to proceed to the school with Neil a couple of paces behind me. It had become our daily routine, so much so, that as soon as I heard his rhythmic clangs of the gate, I'd finish up whatever job I was doing and start making my way there. If we were on the farm, we were always found together. There was rarely a time on the farm that we weren't side by side, either at the school, or by my stable. Sometimes we'd even be in Anne's stable if she was riding, whilst we pretended to finish her jobs on her behalf. If I ran behind on my job list, Neil would grab hold of my wheelbarrow and empty it whilst I moved through the rest of the tasks I had to do. There was a need to get my jobs finished as quickly as possible, so we could maximise the time together before the evening drew to an end.

Neil and I would spend the evening in each other's company, every evening. It had only been a couple of months since Neil and I had that first conversation about smoking, but since then, there hadn't been a day where we hadn't spoken. I wondered how two people could know each other so well, in such a short amount of time. He could read me like a book. He instantly knew when I'd had a rough day. If I sat quietly for a minute, thinking about something else, he could tell where my mind had gone. He was so perceptive, there was no hiding from him, I was as transparent as crystal. I was touched by the level of genuine interest someone showed in me; the way he sat listening to anything I had to say. He told me that I was special, that I would go on to do incredible things. That I could be anything I wanted to be. That he'd never met anyone like me; never formed a connection as deep with anyone as he had with me. I floated with euphoria, completely enchanted, encapsulated by his feelings for me. I yearned for his words, for his attention, for the way he would gaze at me with such unrelenting curiosity. It wasn't that he fancied me, he was in love with me, and I was in love with him. Over the course of a few weeks, the shame and guilt for being a slag begun to lift and all I could see was what Neil saw in me. *Maybe I am special, maybe this is special?*

Anne would leave the farm by car, and he would follow her up on foot a while later.

"You two still here?" Geraldine bellowed from across the farm one night as she made her way around the stables to turn off the lights.

"Yeah, I'll be heading off in a bit," Neil shouted in response and gave me a sly wink as he turned back.

We would sit and talk about music, films, or pretty much anything; nothing was out of bounds. He would gush at me endlessly about my hair, or my 'big blues', or the way I walked, or how intelligent I was. He would tell me how incredible I was; how he could talk to me about anything. He'd tell me how perceptive I was, how in tune we were. When I spoke, he listened so intently, never taking his eyes off me, even when I broke the tension to look away. Despite the forty-two-year age gap, it felt like we were the same person. He would say how our thoughts were the same, but he worried that eventually, I would 'outgrow' him. My heart broke a little when he said that; that he thought so lowly of himself that I would no longer want him. I didn't believe that could ever be a possibility. He was my soulmate. I could never get bored of him, he was so attentive and complimentary, and it felt as though he was cradling my soul. He would say that it didn't matter who I found after him; nobody would ever love me the way that he did. It was said with so much sincerity that my heart would burst.

Once everybody had left the farm in the evening, we took advantage of the dusk and used it to move to the hidden corners. Anne's stable provided us with the most security, nestled deep in the corner of the dark barn. We could see if Geraldine or her husband had come out to do the final checks because they would trip the security light, and the momentary dazzle offered us the opportunity to innocently look busy. I would stand behind Anne's stable door, hidden from view, whilst Neil checked that the coast was clear. Then he'd move towards me, maintaining eye contact as he pulled me towards his mouth. Sometimes he was tender and sweet, stroking my face and gently tipping my chin towards him so that he could softly meet his lips with mine. He would pause to pull away and look at me, before returning to my lips. Other times, he would hold me tight and drive me into the stable wall, wrapping my hair in his hand and pushing his tongue into my mouth as he held onto me tight. I no longer felt panic when he kissed me, instead, I was driven by longing. I loved that he couldn't get enough of me, and I would actively respond to his advances. When he was sweet and kind, I felt loved, adored, and cherished. Neil was in love with me, and I felt like the single most important person in the world. When he was passionate, I felt coveted like a prized possession. He wasn't just in love with me, but he also wanted every inch of me. He would kiss me with such hunger and fervency, pulling my pelvis tightly into him as he forced his way into my mouth. I could feel his urgency as his groin pushed into me, feeling his erection as it pushed into my abdomen. He groaned into my mouth so that I could feel his lips vibrating on mine. I filled him with white-hot intensity, and he couldn't get enough of me.

We would part ways after we had finished. I'd wait for a few seconds whilst he left the Barn and made his way up through the yard. He would look back as he reached the gate to see me walking back to the school to wait for my lift. He never waved, not wanting to draw attention to my presence on the farm to Geraldine or her husband. I would sit at the side of the school for a short while, elated with passion, craving, and love. I'd replay him kissing me, over and over, thinking about his taste, his touch, and the way he had made me feel. I felt drunk on his attention, but then the sadness would creep in as I realised that he was walking home and I was alone, with only my memories for comfort. Each day, as soon as he left, I missed him.

At weekends throughout the summer show season, we would be out with Julie and Liam. We had become a bit of a five-some at the weekends, travelling to the shows together. Either that, or Anne and Neil would follow behind shortly. Neil used to get impatient with Anne for not finishing her morning horsey jobs quick enough as he worried about missing 'all the action'. This couldn't be further from the truth though, as Neil and I rarely saw the ringside 'action'. Instead, we would hover around 'base camp', smoking and talking, whilst Julie, Liam and Anne went to watch the classes. On the occasions that Neil and I attended the ringside with the others, he'd always find a way to position himself next to me, even if it meant he had to squeeze himself in a small gap.

Neil couldn't leave me alone, even around the other three. I understood why he wanted to be so close because it gave us the opportunity to 'innocently' touch. If he sat at the side of me, it meant that we had the opportunity to brush legs, or our fingers without anyone noticing. Often the ringside was cramped, so we had plenty of chances and excuses for being in very close proximity to each other. I never felt like we looked out of place; we had become pretty astute at remaining inconspicuous, or so I thought. The atmosphere between us was intoxicating. He'd offer me a cigarette, and our eyes would lock as he reached forwards to light it, his fingers wrapping around my hands as he 'shielded the flame from the wind'. The stolen moments became the highlight of our days. It wasn't often that we'd get the chance to kiss or touch sexually at the shows. We were never quite sure who was around, and the horsey world is small, but Neil seemed to revel in the thrill of hiding in plain sight.

The second reason why Neil would always position himself next to me became apparent after a few weeks. Neil was jealous of Liam. He was adamant that Liam 'had a thing for me' but it didn't matter how much I laughed it off, he was never satisfied when I said that Liam hadn't tried it on. He hadn't at all. Not even so much as an inappropriate joke had been shared between us. It was a completely innocent friendship. Sometimes my friendship with Liam resembled that of big brother, little sister, but I never *ever* got a vibe that there was an element of attraction. We'd take the piss out of each other, and banter, but it was never flirty. There was nothing there for either of us that would have suggested otherwise. From the outside perspective, the only thing someone could potentially frown on was that Liam, or Julie, would give me a can of lager. Neil never had a problem with me having a drink though- it made me extra flirty, so it wasn't the alcohol that he had taken exception to, but rather the friendship. Neil's thoughts were unfounded, but as much as I got annoyed by it, because I loved being with Julie and Liam, I was also flattered that he was jealous.

Neil told me of his jealousy of Liam one evening, as we sat by the school, sharing a cigarette.

"He's got a thing for you," he said, nodding discretely in Liam's direction. "He wants in your box."

"My what?" I said. "Box?"

"Yes, your minge,"

I hated that expression. I wasn't sure what he could label it as without being either clinical or crude, but the word *minge* just went through me. I'd got used to him calling my various body parts by a euphemism, and in fairness, minge was probably one of the least graphic, but it still made me feel uncomfortable.

"I'm jealous that he gets to spend time with you without raising any eyebrows from that lot," he continued. "Given half the chance, I think he'd try it on."

"Nah, he wouldn't," I said, trying to suppress a laugh, but failing and puffing out a snort at the ludicrousness of his thoughts. "He's not into me like that, you're reading too much into it. We just have a laugh- normally at his expense."

Neil dropped the conversation, but my mind wondered what on earth he could see what I couldn't. I was genuinely shocked that he thought that Liam was attracted to me, as I had never had that feeling, and I had become somewhat of an expert in picking up on vibes.

For some reason, that evening felt tense. Not just the conversation about Liam, but Neil's mood on the whole. Our conversations weren't as natural and free-flowing as they normally were. We experienced a few pregnant pauses throughout our chat, and the atmosphere felt heavy and claustrophobic. I felt as though Neil had something else on his mind.

I sat and stared off into the middle distance, pretending to be interested in Anne on Apollo as they periodically crossed my vision in the school. I looked over to my right as I sensed Neil was brewing up to say something. He sat hunched forward towards the fence, with his elbows on his knees and a trail of silver smoke rising from the cigarette in his right hand. My mind wandered to the cigarette, and I became aware that the oppressive atmosphere had heightened my craving for a drag. Unfortunately, there were too many people walking about the farm for me to reach for it, so I forced myself to relinquish the urge. He sat back in the chair to mirror me, and I averted my gaze back to the school. As he breathed out a plume of smoke, he said that he had something to tell me, and I held my breath in anticipation. *Oh god, this is it, isn't it? He's going to call time on this. He doesn't want to take any more risks.*

"There's something you need to know," he paused, and my heart felt like it was falling to my feet.

I braced myself against the expectation of heartbreak, and the last few weeks played through my head like a reel of film. I was immediately sucked into a vacuum, the vortex flashing scenes of our past. The bile rose from the pit of my stomach as I awaited my fate. *I knew I wasn't going to be enough for him. I knew he couldn't do that to Anne.* The nausea enveloped me as I drew the connections between the Neil, Anne, and I triangle. The break in his speech felt as though it had lasted for hours rather than seconds, but as I anticipated that he was trying to cool things off between us, I didn't try to rush him along. I sat in silence, *please don't do this to me, please, please don't leave me.* He took another drag of his cigarette, and I wanted one even more as I prepared myself to receive a cataclysmic knockback. He moved his eyes to the floor as Anne trotted by us.

"I've been on medication for a while, and I've spoken to my doctor about it, and she thinks that the years of blood pressure tablets have given me erectile dysfunction," he whispered in one long breath, before putting the cigarette back to his mouth and drawing another huge drag.

Is that it? Is that what you've had me panicking over? Relief washed over me, and I had to do everything in my power to hold in a laugh as the torture left my body. My body readjusted back to normal. I had been so flustered at the thought that he was having second thoughts, that what he had just disclosed to me had gone right over my head. I didn't care if he had erectile dysfunction; I just didn't want him to leave me.

"I get four blue pills a month on prescription, which I don't think is enough, but it's all I can have."

I sat in silence, but I shifted in my seat so that I could rest my feet on the bottom of the fence as I bought myself time to think of what to say. The stress in my body was replaced by awkwardness. I didn't feel embarrassed, but I didn't know what to say. What could I say? I hadn't the experience to relate to what he was telling me, nor could I empathise with his situation. Although I felt awkward, I felt touched that he could talk to me about something that had clearly been a sensitive topic for him to approach.

I had an idea of what erectile dysfunction was, but obviously, I had no experience in the area. I thought it was the inability to get an erection, but I knew that this wasn't the case with Neil because I had felt *his* pressed into me enough times to recognise that getting hard wasn't a problem. I didn't want to ask, in case I looked stupid, but I didn't need to as he started to fill in the blanks. He told me that he could get an erection and that the urgency was there but that he had difficulty sustaining it for a length of time. I sat and nodded my head, engagingly, to try and show that I didn't care and wasn't remotely bothered by his impotence. I found it difficult to know what to say. I was just so relieved that he hadn't changed his mind about us, that I'd have accepted anything over that scenario. This was the first proper sexual-related discussion we had, other than the odd remark about eventually having sex, but it wouldn't be the last.

The following weekend we sat at the farm, taking shelter from the sun's beating rays. The air was sticky and the dust from the farm clung to my sweaty body, it made me feel grubby and disgusting. I sat on the floor of the horse trailer, pressing my bare back against the cool metallic surface in the hope that it would offer me some relief from the heat, but it was of little help. The wall heated up as soon as my back pressed against it. Neil sat to my ten o'clock, in the same manner, desperately trying to find a moment's relief from the blistering heat. He'd kicked his shoes off and sat cross-legged on the rubber matting. We were sat, comfortable with each other's silence. It was something I had long thought was overrated- a comfortable silence, but I was starting to appreciate it as time continued.

"What do you do when you get frustrated?" He asked, out of nowhere.

I sat there, bemused, for a second or two before the penny dropped. *Oh no. Please no, not this.* I felt my face pulsate with embarrassment and hoped that the heat and sunburn had rendered my cheeks red enough to hide my blushes. Like a rabbit caught in the headlights, I wracked my brain at warp speed, weighing up my options for escape. *Do I tell him? I can't tell him!* I didn't know whether to answer honestly or fall back into the teenage default of denial. He was asking me about sexual frustration and masturbation. Of course, I had experienced sexual frustration, I was a hormonal teenager involved in an illicit affair, but masturbation was a topic of shame, and I had never discussed it with anyone. I didn't want to tell him that I had masturbated, but I also didn't want to tell him that I hadn't. I didn't want him to think that I had lied to him or was such a little girl, that I didn't know what he was talking about. Instead, I opted to be truthful.

"Well, you know, sometimes… I relieve the pressure" I said shyly. Using the phrase 'relieve the pressure' distanced me from the shame.

"Masturbate?" He mouthed at me, his eyes popping out on stalks.

I felt embarrassed and wished for the ground to swallow me up. I'm not sure if he was hoping I would say it first or whether he was surprised that I had admitted it, but he was excited and adjusted himself accordingly. He was jittering about like a lid on a boiling saucepan. He couldn't contain himself at my revelation, though at the time, I did think that he was trying to lead me into saying it aloud. It felt like a bit of a test, whether I would be frank with him and say yes, or whether I would deny it and be embarrassed. Of course, I *was* embarrassed, but also, I was pleased that my answer made him horny. I got a lot out of pleasing him. I was glad that I turned him on. I was 14.

*

I had started going out towards the end of Summer. My first 'night out' was for Sara's sister-in-law's birthday. Sara was allowed to invite a friend to the private birthday party held in a nightclub, and she chose me to be her plus one for the night. It was my first experience of drinking and dancing in a club atmosphere, and it felt like a big deal, like a rite of passage into adulthood. I arranged the logistics of it all with my parents, and they were fine with it as long as I sent them a text when we got back to Sara's house after the party. It was a safe environment to pop our 'going out' cherries; the club was full of friends and acquaintances of Sara's family. We both drank way too much for our unaccustomed bodies, back in the day when we were lightweights and alcohol was cheap! We danced all night, and I had the best time.

I was on a high. I had successfully managed to pass as an adult (though, I suspect, the bartenders policed laws far less during a private event). I had experienced a double taste of being a 'grown-up', firstly Neil and now, going out. Sara and I had talked about the party at school, and shortly after, we arranged to go out again a few weeks later, but this time for my 15th Birthday.

My 15th Birthday arrived and the stark contrast between that and my previous birthday hadn't gone unnoticed by me. I'd spent the previous year at the cinema watching a family-friendly film with my parents and my little brother. But my 15th birthday had seen me turn into an adult- celebrating in the bars and nightclubs of the Big Town! *My birthdays are getting bigger each year*, I thought as I emptied all the clothes from Sara's wardrobe onto her bed along with several pairs of shoes for analysis. I had a vast shoe collection and I absolutely loved stilettos, so I nearly always supplied the shoes for non-uniform days at school. As I was only short, heels gave me confidence by adding an extra 4 or 5 inches of height. *If I look taller, I'll look older and we won't get asked for ID*. I picked out one of my own tops, Sara's denim skirt and a pinstriped suit jacket to keep my back covered. I wore my big curly hair down because Neil had complimented me on it so many times; *he loves it, it must make me look older*. We slapped on our makeup to hide our baby faces, slipped on our shoes, and hit the town.

We were out, drinking and dancing until our feet bled. It made me happy. I felt alive. It was liberating to forget everything for a short while; to forget Neil for a few hours. It allowed me to step outside my head for the night, to be carefree and blow off steam. I would flirt, dance, laugh, drink, and smoke, but it was something that didn't require secrecy. My only concern was the bouncers turning us away because we looked like children. It happened a couple of times that night, which was mortifying, but as we got drunker and drunker, the confidence oozed from us and we were let in without question.

*

By the end of the show season, Neil and I would talk on the phone for a couple of hours each day- generally during my lunch at school, but if I was at the farm, I would disappear off up to the fields. He always started the phone calls. He would 'drop call' off his house phone, and then I would ring him back on a withheld number so that Anne wouldn't suspect anything. I'd sit at the top of the fields or by the school if the workers were inside for lunch. He would say how much he missed me and that he couldn't wait to see me later in the evening. We would briefly talk about what we had done in the day, but I'd often be a bit vague about if it was a school day. I didn't like to discuss school much with him, so I didn't volunteer it in conversation. He often asked me what I was wearing because he wanted to picture me when we were on the phone. He said it's because he wanted to imagine being with me. He liked my uniform and confessed to having a fantasy of fucking me in it. I felt my face flush. I wanted to fulfil his fantasies. I wanted to please him in any way I could. I was flattered that he found me attractive in my uniform as I had always thought it had made me look frumpy. He would ask me what underwear I was wearing. He asked me not to wear knickers as he wanted to imagine me walking around the school without them. More often than not, I told him a white lie and let him think I wasn't wearing them; I didn't want to spoil his illusions, but I also didn't want my bits on display if a gust of wind took my skirt.

We had also met up away from the farm several times through winter. We would go back to Falmer's Woods and sit in the car and kiss and cuddle. We exploited the cover of winter, as the wind and rain usually kept the dog walkers at bay. He would fondle my breasts, both outside and inside my clothing. We would sit in the backseat of his 4x4, him to my right, behind the driver's seat. He would drape his left arm over me and slide his hand down under my top. He would stroke my genitals over the top of my trousers. He would kiss me passionately and with longing. I enjoyed feeling close to him. I enjoyed having his undivided attention. He was so attentive and gentle but touched me with such confidence and urgency. We had talked about sex, and Neil told me that he didn't want to have sex with me until I was 16 as he was worried it would get him 'in the shit'. I was OK with that. I was happy with the pace we were going at and didn't want to rush things any more than the lightning speed in which it had already gone.

I hadn't touched him by that point. I could tell he wanted me to. Although he hadn't asked me outright and I didn't have the confidence to instigate anything. I was worried that he'd suddenly develop a conscience and change his mind and tell me we had to stop. I was also worried that we'd get carried away and take things too far. He would pull me close to him so that I could feel his genitals pressed up against me, but although I never pushed him away, I never reached to touch him. If he had wanted me to, he would have had to ask or physically guide my hand. He hadn't by that point.

On school days, I would scurry down to the farm to be with Neil as soon as I could. We would sit and talk for the entire evening. He started to invite me up back to his house for a 'brew' once we'd finished at the farm. I think a few comments had been made about the amount of alone time we had down on the farm, so Neil thought it would be less obvious if everyone thought Anne was with us. I don't know if Anne had said anything to him, but our long solitude evenings were replaced by the three of us going back to their house once Anne had finished. We'd either bundle into her car or follow Anne back on foot.

Neil had 'his space' on the settee. I'm not sure if Anne had her own space or not. It was hard to tell whether I had taken it, or if she was more of a floater. A small 2-seater settee sat under the window, perpendicular to the one Neil and I were on; that is where Anne would sit. Neil always sat in the middle of 'our settee', directly in front of the TV. It was logical that we'd sit together. We were both smokers, and Anne wasn't, so it wasn't as though it would have raised suspicion that we were sat side by side because we shared an ashtray. Anne, Julie, Liam and Neil were the only ones I'd smoke around, except Cleo and Rebekah. We were friends, and they knew that Marilyn or my parents couldn't know. Anne would make drinks, and Neil would put music on. Most of the time, Anne would be pottering around doing odd jobs in the house, whilst Neil and I would sit there, listening to music and dropping our voices if the conversation became a bit risqué. Sometimes I'd eat with them, or sometimes I'd go home before they ate. It was all very casual and relaxed, and when all said and done, it did us a favour, as it gave us many more hours together. For the next couple of years, that set-up continued. I'd be invited up every evening by Neil to sit and talk, whilst Anne hovered about, nipping in and out of the room occasionally.

CHAPTER 5

Christmas 2004 came and went. I hated every minute of it. I only saw Neil every other day because the holiday had messed up everyone's routine. Anne was off work, as was my family, and the spontaneity of my parents meant that my days were thrown off-kilter. I couldn't even talk to Neil much because he didn't know how long Anne would be out, so he didn't want to risk her reappearing unannounced. I missed him. *What is he doing right now? Is he feeling the same way I do? Is he thinking about me right now?*

It's not that I didn't love my family. I loved them dearly. I hardly ever got to see much of them the rest of the year. Christmas was a time for family, a time for togetherness, but I just couldn't shake off the feeling of isolation. *I feel so alone, nobody understands me the way Neil does. Should I try ringing him? No, I can't. Everything will go to shit if I get caught.*

I felt lonely, despite being surrounded by the people I loved. I felt myself grappling with a sense of guilt because I couldn't enjoy my time with them. I just couldn't wait to get back into more of a routine. I couldn't wait to be able to talk to Neil freely. Christmas day was the worst day of them all and I spent Christmas day sitting at the table, wishing Neil was there with me. It was depressing.

I didn't do anything for New Year's Eve, but I spent New Year's Day with Rebekah. We did the farm jobs and we walked up to her house in the evening. Marilyn had bought me a bottle of Baileys for Christmas because I had once mentioned that I loved it in hot chocolate. I just wanted to get out of my head for a while. I want the feelings to stop. I wanted a few hours where I couldn't feel anything. I felt so overwhelmed, so out of control, such a massive disappointment. Such a whore.

I needed Neil so badly that my body ached from the constant turmoil in my mind. *He'll make it stop, he always makes it stop. The only time I ever feel like this is when he's not there.* I needed an out. I needed to pause the merry-go-round and take a break from the reality I had found myself in. I needed to get drunk. *That always works.*

I drank the whole bottle that evening, the creamy pungent alcohol coated my stomach like a cloth. It replaced the void in my body, dulled the pain, and masked the loneliness. It was the first time I had been drunk to the point of vomiting, so it came as a bit of a surprise when I hurled my guts up through Rebekah's bedroom window onto the bay window below. The whole time, I thought about walking up the road to his house to see him. *It's not far, literally 200 yards. He might even walk past with the dogs. Let's go out. What's the worst that could happen?* But, even in my most inebriated state, I couldn't convince myself that it would all be ok. Even at the drunkest that I had ever been, I couldn't truly let loose and throw caution to the wind. Even during the time when I thought I had no impulse control, my brain wouldn't switch off. I still had a battle between good and evil playing out in my head. It was exhausting.

A couple of days later, standard service resumed, and the black cloud lifted. I was back at school and Anne was back at work, so like clockwork, Neil's number appeared on my phone during lunchtime. We weren't supposed to take our phones into school during years 7 to 11, so I had to disappear out of sight to ring him back. We spoke for the whole of lunch, which, again, wasn't unusual at that point. We both said how difficult Christmas had been. Neil had started explaining that things between him and Anne had been strained.

"She's all picture, no sound," he said one afternoon. "She's there all the time, but she's never there. She comes home and falls asleep in front of the TV and I don't get a minute's distraction from you."

So, she doesn't want him, but has him. I want him and can't have him. Woah, Tanya, get a grip. She's your friend! A pang of guilt wound like a vine around my chest. *Don't think badly of her.* I wanted to say to Neil. *Wait? Why am I defending her? What's wrong with me?* I was so confused by my feelings. *Am I supposed to hate her? I don't hate her, I like her, I think? But why do I feel jealous of her? Does she know something is going on? Has she heard the gossip at the farm? Is she giving him the cold shoulder?* My blood ran cold at the thought. *I don't think she suspects anything; she's been fine with me.* Neil hadn't told me that anything had been said, so we were probably in the clear. It was the first time he had moaned about her and it left me feeling uneasy. I didn't say anything but moved the conversation on to lighten the mood.

*

We carried on as expected over the next few months. We spent every possible moment with each other and talking on the phone whenever possible. We met up several times for the usual kiss and fumble. We would sneak from the side of the school if nobody was around and go into the barn for a cuddle, kiss and a grope. It was exhilarating. Neil made it feel romantic, *stolen moments* between us. We went out with Julie and Liam over the winter. Anne and Julie would ride their horses, and Neil, Liam and I would take an alternative scenic route on foot. We'd smoke, flirt, and joke in front of Liam, and Liam was utterly oblivious.

We shared private jokes that Liam didn't understand, his quizzical expression regularly revealed his confusion. We were spending so much time together; it was as though we were an extension of each other. People expected us to come as a pair. There was quite a bit of gossip going on at the farm about it, that I had come to find out about from Cleo and Rebekah. Cleo had started coming out with Sara and me, so as soon as she'd had a few drinks, she'd bring it up.

"Everyone wonders what you are getting up to when you walk off alone, you know?" She'd slur her words together as though speaking in cursive.

Cleo had insider knowledge on the gossip at the farm because her older sister had started working down there. *Do not say anything. Do not trust her Tanya, she'll tell them.* I didn't offer anything in return, but just shrugged my shoulders. *She's just fishing* I told myself. Nobody knows, somebody would have said something.

Cleo, Rebekah and I were starting to fall out at the farm quite a bit. They thought I was getting ahead of myself, *constantly hanging around with the adults, pretending to be better than them.* I thought Cleo would use the information about me as a weapon, so even after I'd had quite a bit to drink, I knew I had to keep my secret safe. Sara had noticed, though. Even without Cleo's interference. She would see me looking longingly at my phone and noticed that I had withdrawn on our nights out. She knew that my mind had taken me elsewhere. Even when we were both blind drunk, Sara could see that I had someone on my mind. I couldn't keep it to myself any longer, I needed to tell someone, so I told her that I had been seeing somebody, a married man, but I was intentionally sketchy about the details.

*

At the end of what seemed like a very long winter, I started going to shows again. Sometimes it would be just CJ and Marilyn, sometimes it would be a whole entourage consisting of Neil, Anne, Julie, Liam, and my family. Sometimes I'd go alone with Julie and Liam, Anne and Neil. After one show as the fivesome, Neil, Anne, Julie, Liam and I arrived back to the farm and began unloading everything. I was completing my odd jobs and had just finished emptying a wheelbarrow when Neil walked up to me.

"You should listen out for a song," he said. "You're beautiful, by James Blunt."

He clutched his hand to his chest like it had struck a chord with him and insisted that I should listen to it too. I assured him I would, and when I got home that night. I did just that. I found it on LimeWire, and it broke me as the lyrics flowed. I sat in the bath for over an hour, listening to it on repeat, sobbing my heart out. *I'll never be with you... What does that mean? I thought we were going somewhere, I thought we were just waiting until I turned 16. He doesn't want me. Is he walking away? I can't be without him. I can't live without him. He is everything. He said everything would change when the law didn't stand between us. I'm the one he wants; he says it all the time.*

The song devastated me. All that time, all those feelings, all those promises that things would change when I was 16, and I felt as though he had burned them down. *Was he having second thoughts? Was it not going anywhere?* I had been told that things would change once I was 16, not just the sex but the commitment. I would be legal, and we could be together. *Is that song his way of telling me things aren't going any further? Are things coming to an end?* It was the first time that Neil pulled the rug out from under my feet. The water rose in the bath, pulling me under, suffocating me, drowning me. Nothing made sense. I felt black, hollow, crushed, broken.

As I lay in bed, the lyrics etched in my head. The words cut deep into my brain- bloody, gory, fatal. It felt like someone was sitting on my chest. I couldn't swallow air; I couldn't fill my lungs. I was pulverised. It was my first heartbreak. I couldn't function in class the following day. I didn't even pretend to know what was going on around me. None of it was important. *Nothing else matters if I can't have Neil.* He rang me at lunchtime, bright and chipper.

"Did you listen to it? What did you think? It's good isn't it?" He asked, cheerily.

"Umm, yeah it's good," I responded. *Please don't say anything else, please, I'm begging you.*

Neil mentioned nothing else about the song and moved the conversation on. I felt as though I'd dodged a bullet. I was relieved, and by the end of the conversation, I had perked right up. *Things are OK between us. Life will continue. We just have to wait until my 16th birthday, and then everything will work out for us.* There were just a few months left.

A couple of weeks later, the five of us went to another show. It was a local show, and Neil had been able to park his car at base camp. It was a sweltering day, and as I wasn't riding, I didn't need to wear horsey clothes. Instead, I dressed to keep his attention, donning a black rara skirt and a white button-up, sleeveless blouse. The skirt was very short and complemented my dancer's legs. The weather provided me with the opportunity to flash a little flesh without looking desperate. Thankfully the gamble paid off as there were plenty of people at the show in denim hotpants and vest tops, so I didn't look out of place.

Anne and Liam went to watch Julie in her class, and I stayed in the open boot of Neil's 4x4. The both of us were trying to keep from crisping up in the sun. Neil had removed the rear seats of the boot, so there was plenty of room. We comfortably sat together without looking too suspicious and there was plenty of room to stretch out. I was sitting right at the back of the boot and leant on the interior wall of the car with my hands propping me up as my legs stretched out in front of me. Neil sat further forward, facing me, with his back against the rear passenger door and his legs crossed like a schoolboy. We shared a cigarette.

"Nice skirt," he said, and raised his eyebrows as I leant forward to pass the cigarette back to him.

"Ha, thanks. It's got built-in pants!" I bragged to hide my blushes, flattening the skirt over the front of my thighs.

He readjusted his crotch, wincing, and appeared uncomfortable. I trusted that to mean he had got an erection.

"Give me a look."

Oh, no. I wanted him to wonder, not actually see. I wracked my brain. Is *there any way I can get out of this?*

I felt uncomfortable and vulnerable, but there wasn't an escape route without looking like a frigid little girl. *Ok, fine, what's the worst that could happen? Just a brief flash and he'll be satisfied.* I pulled my legs up towards my chest and parted them a few centimetres, just enough for him to get a glimpse of the built-in black pants before I closed them again. I felt shy and exposed, but I didn't want him to see that. He let out a whine, and I knew he was aroused. He bit his bottom lip when he became aroused. That much I had come to learn over the past year. With that, he twisted around and opened the passenger door and got out of the car. *Was that a mistake? Should I not have done it? Where's he going? I've frightened him off.* I couldn't work out why he was walking around the front of the car, until he walked all the way around and appeared at the back where I sat, my knees up as he had left me. He lifted the boot's tailgate and the snap of the metal jolted through me.

What's he doing? I don't understand. He slid his left hand below the level of the tailgate and under my left leg, stroking my vagina through my pants. *No please stop,* I wanted to ask. He pushed his middle finger under the edge of the seam. *No, no, no, please, I'm not ready. He's going to touch me. Please don't. Someone will see.* He slowly pushed into my vagina, letting a groan out as he did so. *Oh god no, please, no.* I sat there in silence, *what do I do? What do I do?* I had frozen to the spot, unable to verbalise anything, unable to move, unable to breathe. My head flashed back to the feelings I had the first time he kissed me. How detached, and uninvolved I felt. How my body got up and walked off without me, and looked at me disapprovingly from a distance. *But I want him to want me, and this shows that he wants me, and I've let him want me.*

The whole experience lasted seconds, just 10 seconds if that. Neil pulled his finger out of me, lowered the tailgate, and moved away from the rear of the vehicle, disappearing from my sight. *What on earth was that? Did that just happen?* I sat there for a couple of minutes unable to move, unable to process every emotion that I had felt. The sounds of Anne and Liam talking snapped me out of it. Their voices getting louder and louder as they returned to our base camp. My head was all over the place. *Can they tell? Relax your face, they'll see it.* I thought a secret as big as this would have been obvious. I felt as though it was written in big, bold letters above my head. I got out of the car looked up, accidentally making eye contact with Neil when he stuck the middle finger of his left hand in his mouth. *Urgh.* My insides fluttered, partly with disgust, partly with excitement. His finger had been inside my vagina just moments before, so my response seemed reasonable.

*

A few weeks passed, and I was undertaking work experience on the farm. It was early July 2005. I remember the events vividly, as it was the week of the London bombings and the week in which CJ has his life-changing accident. We watched the aftermath of the bombings on the TV during breakfast in the farmhouse. It was horrific, and everyone was talking about it as it unfurled. I didn't appreciate just how big of a deal it was at the time; I was young, and it didn't grip me like the adult workers. We did the morning mucking out and turned the horses out as quickly as possible as it was a Thursday. We collected the shavings from the city on a Thursday. All the workers, me included, bundled into the double cab of the farm lorry. The radio was on, but the continual updates from London replaced the usual music. We sat in silence during the journey there and back, the atmosphere was sombre.

Once we arrived back at the farm, we quietly continued with the day's jobs. We tidied the yard, and then we moved on to the bed-down routine. Unfortunately, this occurred at a similar time to Neil's arrival, so it ate into our time, but we sat together once I'd finished and spoke about the events in London. We disappeared into Anne's stable to hold each other in silence.

The following day, after finishing the work experience for the day, I had to bathe CJ as he was a guest at a wedding on Saturday. Marilyn's colleague and friend (and thus my friend) was marrying her soul mate. Since being a little girl, she'd had an enormous horse interest but had never had one of her own. Once we got CJ, she came down to ride him every couple of weeks, and spoiled him rotten with a bag of veg each time. She loved him, so when she organised her big day, she asked if CJ would go to the wedding and have his pictures taken with her. Liam was the photographer for the day, so it was a perfect fit that the photographer was familiar with horses and knew how to get the most out of the pictures.

I spent the evening bathing and plaiting CJ's mane, preparing for his centre stage appearance at Daniella's wedding. It took me hours to plait him, as I was still inexperienced. Marilyn had arranged for Geraldine and Samantha to take CJ to the wedding, as Marilyn and I were guests. Geraldine's offer meant we wouldn't have to rush around in the morning, and we could concentrate on getting ourselves ready. The wedding took place at a grand hotel on the edge of the National Park. We had asked Geraldine to drive the lorry to the car park so Daniella and her new husband would be able to come outside after the ceremony and have their photos taken.

The morning of the wedding arrived, and Marilyn and I made our way to the hotel. As the ceremony ended and the wedding guests made their way outside for drinks, Geraldine came rushing in to find us. She was completely ashen faced. She told us that CJ had spooked in the car park and had stepped back into the edge of the lorry ramp, cutting the back of his rear leg on the sharp edge. I hadn't appreciated how bad the prognosis looked at the time. However, Geraldine was very experienced and knew the location of the injury could be devastating to CJ.

Geraldine and Samantha loaded CJ into the lorry and rushed him off to our local veterinary practice whilst Marilyn and I flapped about, hanging back just long enough to feature on a couple of photos. As we rushed home to CJ, the phone rang.

"Hello," I tentatively answered.

"Tanya, it's Geraldine," I didn't get the chance to draw a breath before she continued. "CJ has been referred to the hospital in Newmarket. The vet thinks it's his best opportunity. He needs to be under specialist care. You need to take him tonight, the vet on-call is expecting him there as soon as possible."

I relayed the message to Marilyn frantically.

"Ask Geraldine where they are now, and we will meet them in our lorry."

"They're at Margaret's practice," I responded and diverted back to Geraldine on the phone. "We are heading back now and will collect our lorry. We'll be with you in about half an hour." I paused for a second, listening to a three-way conversation, but not absorbing any of the information. "OK, we'll see you soon. Bye. Bye." I hung up the phone.

We arrived at the local vet practice within an hour, after madly rushing around, trying to make sure we hadn't forgotten anything. *Phone. Purse. Keys. Yep. Ok. Let's go.* CJ was heavily sedated and required the vet's help getting loaded into the lorry. The journey down to Newmarket took about 3 hours in a car, so it would be a considerable while longer until we could get CJ to the specialist. Whilst at the local vet, Geraldine and Samantha had offered to come with us on the journey in case something happened in transit. As we knew it would be a long night, having an extra driver was a wise decision, as the round trip would take well over 10 hours.

Our lorry was a 7.5t Ford, with a separate cab and lorry body. The lorry's body contained living quarters with a sink, oven, hob, table, and a fitted leatherette bench that backed onto the vehicle's front. It wasn't a cut through the cab, so the living and horse parts were in a separate box, loaded onto the lorry axle. Geraldine and Marilyn sat in the cab, and Samantha and I sat in the living, with the door between the living and the horse open so we could see CJ. The vet had heavily sedated him as he was in so much pain that his fight or flight response was too heightened for us to handle him safely. The journey was long, and we were well into the dark hours of the summer night.

We arrived at the veterinary hospital at about 11 p.m., and the on-call vet saw us quickly. Our local vet had already x-rayed and scanned CJ and forwarded her investigations to the hospital. The damage was worse than we thought. The outlook was bleak, and we were told, the best outcome was that CJ's ridden career was over and he would have to remain a companion horse. The examination hadn't convinced the vet that CJ would even achieve that level of soundness and advised us that euthanasia was probably the best choice. We vowed to give CJ a fighting chance at a recovery and opted for surgery. With that, we left him in the expert hands and drove back up to home through the night eventually arriving at Marilyn's house about 4 a.m.

*

Marilyn and I had a huge row the following morning. I had arranged to go to a show with Julie and Liam before CJ had his accident, and I had no intention of missing it. Marilyn was devastated by CJ's accident and wanted me to stay with her, but I was adamant that I would cope better with the distractions of a show *where Neil would be,* though I refrained from saying that out loud. She was gutted that I wanted to be with my friends and not with her but took me to the farm, regardless.

The usual five of us made our way to the show. Julie and Liam had warned Anne and Neil so, they were aware that I would likely be upset. We parked up at the show and went through the usual routine. I had helped get the horse ready, and Julie went off to her class, with Anne and Liam in tow. I stayed back with Neil. We sat in the car, Neil in the front and me in the rear seat. He asked me if I wanted him to sit with me. I did. *What took you so long to ask?*

"If anyone says anything, I'll just say you were upset over yesterday," he said.

I scooted over to let him in. He put his arm around me and hugged me, lifting away all my sadness in the process. He was like a warm comfort blanket and immediately made all my worries disappear. He had that effect on me. He made me feel safe and loved, even though there were times when he made me feel exposed and vulnerable. He kissed me, slid his tongue into my mouth, and held me tight. When he pulled back, he looked partly alarmed and partly thrilled. Immediately to our left, something we had failed to consider, was a horse lorry. It wasn't anybody we knew, but their living window was positioned right above our window, where we had just been kissing. He was concerned that we had just been seen and sat facing forward, looking 'proper'. He was equally elated by the risk and also shitting himself as it had the potential to blow up in his face. I didn't care.

The five of us drove home later in the day. Nothing had arisen from the possibly viewed kiss, so we were in the clear. I was sat in the back seat with Julie and Anne. I rested my head on the seatbelt as I hovered in that blissful place between asleep and awake when I became aware of the conversation around me.

"Partners in crime, these two." I heard Julie say. "Both fast asleep."

She was right. We were partners in crime. Soulmates. I smiled internally.

*

I was still on work experience down at the farm the following week. I was finishing up the jobs when Neil arrived. Marilyn, Dad, and I were going to visit CJ at the weekend, and I had planned to ask Neil if he wanted to come with us. Of course, he jumped at the chance. Anne would be working on the farm on Saturday, so at least it *'would get him out of the house'* whilst waiting for her to finish work.

The following day we drove to the veterinary hospital in Marilyn's car. She and my dad were sitting in the front whilst Neil and I occupied the back seat. Before we left Marilyn's house to pick the others up, I wrote 'I love you' on a small piece of paper that I had planned to give to Neil at some point in the day. We had already told each other we loved each other plenty of times, so this wasn't something new, but it would provide us with a private moment when we couldn't say it aloud.

When we got to the hospital, we went in search of CJ's stable. I opened his door and buried my face in his neck. His familiar smell warmed my nostrils and replaced the clinical odour of the hospital. Dad and Marilyn went off to find the vet for an update on his condition, whilst Neil and I stayed with the him. I came out of the stable once CJ had finished his pack of mints and sat next to Neil on a bale of bedding that had been left outside.

"I love you," he said.

"I love you too," I smiled at him.

"It's been feeling one-sided lately."

What? Where has this come from? My heart plummeted to my feet. *What have I done wrong? I'm always telling him I love him. I'm always flirting with him. I'm with him all the time, how can he say that it's one way? I even arranged for us to spend today together. Granted my dad and Marilyn are here, but I'd have been coming down anyway, even if I hadn't invited Neil.*

I felt hurt.

"What? No," I pleaded, "I don't understand. It's two way. I don't know what I've done to make you think it's not."

I'd still got the piece of paper in my inner jodhpur pocket, but it didn't feel like the right time to give it to him, especially once he stone-walled me. His comment stung like a hornet. I felt like I had done something wrong, but I couldn't understand what I'd done.

I waited until we were back in the car before giving it to him. He looked down as I discreetly slid it into his hand out of the view of dad and Marilyn. He looked down at it and smiled. It was reassurance for the both of us.

Tanya Pursglove

CHAPTER 6

A week later, CJ was due to come home from the vet. We knew that he would require strict rest when he got home and he would have to go back for follow-up scans at a later date, but I couldn't wait to get him home. It had been arranged that Dad and Marilyn would share the driving, and I would sit in the back of the lorry to keep an eye on CJ. I'm not sure whether it was my idea or not, but I told to Marilyn that I had invited Neil along to keep me company. She hesitated. *What was her problem? It was fine for Samantha to travel in the back with me, what has she got against Neil doing the same?* Eventually, after I threw a tantrum she conceded, so, we picked Neil up and headed on the long journey down to Newmarket.

Neil was ecstatic about being alone with me in the back of the lorry. As soon as we pulled away and were out of spying eyes, he started kissing and touching me. His hands ran over the top of my clothes unable to contain his excitement of being completely isolated.

"I want to make you come," he said.

I experienced a plethora of emotions. Nervous excitement, hesitancy, wanting. My feelings were all over the place. *It will make him happy and you might even enjoy it,* I told myself.

"Take these down," he tugged at the waistband of my jeans and I reluctantly did as he asked.

Just be confident. It will be fine. Your nerves will go, and it will all be ok. He pushed his right hand between my legs and slid his middle finger straight into my vagina.

"You are so wet and tight," he took a sharp intake of breath.

Ouch! Relax Tanya, relax. I felt my body become heavy. *Ok, that's better, that doesn't hurt. It feels ok. Just don't tense. If you don't tense, it won't hurt.* Neil kept pumping away inside of me. It didn't hurt anymore, but I knew there was zero chance of an orgasm. I wasn't even close. *What is wrong with me?*

I didn't have the heart or confidence to tell him it wasn't going to work. *What if I offend him? He really wants to get me there, and I'm letting him down.* We'd periodically stop to smoke and get our breath back before starting again. Neil wanted to look at me, so he undid the buttons on my sleeveless blouse so he could look at my breasts as he fingered me. Whilst we were on a cigarette break, he asked me to sit there with my top open for him so he could 'take it all in'. I felt awkward; exposed. I was on display and vulnerable. I didn't feel sexy; I felt ogled at, but I didn't have it in me to tell him no. *He wants this, the least you could do is let him look at you.*

"Hang on," I said. "What's happening?"

I felt the lorry pull off the main road and onto a slower side road. I couldn't see a great deal in the back of the lorry as there was only one small window that overlooked the offside of the road. I got up and pulled up my trousers up from around my thighs. I leant over the sink to look out of the side window as I did up the buttons on my blouse. The lorry pulled to a stop and the reversing beeper kicked in as I realised that we had pulled into a service station. As soon as the engine died, Neil opened the jockey door and I climbed out.

"I need the loo," Marilyn said as she stepped down from the cab.

The four of us got out of the lorry and walked over to the service station. It was further than expected as we had to park in the lorry part of the services. I felt swollen and slippery between my legs. I walked behind the others, and as I did, I loosened the crotch of my trousers as I was worried a wet patch would show through. Also, I was paranoid that they would smell the cigarettes on me, so

I popped in a couple of mentholated chewing gum and began crushing through the coating, in a vain attempt to disguise the smell. *Of course, they'll smell it on my skin, it's no secret that Neil smokes. Just hide your breath.*

Once we returned to the lorry, Neil and I got in the back again. We still had an hour left before reaching the vet, so there was still plenty of time together. We knew it would have been a while before we got that kind of opportunity again, so Neil wanted to make the most of it. Given that we were travelling at 50 miles per hour down the main road we were the most secluded that we'd ever been. There was no chance of someone coming up and banging on the window, or at least we had plenty of warning before someone could open the door.

Once we were back inside and felt the lorry pulling away, Neil asked me to lower my trousers again. It wasn't quite as slippery this time, and I started to get sore with his constant plunging.

"Sit up here," he patted the table in front of the bench.

It was a small rectangular table, so I had to lie down diagonally across its cold surface, with my trousers around my ankles and my knees on either side of one of the corners. He let out a dirty groan as I lay back, and he pushed his face into my vagina. *What the fuck? No, no. Please stop. I don't want this.* I wasn't expecting it, but the moistness of his mouth made a change to being pumped with his fingers. He used his tongue to try and make me climax, alternating every few minutes with his finger and using his free hand to reach up the table to my breasts. I couldn't focus. *What if they find out? They are literally three feet away from us, separated by two thin walls. No, please don't, please stop.* My body was limp, my shoulder blades pushed into the cold hard table. My head teetered on the lip around the edge, it was painful. There was too much to concentrate on. I knew it wasn't going to happen. There were too many thoughts moving through my head, and his technique wasn't touching the helpful spot. Although more pleasant than being pounded, it was another fruitless attempt. and I felt so disappointed that my body hadn't worked for him. *What is wrong with me?*

We arrived at the veterinary hospital and took our instructions about CJ's care before we loaded him up for the journey home. My dad had said he would travel in the back with me on the way home. I was partly disappointed, partly relieved; at least I would get a bit of a break. I was sitting with my iPod headphones in and contemplated why my body had failed me. *I don't struggle to climax on my own, and I want to for Neil, but it just won't happen.*

We weren't on the road for an hour before we had to fill up the tank, so Neil used the chance to jump in the back again. My dad was a rubbish passenger, and so he wasn't disappointed to get back into the cab of the lorry. It was preferable to travelling backwards or being unable to see the road ahead. Neil got into the back and asked me to undress again. *Again?* This time he had me lie back on the bench. My skin stuck to the leatherette and the unforgiving bench offering little cushion to allow for the natural curve of my back. He didn't pause before pushing his finger deep inside me. I was dry and it hurt. He pumped and pumped at my vagina, trying to get me there, but it was no use. I was too sore, too dry, and too despondent at my failing body. He became increasingly frustrated and his face couldn't hide it. Another finger, another finger. *No stop, please, I don't like this.* I blinked rapidly to disguise the tears in my eyes. *Just relax like the last time, it will stop hurting if you just relax.*

I thought I might tear. My perineum stung from the eye-watering stretch. I flopped. I disappeared into a trance and left. My mind was black, void of anything. My body heavy and unresponsive lay there as he continued to pump me. I drifted between complete absence of thought and total focus on my burning vagina. He eventually recognised that I had gone elsewhere.

"Do you want me to stop?" He asked.

"Yes." I was surprised that I'd said it. I wasn't sure I'd be able to verbalise anything.

He patted my knee, obviously exasperated, and admitted defeat.

"I'm sorry, I'm too distracted," I apologised.

I sat up and hitched my trousers. As I repositioned myself next to him, a deep exhale of breath escaped my lungs. I wasn't prepared for it, and the noise was audible, as I scooted my bottom on the bench. I felt bruised, marred. I was too dry. Even sitting on my vagina felt like I had been filled with sand. My body felt broken. I felt broken. *Why? Why can't I just do this for him?*

He asked me to touch him and opened his dark green trousers and exposed his penis. It was semi-erect, so I wrapped my right hand around it as I sat to his left, he was touching me the whole time, but I was just pleased he was no longer inside me. My shirt was still open, and my bra was still on display, so he moved his hands up to grope at my breasts as I held, motionless, his semi-erect penis. We were like that for a few minutes as he groped at me, burying his face into my neck.

"Will you pose for me?" He asked.

I shook my head. I didn't want him looking at me, I felt a let-down. I'd let him down. I wanted out of the lorry and wanted to be in the security of my own bed. I was tired, sore and just wanted to be on my own. Nobody had ever asked me to pose for them. The whole idea gave me chills and the hairs on the back of my neck stood on edge.

"You probably don't feel sexy anymore, do you?" He asked.

I had confidence, but not to that degree. It would have felt forced and unnatural. Thankfully, Neil accepted my reluctance and slumped back in the chair. He was right; it was like he read my mind. What I didn't tell him is that bodily fluids made me feel sick. I hadn't seen semen by that point except for the fake semen scene in Something About Mary. I remember feeling nauseous at the thought of being exposed to it, but I couldn't tell him. He would think I was frigid and childish. So, when he suggested that I probably didn't feel sexy anymore, I saw my opportunity and jumped on it. We both redressed and sat listening to my iPod for the remainder of the journey.

*

After the 'lorry incident,' the fundamental dynamics of our relationship changed. It became almost entirely sexually motivated. Virtually every time we saw each other, there would be some degree of sexual contact and activity, often multiple times throughout our time together. We hadn't had full sexual intercourse and didn't for a few more months but that didn't stop him using alternative means of exploring my genitals.

During the remainder of summer 2005, after the lorry incident, Neil had started working on Marilyn's garden. I still don't know how he managed to pull that one-off, but I suspect it was Marilyn's way of helping a bored bloke out, cash in hand. Luckily for us, it enabled him to spend more time with me. I was delighted as Marilyn lived about 200m from my family home, so I could walk up there to see him whilst he was 'gardening' and Marilyn was at work. I was off school for the summer holidays, so I had an unlimited number of hours to fill before I could see him otherwise, so naturally, I jumped at the chance when he rang me to tell me he was heading over to her house. I walked up the road in a denim miniskirt and a pair of wedges that I'd owned for a few years. They were too small but had an open toe, so they forgave my growing feet. I got up to Marilyn's house and was greeted by Neil at the end of her garden, gesturing towards her shed.

The term 'shed' is an understatement. It was large, probably 12ft by 10ft, and in true Marilyn style, it was kept immaculate. Everything had its place, and a large part of the floor was empty, so there was plenty of room to sit. Marilyn kept it padlocked, but as Neil was there gardening, she left it unlocked. Neil got out two garden chairs inside the shed and set them up in the middle of the floor. He positioned the green and cream, striped chairs, with one facing the door and the other just to the side, shielded from view. Neil chose the chair that gave him a good view of the outside, and I sat in the other. We were talking and flirting until my phone rang. It was Marilyn. I answered the phone and played oblivious when she said that Neil was working on her garden.

Meanwhile, upon hearing that Marilyn was at the end of the phone, Neil leaned forward and slid his hand up my inner thigh into my knickers, where his fingers found their way into my vagina. It had been made clear by that point that he got off on the danger and risk associated with doing naughty things when other people were nearby. That wasn't the first time. Previously, we had walked down the neighbouring track to the farm, and a similar incident had occurred where my phone had rung, and he was straight in my knickers. One of those times, we followed Anne on Apollo, and Neil took the advantage of a bend in the path to put his hands down the front of my trousers.

Neil was trying to get me off whilst I spoke Marilyn. I knew it wasn't going to happen for a couple of reasons. Firstly, I was on the phone with Marilyn, and my brain was certainly not going to allow that to happen. *Weird.* Additionally, I'd realise that his skill was less than adequate as there were zero stimuli to my external genitals. I feigned enjoyment as I knew that would please him, and although not unpleasant, I was about as close to coming as Christmas in July. After the phone conversation, he continued to try and get me off. Over the previous weeks, I worked out how to get him to stop, so I faked an orgasm just before I got sore. I had got good at that. He never questioned whether I did or not. Though, thinking back, it was about as obvious as the café scene in When Harry Met Sally, but it meant that he would stop for a few minutes, so I took that to mean that he believed it.

He noticed when I was on the phone that I was wearing white pants. They were plain white cotton. Not quite Bridget Jones' but just plain white cotton briefs. They turned him on. *Why?* I thought. They weren't remotely sexy, but I hadn't put them on thinking that we would have sex. I had thought we would be out in the garden and I had forgotten about the shed when I got dressed that morning. He asked to see them and gestured to me to stand up behind the door. I obliged and stood, lifting my skirt to my waist, and turned my back to him so he could see my bum. I felt admired. I felt adored. Even in these plain white, ugly knickers, he still wanted me. It made me feel sexy and desired.

He told me he had Viagra in the car, and he wanted to have sex. I was taken aback as he'd maintained to that point that he didn't want to have sex with me until I was 16. *What? No!* I didn't want to, but I didn't want to look nervous. I also didn't want our first time to be on the floor of a shed. I wanted romance and a gradual progression throughout an evening, not a dirty romp on the floor. I said it was too risky and tried to navigate my way out of the situation without looking frigid.

"Oh come on Tan," he begged.

"No, someone will come, it's too risky."

He sulked for a bit but eventually relented, so I made excuses to get out of the shed. I didn't feel unsafe. I didn't think he would force himself on me. Instead, I felt bad. I felt guilty that I had said no to him. He had been patient up to that point and had held out for over a year, but *I* had decided that it wasn't the right time. I was also disappointed. Not because I wanted to have sex with him, but I was disappointed that he didn't want our first time to be anything more than a shag in a cobwebby shed in my aunt's garden. I felt like a tease, not the flirty fun kind of tease, but I was left with burning guilt and shame. He thought he'd made me climax all these times, and I felt guilty that he wouldn't be getting it in return. It left me feeling uneasy and cruel, but regardless, I did not want our first time to be on the *FLOOR OF A SHED.*

The hours passed without incident or more pressure to have sex. We were in and out of the shed. Smoking and fingering, fingering and faking, followed by a bit of weeding and tidying in the garden. One of the times we were in the shed, he asked me if he could put his toes in my vagina. *No way! Urgh! Feet!* Again, I declined. I did not want sweaty dust feet anywhere near me, never mind inside me. *Why would I want to do that?* Again, I said no. He asked why I explained that the idea of feet in my foof didn't do anything for me. He dropped the subject, then our cycle of weeding, smoking and fingering - and faking - resumed until it was time for me to walk back home for a lift to the farm.

*

Anne, Julie, Liam, Neil and I had come back from one of the country shows after a long day in the beating sun. The sun had been glorious and Julie had won her class, so she had come back to the farm on cloud nine. She wasn't much of an optimist, and seemed to like beating herself up, so it was lovely to see her excited for a win.

"Are you coming back to ours then?" She asked me.

"Yep, got nothing else planned," I replied.

"Goody, we'll get a few cans out then."

"Beer party? I'm game!" Neil interrupted, inviting himself up, though the invitation would likely have been extended to him and Anne anyway. Julie, Liam, Anne and Neil had been a foursome long before I got involved.

We made our way up after I checked that CJ was set for the afternoon. I bundled into Anne's car with her and Neil, and we walked a few houses up to Julie and Liam's place. Liam had been working in the garden, creating a beautiful, natural-looking, but tidy landscape to photograph any birds and insects that visited his home. We pottered around the garden, and he showed me the plants he had put in or relocated to give it an aesthetically pleasing, groomed finish.

Once he had finished the tour, I made my way to the bench and sat next to Neil. He passed me a cigarette that he had lit in anticipation, whilst Liam disappeared off into the house. I leant forwards and braced myself against my elbows as I drew on the cigarette. The silence was peaceful, comfortable. It was just Neil and I, sitting in the shade, soaking in each other's company. No conversation, no flirting, just pure contentment as I squinted my eyes down the length of the garden.

"I love you," he whispered, as he leant forward onto his elbows, so to disguise what he'd just said.

"It's rude to whisper," Liam's voice appeared over my right shoulder.

We hadn't realised that Liam had made his way back outside and was stood no more than three feet away. *Fuck!* I tried to mask my face, but I was sure that Liam had seen the guilty shock flash across my expression.

"But it is hot isn't it?" I mockingly whispered, hoping that Liam would convince himself that he misheard Neil. He smiled and raised his eyebrows before nipping back into the house. I looked over at Neil and saw his wide eyes turn to face away from the door. *That was a close one.*

CHAPTER 7

My birthday was fast approaching. In September 2005, I would turn 16, and *everything* would be different. The countdown was on, and I was so excited. It would be legal. We would be a couple, as he had promised me, almost daily. No more sneaking around. I had moved into my final year of compulsory education, Year 11. I felt as though the people at the farm gossiped about us relentlessly; giving me the side eye every time I turned the corner. I could feel the atmosphere as soon as I stepped foot on there. Neil and I were together all the time. All the time. We came as a pair. The names 'Tanya and Neil' rolled off the tongue even more so than 'Anne and Neil'. It was always us, together, disappearing off for a quiet minute, and the routine we had found ourselves in had been like that for a couple of years. If I was in one area of the farm, Neil would follow shortly behind me, or we'd be found together, in cahoots somewhere quiet and away from prying eyes.

My 16th birthday fell on a Sunday. I went to the farm in the morning. I had fallen out with my mum over the lack of interest in my family life, so I felt miserable. Anne and Neil came down to the farm in the morning and my heart jumped when I caught his eye as he walked through the gate. He discretely handed me a letter through CJ's door, and I hurriedly took off down the neighbouring bridal track.

He'd put a yellow rose inside the envelope and my heart melted. Whenever I showed CJ, I always wore a fresh yellow rose as a buttonhole on my jacket. *He always notices the smallest details.* I ripped open the rest of the envelope and pulled out a small piece of paper, the size of a compliments slip.

Tan,

Well, we made it. You mean the world to me. I can't wait to celebrate your birthday with you.

I love you,

Nx

I clutched it to my chest before opening it to re-read it. *You mean the world to me, too.* I lit up a cigarette and put it to my mouth as I gazed at the letter over and over again. *Nx? That's the way my grandma signs off on her text messages.* I smiled at the connection I had drawn. *If anyone finds it, it wouldn't take them half a second to work out who Nx was.* As I drew the last breath from the cigarette, I tucked the letter and rose into my green and navy Adidas jacket. Its zipped pockets would keep it from falling out. Then I made my way back to the farm.

Neil invited me back to their house for something to eat. Julie and Liam were away, so Anne and Neil had agreed to keep an eye on their house whilst they were absent. The three of us walked around to Julie and Liam's place to check on it. Neil slid a can of lager across the kitchen counter in my direction.

"Here y'are," he said as the can slid into my hand.

The air escaped as I opened the can with a violent hiss. I put the can to my lips and sucked in the spray before I continued to crack open the ring pull. Its nectar slid down my throat more smoothly than I had anticipated. We walked outside to sit on the bench and lit up a cigarette. Somewhere in my periphery, Anne had mentioned that she was going to head back to their house to start dinner and left us enthralled in each other's conversation. We only noticed that she'd gone by the time we hit the bottom of our cans.

We headed back inside where Neil continued to offer me can after can of lager. As I rubbed my nose, I realised the alcohol had started to dull my senses. The euphoria hit my body and I felt as light as air, my mind free from interruption, my chains unwound. I leant against the kitchen countertop and was aware that my feet didn't want to coordinate with my brain. Neil held my eye contact as he moved towards me, bending down to meet my mouth with his. His hands slid from my waist and cupped my bum, squeezing it and pulling my body towards his. I could feel his penis pulsating on my abdomen as he held me tight against him. He moved his hands further down the back of my thighs and in one smooth movement, lifted me onto Julie's counter. He pushed his way between my legs, pulling my knees tightly into his hips, and anchored himself against my groin.

"Can I give you your birthday present?" He asked as he pulled back a couple of centimetres away from my face.

I turned my head to look over his shoulder.

"Anne could walk back any minute," I responded, feeling partly relieved I had an excuse to say no, partly disappointed that I had to turn him down again.

"Let me go down on you, instead."

"No, we can't, we'll get caught!"

I was drunk enough to lose the concept of time but not so drunk as to lose myself completely. My senses were numb, and I couldn't rely on them to alert me to anyone arriving back at the house. Neil had also had a couple of cans; not enough to be drunk, but enough that made me think that his judgement was impaired. *Does he want to get caught?*

Anne arrived back a short time later. We were sitting outside on the bench in front of sliding French doors when she turned up. Thankfully the need for a cigarette break had drawn us out of the kitchen, or who knows what she'd have walked in on. Lunch was ready, so we locked up the house and went to Anne and Neil's house. The roast chicken dinner worked to sober me up a little. Neil and I sat next to each other on the settee to eat, whilst Anne sat on the other. After listening to music and talking for a couple of hours, it was time to head to the farm for the evening jobs. I walked down with Neil, Anne a few paces in front. It had become customary that if the three of us went anywhere together, Anne would be ahead, and Neil and I would tag along a few paces behind. As I have mentioned numerous times, it was expected that Neil and Tanya would come as a pair.

Anne had marched off ahead and got to the farm a few minutes before we arrived. She'd closed the gate behind her, so as Neil opened the gate and I stood slightly behind him, I put my hands in my pockets so I didn't feel awkward about having the gate opened for me. As I looked down the yard, I saw Geraldine nudge Kelsey, and they both looked up the farm at Neil and I coming through the gate. They turned to look at each other and I saw Kelsey raise her eyebrows before Geraldine gave an all-knowing look that said *I told you so.*

Marilyn was at the farm when we got there. I had finished most of my jobs in the morning, so there was only the quick bedding down left to do. At least she couldn't moan at me that I'd gone off gallivanting without seeing to CJ first. Neil told Marilyn that I'd had a row with Mum and he seemed proud of himself for 'softening the blow' as he offered his hand to his mouth with the action of drinking. I don't know if my perceptions were off, but Marilyn didn't seem to mind. Besides, after consuming food to counteract the alcohol, I was almost sober by that point. I finished the bedding down before leaving with Marilyn for home. It had been a good day, after all.

*

My school friends and Cleo had arranged for a night out to celebrate my birthday the following weekend. My enthusiasm for going out had depreciated some over the previous months, but I was looking forward to celebrating my birthday now that I'd already celebrated it with Neil.

"I'm off out with the girls tonight. We are going up the town, so hold back ringing in case I'm not the first one to look at my phone," I said to Neil.

"Fine. Don't worry about it," he sniped.

Please don't be sharp with me again. I hated it when he went cold on me. He didn't do it very often, but on the odd occasion that he did, it felt as painful as a slap to the cheek on a cold day. I dropped my eyes to the floor and kept my mouth shut as Anne rode past us in the school.

"I'll be home by lunchtime, so I can be down here any time after 1 p.m. if you fancy it?" I said once Anne had made it far enough away so that she didn't overhear.

"No, I'm thinking of going to see my son, so don't worry about it."

He is giving me the silent treatment. He never goes to see his kids. This is because I'm going out.

I sat and tried to move the conversation on, but Neil wasn't budging. I gave up and went over to my stable to finish hanging the nighttime hay nets and check the water level. *What is his problem? What have I done wrong?* I thought, as I hauled up the hay net above my head and pushed my body into it to support its weight as I scrambled for the string to tie it. I patted CJ on the chest as I looked in the corner of his stable at his water bucket. *I'll top that up again.*

I ducked beneath the rope that straddled the doorway of CJ's stable and looked up at the school to see Neil still sat there, staring into the abyss. As I reached the hosepipe reel, I pulled the loose end of the hose and dragged it across the yard into CJ's stable and dipped the end into the bucket, before leaving to turn it on. Geraldine hated when the water splashed all over the dust on the farm, as it always made it look a mess, so I didn't like walking backwards and forwards with the hosepipe running. I ducked back under the rope and picked up the end of the hose so the splashing of water drowned out my thoughts. I stood facing the corner, trying to remain inconspicuous and invisible. I drew a figure of 8 with the pouring water and as it fell into the bucket, I watched it create a trail of bubbles on the surface. The whooshing, rhythmic sound of the hose pipes breaking the surface water felt calming, almost cleansing. CJ made a rocking motion and I felt his side push against me as he made his way to the door. *Ah, the mint man.* That's how CJ viewed Neil. Neil always carried mints for CJ.

Neil ducked under the rope after thrusting a mint at CJ and pushed his way into my body, forcing me back in the corner of the stable. I lost my balance and shuffled my feet quickly to avoid stepping into the water bucket as I sought the ground underneath me. His weight leaned against me, his hand grabbing me by my ponytail as he pushed his tongue into my mouth. *I knew he wouldn't be angry with me for long.* I kissed him back, relieved that he didn't hate me. He drove me into the wall, the urgency in his pelvis becoming more apparent as he pushed into me harder. He pulled back and gazed into my eyes.

"Don't forget about me, will you?" He said, but he didn't give me time to reply before he ducked back under the rope and made his way up the yard.

I wiped my mouth before leaving the stable to turn off the hosepipe and wound it back up. *Don't forget about me, what does that even mean?*

A short while later, my dad collected me from the farm and dropped me at Sara's house to get ready. I always wore a skirt out, knowing that if I'd flashed a bit of flesh, being asked for ID was minimised. We plastered our makeup on whilst fighting for mirror space and sang outrageously to The Killers. I didn't particularly know any of the songs, but Sara and Cleo loved them, so I feigned enthusiasm as I tried to join in on the choruses.

Don't forget about me? Don't forget about me? I couldn't wipe Neil from my mind, even after a few pre-drinks. Whilst in the taxi, I looked down at my phone to see a missed call from thirty minutes before. *Shit. Anne will probably be home now. I can't ring back. Shit.* I tried to brush the thought aside but made a mental note to worry about it in the morning.

As we pulled up in town, we got out at our usual jaunt and teetered in our stilettos across the cobbles. *Straight in, not even a look*, I thought as I turned back to check the bouncers. Cleo elbowed her way to the front of the packed bar and ordered a row of shots. I prepared myself for getting absolutely shit-faced. *Just get it out of your system, Tanya.*

We knocked back the shots between us and followed them down with WKD, the blue one, obviously. I got drunk quickly and my dancing feet took over my body, dragging me to the dancefloor, and I did little to try and stop them. As we danced with our bottles over our heads, the DJ brought out the old mixes, strategically overlying old music- my music- with modern beats.

"I fucking love this song!" I screeched over the top of George Harrison's Got my Mind Set on You.

I was in full party mode and threw my head back in glee as the three of us dominated the dancefloor. The music kept rolling and the drinks kept pouring, and I found myself lost in a plethora of drunken bodies. I didn't care that my body didn't belong to me anymore, as I was pushed backwards and forwards over the dancefloor. I was so happy to be out, I was so happy to be with my friends, I was so happy to feel so free.

I looked up, completely aware that my senses had left me. My mind belonged to my friend Jack Daniel's. I made eye contact with a man in his mid-twenties crossing the dancefloor towards me. He was quite drunk, but I could see that he was attempting a seductive pass, and my body froze. He reached forward and pulled me towards him and wrapped his arm tight round my waist. I pushed back and lifted my left hand to his eye line to flash the ring I put on before every night out.

"Sorry, I'm married," I yelled over the music.

He held his hands up in defeat and backed away, leaving me dancing with my friends.

Don't worry Neil, I didn't forget about you. I finally understood what he meant.

*

Things went a bit crazy from that point. In year 11, I was allowed out of school for lunch - something forbidden in the lower years - so I didn't have to *sneak* off the school grounds to meet with Neil. Neil had also got a mobile phone, so communication became easier. We were no longer worried about what his phone bill would reveal. With the increased freedom came an increased number of meet-ups away from the busybodies at the farm. Neil would ring me up in the morning to tell me what time to walk to the nearby nature reserve and he would meet me on the way in his car.

We had been meeting at lunchtimes for a while, so we'd get down to business straight away. I no longer felt shy or nervous. There had still been no penile penetration, but Neil had explored plenty of positions for fingers and tongues. He liked me to bend over the space between the two front seats so that masturbate himself to a climax whilst inside me with his left hand. Pumping me would only stop if he achieved orgasm. If there was time, he would go again and again. He didn't seem to need much down time between ejaculations. *Again?* I would think as he slipped his hand towards my vagina. Sometimes it would go on for what felt like ages, and I'd get sore. If it took multiple positions, I would get a pain in my hips from the constant spreading of my legs.

I was always on full display for him; he didn't want subtlety. He liked it the wider I could get my legs, the further over I could bend and expose myself. He would start with one finger inside me; two, then he'd add more until his whole hand was inside there. It hurt, and my body would tense beneath me, but I was just relieved that he couldn't see my face blinking away the tears that had risen in my eyes. But, he liked it, and I wanted to please him. It became expected, predictable. If he struggled to reach ejaculation, he would ask me to masturbate in front of him whilst he knocked one out. I felt uncomfortable the first few times, having only ever done it in the privacy of my bedroom, but he managed to talk me into it. It all became a new normal and there wasn't much in the way of boundaries at all. I couldn't achieve an orgasm in front of Neil, there were too many distractions. I couldn't relax, but when I knew he was getting close to ejaculation, I'd moan loudly and fake one to get him over the hurdle. I knew my battered vagina would get a rest for a few minutes before he'd want to go again.

Most of the time, he would try to catch his semen as he came. The first time that he ejaculated in front of me knocked the wind out of my sails. I couldn't look; I felt so sick. The smell was like nothing I'd smelled before, the mixture of stale and fresh tobacco, vaginal secretions, and freshly sweated bodies. I had to fight the urge to wretch whilst simultaneously passing him the tissues and turning away. I didn't want him to see my face as I swallowed the bile that had risen to my throat. I hadn't known that sex had a smell, but I grew to acknowledge that sex had a distinctive smell. It was unmistakable.

Neil loved my uniform, and this unfortunately caused quite a big problem for me. *Does he feel like he's fucking a schoolgirl in it?* I couldn't deny that I had mixed feelings. Part of me felt flattered that he fantasised about me in it, the other part of me thought it as a bit perverted. It wasn't my only worry about having sex in my uniform. It was navy blue and the heavy cotton skirt often ended up splattered with escaped semen. The colour and the material were not conducive to disguising my extracurricular activities. I'd return to school after lunch and my friends would wind me up about the spots of creamy white on the navy canvas. It became a running joke. They'd ask me questions, and we would talk in great detail about sex, positions, orgasms and oral. Quite a few of my friends knew I was having *'an affair with a married man'*. They loved to gossip, and I loved talking about Neil even if I hid his full identity, so it was win-win.

*

Away from school, I pulled away from my friends. I had gradually reduced the number of nights out with Sara and Cleo. Neil didn't like me going out. Although he never told me explicitly the atmosphere changed between us whenever the conversation came up. He would give me the cold shoulder and I wondered whether he thought I was copping off with other men. He eventually told me that he didn't like other men looking at me. It made him jealous that they could see me in all my glory, and he couldn't. He couldn't watch me dance, get drunk and have a good time. He told me that he would sit in his lounge all night, unable to sleep because he didn't know what I was doing. I couldn't do that to him anymore. I felt guilty that I was out getting drunk and dancing until my feet bled, whilst he was sat at home worrying about me.

Whenever the subject of going out came up at school, I'd play along. I'd arrange to go out and then bail out on the morning before. I couldn't put him through it. I knew he would be upset because he worried about me. It wasn't fair on him and the guilt would swell like a torrent inside me. My anxiety increased to the point where I stopped completely.

I arranged for Cleo to get ready at my house one evening, which meant that I could see Neil at the farm first and bring Cleo back with me. We got ready, our glad rags on, our faces plastered with makeup, and my dad drove us to town. I got progressively more anxious as the 40-minute journey continued. I feigned joy and excitement, but inside I was twisted like knots. As we pulled up to the side of the road where Sara stood, Cleo flung open the door and leapt out. I couldn't.

Guilt fixed me to the seat, and I burst into tears. Sara and Cleo stood in front of the open door; their faces were completely bewildered.

"Tanya, what's wrong?" Sara said, her face softening into gentle concern.

"I just can't, I'm sorry, I just can't." The tears were out in full force. My cheeks were soaked as the salty tears ran into my mouth and under my chin.

"Just come out for a bit, ya dad can fetch you later if you change your mind," Cleo suggested.

"I'm sorry. I can't. I'm so sorry," I forced out between the sobs.

I had always been able to provide an excuse for bailing on a night out, but I missed my window of opportunity that time; I was dressed and ready to go. I apologised over and over and said I'd see them on Monday before I urged my dad to take me home. We drove home, I was a blubbering wreck in the back, and my dad was completely perplexed in the front. That was the last time I tried to go out. I was 16.

*

I barely held myself together in school. Thankfully my grades hadn't slipped, but I had become well-versed in finding excuses for late homework and assignments. I'd hide away at lunch and break times, waiting for his call to tell me where to meet him. I had no interest in people and found myself on my own most of the time. I felt the sadness creep into my bones as I realised that Neil and I still had to be a secret. The ache of the loneliness, the desperation, followed me around and gnawed at my joints. *Why? I'm 16 now, it's not illegal anymore.* Neil told me that if our secret came out at that point, it would look like it had been going on for a while, so we would need to wait a bit longer. I felt jealous of Anne. *Really* jealous. I'd bubble up in rage every time I thought of her and Neil sat on the settee all night. I used to admire her, but I could only see her as an obstacle by that point. *My age isn't a problem anymore, I am 16, I can do whatever the fuck I want.* But Neil was right, it would look like it had been going on for a while. Which would mean that he wouldn't be able to be with me anyway, as he'd be too busy spending time at *Her Majesty's pleasure.* I was disappointed, but I knew I had to protect both of us. There was no alternative but to carry on in secret and wait until I was much further past the age of consent.

I had to decide what I was going to do after school had finished. The pre-Neil era had seen my future planned out. I'd do my GCSEs then my A-Levels in 6th form, then after that, I'd go off to university to study medicine. I'd always wanted to be a doctor. I hadn't seen an alternative career. The only thing that rivalled my obsession with medicine was my obsession with Neil. I knew I couldn't have both at that point, and I wanted Neil so desperately that I'd have given up medicine for a home with him. Going off to university would have meant the end of Neil and me; we would hardly see each other. It would be probably limited to weekends at best, and during the holidays at worst, assuming, of course, that I kept the horse and my ties to the farm. So, it seemed logical that there was no point in doing my A-levels either.

My parents and I butted heads over that. They wanted me to stay on for another couple of years at the school to do my A-levels, but I couldn't wait to get out of education into the real world. I had fantasised about earning a wage and moving out of the family home and into a home with Neil, as he had promised. I attended the 6th form open evening to keep the peace, and I reluctantly agreed to stay. I resisted, but deep down, I knew it was the right decision. It didn't look promising that anything between Neil and I would develop at a faster pace. We had talked about it quite a bit before I turned 16, but it had hardly come up at all post-16. In fairness, there was too much sexual stuff going on so there wasn't a great deal of time for us to talk in private. We'd talk down on the farm, but it was always difficult when we didn't know who was about. The conversations weren't a heart to heart anymore either; Neil mainly focused on sex or *'did anyone ask you where you were?'*

My parents had noticed my change in attitude towards school. I used to thrive in school, I only had to turn up to fly through the exams. The brain that once absorbed every piece of information in class had left me. I used to look forward to parent's evening at school because I knew my parents would come home gushing about how brilliant I was, but for the last two parent's evenings, I was left feeling sick.

Although my teachers had never complained that my grades had slipped, it was mentioned that I was repeatedly handing work in late and that it wasn't up to my previous standard. They noted it was rushed and that it looked a mess. It was true. I didn't care about handing work in anymore. I feared getting in trouble, so I made many excuses as to why I was late, and I cannot even begin to count how many imaginary relatives I had lost during Year 11. Nobody ever questioned the grief of a teenager.

I knew my parents were right; I had grown lazier at school. I needed someone on my case to keep me focused. I spent the time wishing the day away, waiting for lunchtime to see Neil, and then I would think about our escapades all afternoon until I got to the farm. He didn't meet me every lunch, but he'd make his way up to the school most days. He couldn't meet me if Anne was on "earlies" as she'd wonder where he was. Nevertheless, it was never enough time together. We would only have time for sex, never for affection or cuddles, so once again, I used the time for 'education' as a stop-gap between 'Neil time'.

I felt sad when I wasn't with Neil, or if the stars had aligned incorrectly, and somehow, we had missed each other. It wasn't often that we wouldn't see each other as we had fallen into a full-time routine. We were virtually guaranteed to have several hours together most days. I missed him when he wasn't with me. The loneliest period was nighttime. Anne was at home, which meant that he couldn't ring until she had gone to bed, and my nights were starting to resemble those of a night owl. I struggled to sleep because all I could think about was Neil. I would look longingly at my phone, willing it to ring. One evening, I sat looking at my phone as a text message popped up with his name.

I got butterflies, but then a sense of doom washed over me as I knew Neil couldn't text. It was from Neil's phone, though. He had gone out with his friend, Peter, a social worker from my town. Neil was out at the pub with Peter, and he had asked Peter to text me. I was relieved and pleased as that meant that another line of communication had opened. It also cemented my feelings that he spent the evening thinking about me as much as I did about him. They weren't dirty texts but clearly of an intimate nature. He got Peter to say things like 'I'm missing you', 'I love you', or 'I can't wait to see you'. He already had a photo of me that he had shown to Peter and another friend, but it felt like confirmation that our relationship was progressing. He'd actively got Peter involved in our relationship. It was no longer a complete secret; he had chosen to tell someone. That meant that things were still moving forward and not stuck in a rut as I had thought. It gave me hope that eventually, we would be together.

Tanya Pursglove

CHAPTER 8

It was the 11th of February 2006. We had made the opportunity for a lengthy fondle and grope at the farm. That's what our relationship focussed around. Neil left the farm earlier than the norm. Anne was still working at the farm on Saturdays, so that gave us a bit longer together than in the rest of the week. Neil had made alternative arrangements that Saturday, however, as he was going out for the evening to watch a local band play in the city. He left the farm about 5pm, so after I had finished doing my jobs, I hung around the school for a while until my dad collected me.

"You here alone, where's Neee-ulll?" I looked over my shoulder to see the eye-rolling, mocking face of Liz, one of the older liveries on the farm.

"Oh, he's gone already. Said he was off out for the night or something." I replied, playing oblivious. *Don't try that with me, it will take more than that to get a rise!*

"You not going with him tonight then?" She probed once more.

"Nope, didn't fancy it tonight." I cut her off. *I'll let her think we meet at night- she'll live off that for weeks.* I'd reached a point after so much gossip and so many sly remarks directed at me, that I willingly added fuel to the fire. *They'll never know what to believe.*

I couldn't see the point in hanging around until late. I called my dad to fetch me and made my way to Marilyn's house. Marilyn was away for the night and had asked me to look after her dog in her absence. I'd done this quite a few times, so it wasn't a particularly unusual arrangement. My dad dropped me off at the door as he drove by, and I let myself in to be greeted by the wiggling body and high-pitched yips of her border collie.

"Go on in, good boy," I said to Benson as I squeezed through the narrow gap in the door. His excited body wriggled around my knees, and his whip-like tail bashed the dining room door. "Let me in."

The dog shot up the garden like a greyhound after a hare, as I clicked the kettle on and began shovelling instant coffee into the dainty china cups. *Marilyn always has the most precious trinkets in her house. Most of our mugs come out of easter eggs. Oooh, this is cute,* I thought as I picked up a little chicken-shaped egg timer whilst waiting for the kettle to click off the boil. Benson leapt up at the door, barging it open and trotted into the kitchen, his excitement and energy had subsided.

"Good boy," I said as my hand rummaged around in the bottom of the old terracotta bread bin in search for one of his bone-shaped biscuits and threw them into the dining room for him to find.

I locked the kitchen door and finished making my coffee; *tink, tink, tink* the delicate teaspoon tapped the side of the elegant cup. I slid the cup along the countertop towards the kitchen door. I bent over to unzip my long boots and levered them off, having braced my head against the wall to stop myself toppling over. The instant relief in my feet as they stepped onto the cold tiles, having been cramped in my heavy boots all day. I stood upright to undo the flies on my jodhpurs and pushed them down around my ankles. I was too lazy to bend over again, so I used one foot to push the trousers off the other ankle and then stood on the trouser leg to pull my other leg free. I pushed the limp fabric across the floor into the corner. I dropped my arms and my coat fell to the floor and flicked it up with my foot, to lie in a crumpled heap with the jodhpurs and boots. My T-shirt joined the pile a couple of seconds later. Wearing nothing but a bra and pants, I took my hair down from the elastic and loosened it with my hands, shaking what was left of any shavings or hay that had become nestled in my curls. I retied my hair in a floppy bun on the top of my head.

"Come on then, let's go," I said to Benson as I picked up the cup from the side.

Benson shot from the dining room up the stairs, as he'd done a thousand times when I'd gone to babysit him. I followed him up and turned into Marilyn's bedroom, placing my cup on the nightstand, and removed what was left of my clothes.

Brrrr... Chilly.... I'll have a shower later.

"Budge up fat bum," I said as I patted Benson's bum so I could get in bed at the side of him.

I pulled the duvet over me. I reached for the remote and pointed it at the tiny TV in the corner of Marilyn's bedroom. It came to life, and I began flicking through the channels, eventually settling on soap opera reruns.

Drrr.... Drrr.... Drrr... Drrr...
Drrr... Drrr...

I looked over and saw my phone rhythmically flashing as it edged towards the ledge of the nightstand. I reached over and switched my cold cup with the phone and inspected the screen. *Neil? What? Why? Oh god, has something happened?*

"Hello?" I tentatively answered.

"Hello, it's me, I'm in Whitewell, are you alone?"

"Yes, why?"

"I've got 20 minutes, let me in, I'll see you in 3."

Whitewell was the neighbouring village, just half a mile up the road from us. *He's coming round!*

I jumped out of bed, and the dog mirrored my behaviour and lunged towards the bedroom door. I grabbed a fluffy cream dressing gown off the coat hook and wrapped it around me. Benson raced ahead, nearly taking my knees out from under me as we battled down the stairs.

"Come on Ben," I said as I rushed him into the kitchen and closed the baby gate behind him. By the time I located the side door key and made my way to open it, Neil was standing at the door.

"Hi!" I said, unable to contain my smile.

Neil darted in, closing the door behind him, and he explained that he had parked on the neighbouring street so nobody would see his car outside the house. The dark February night offered him a cloak whilst walking down to Marilyn's. He slid his cold hands inside the dressing gown, against my bare skin and pulled me towards him, greeting me with a kiss. He pulled back after a couple of seconds and raised his eyebrows up the stairs behind me, gesturing for me to invite him up.

I turned around and walked up the stairs, he was followed closely behind. *Are we really going to do this?* We were both silent with anticipation, unsure how to act around each other. *Why am I so nervous?* I got into Marilyn's bedroom and lay my side as Neil kicked off his shoes and dropped his coat on the floor. He lay facing me. *What do I do? Just wait for him and go with it.*

"Are you sure you want to do this?" He asked.

I nodded.

He asked me to take off the dressing gown. It was the first time he had seen me completely naked. I felt shy but tried to disguise it. I could feel my eyelid twitching with nerves and tried to discretely rub it with the back of my hand. He started to touch me, and it felt as though it was the first time all over again. I moved on to my back as he began to pump away at my vagina, expecting that he would get on top.

"No, not like that," he said as he turned on to his back and pointed to his pelvis. "You get on top."

What? I don't want him watching me. Neil began to open his flies and pushed his trousers and pants to his thighs. *Well, it looks like I don't have much choice.* I awkwardly sat up. It was difficult to push myself up against Neil's weight on the mattress. I lifted one leg over his pelvis and sat on top of his thighs. I still couldn't look at his penis, despite having had many dozens of sexual experiences with him, so I felt around for it. He was soft. Barely a semi. I took him in my hand for a minute, but he wasn't firming up, so I offered it around my genitals, thinking that would get him hot. *I think it's working.* I attempted to put him inside me. *Nope, its not.* He was too soft and my body was too tense. I couldn't think of anything that would get him excited enough, besides from the obvious, and I wasn't about to do *that*.

I sat further up him, so I was on his abdomen rather than his pelvis, and he used his hand to masturbate himself harder.

"Try again now," he said.

This isn't going to work, I thought to myself. I lowered myself under his guidance. He was harder, but still not hard enough. He was in too much of a rush to get things moving. He forced his way into my vagina, using his fingers to provide a scaffolding for his semi-flaccid penis. *Is he in? I think so?* I sat upright and feigned a groan- *that always helps him*. I didn't dare make too much movement as I knew he would pop out, so I rocked my pelvis in micromovements for a few seconds, pretending to enjoy myself; pretending I knew what I was doing. *This is as good as it's going to get*. It was awkward and weird, and I didn't feel remotely turned on by the experience. I pretended to orgasm after a minute of gentle rocking as I realised that Neil was never going to get there.

"Have you finished?"

"Yes!" I exclaimed, feigning to catch my breath; tensing my whole body as though I couldn't bear any more stimulation.

I lay backwards, my feet awkwardly under my elbows, his calves on either side of my arms. I didn't want him to see my face for fear that my expression revealed my treachery.

"Sit up."

I sat up reluctantly and his face was ashen.

"I can't believe I've just done that to a little girl."

His words felt like a punch straight to the gut. *A little girl? Wow, thanks for that!* I thought. I didn't say anything, but just dismounted and lay at the side of him, as he pulled up his trousers and began to tuck his t-shirt back into his waist band. *A little girl?*

"I've got to go," he said as he sat up to tie his shoes over the edge of the bed. The bottom of his narrow back faced me. He stood and turned around as he put his arms back into his coat.

"Happy Valentine's Day," he finished as he pecked the corner of my mouth and pulled the door for his exit. I didn't move.

I don't think he wants me to follow him.

I lay there in a complete whirlwind. *Did that happen? What did happen? Was that sex?* I was disappointed by the underwhelming first-time experience with him. I thought it would be romantic and drawn out. We had all evening to touch and caress and explore every inch of our bodies with no prying eyes. There was no back arching foreplay. It wasn't even a mad passionate quicky, nothing, but a half-hearted attempt at a bit of a bonk and failing miserably on both our parts.

He rang me about an hour later once he'd arrived in the city. He asked me if anyone had been, or if I'd spoken to anyone. I put his mind at rest; nothing eventful had happened since he left. I refrained from saying that nothing eventful had happened since he had arrived. He was in the clear and we left it at that. I went back to 'watching' Saturday night television. I stared at a 15-inch screen, mesmerised by the flashing light in the dark, but my mind was elsewhere. There was no focus, no distraction. Neil had etched himself on my mind even further. I started to sugar-coat the whole experience and couldn't wait to see him, to repeat it all over again. *I won't get caught out next time, though. I'll be mentally prepared and perform better. I'll get him so fired up he'll explode.*

*

We didn't have to wait too long for our next attempt at sex. The end of February provided us with the half-term holidays. He arranged to pick me up from home, so I walked to the bus stop at the bottom of our road, and he pulled into the layby. I got in the back of the car and sat reclining on the back seat. I had done that plenty of times. If Neil had passed me on the way to the car park near the school, he would pull in and wait until I slipped in the back before driving off. It was safer that way, given that his 4x4 was much higher than most other cars; I could lie down on the backseat, obscured from the view of virtually any vehicle. Sometimes he would tell me to get me on my knees in the footwell of the rear seats and present my exposed behind as my stomach lay on the chairs.

We headed to a local National Trust house with its vast surrounding woodlands and nature walks. It wasn't far from my house, but it was secluded enough that we were unlikely to bump into anyone we knew, especially in the middle of a workday. We parked up, and Neil paid for a parking ticket before we walked into the woodlands. We had planned to have sex and there was more flirting that time. We stopped to kiss, touch and flirt. I was a little nervous, but I managed to channel the nerves into playful teasing.

Neil pointed up to a thickening in the woods, off the beaten track and despite being at the top of the hill, it looked well hidden. My legs barely carried me up the incline. It wasn't particularly steep, but it was steep enough to trouble my already weakened knees. The nerves had come to the front and although I was not as nervous as the first encounters, my adrenalin still pumped. I felt comfortable around Neil. We'd had too many sexual experiences for that to be nerve-wracking, but I didn't want it to feel like another massive disappointment.

Neil glanced over at a tree. We were still on an incline, so the tree looked promising for counteracting the height difference between us. *I'll lean back on the tree, and he can stand, facing me. Bingo.* I leant up against the tree, feeling the knobbly bark pushing between my shoulder blades. *Yes, I can make this work.*

"No, not that way." He said as he pulled me away and swapped places with me in one swift move. He bent at the knees to lower himself to my height and used the tree for stability behind him. I was faced away from him. *But now I'm even lower down?*

"Bend over," his voice was firm and authoritative.

He pulled up my denim skirt and revealed my bare buttocks before taking both in his hands as I bent forwards. I was unsteady on my feet. He took one hand away and I heard his zip slide open. It took a couple of seconds, so I shuffled my feet into a slightly more stable position. *Yeah, I think that will be ok.*

FUCK! Neil slammed his penis into my vagina. My eyes instantly welled with tears and my jaw flew open, but no sound came out. *Fuck! No. Wait. Stop!* My body clenched beneath me as the sudden shock of him in my genitals sent shooting pains up my spine. I immediately felt a searing hot pain in my pelvis, all the way up deep inside my belly.

I had already been used to having his hand and fist in my vagina, but this time there was no warning. I was dry. There wasn't even a couple of seconds of fumbling for the right hole for me to prepare myself. The pain was immeasurable. My toes curled violently which only made it more difficult to balance on the tenuous terrain. *Stop tensing, relax into it. Just breathe, just relax.* But it didn't work; it felt as though I was about to split open.

Neil pulled back too far and pulled out of me. *Thank fuck. Thank God.* I dropped to my knees to regather myself, my shins hit the floor hard, and the weight of my body thudding the ground forced the air out of my chest in a loud grunt. Neil took my grunt as an invitation and got down on his knees behind me, and sat on his heels, pulling me backwards onto his lap. My moments reprieve was over as he used his hand to put himself back inside me. I didn't move. I needed a minute to acclimatise. I sat there, with one of Neil's arms wrapped around my pelvis and the other underneath my top holding my breast. *Fuck sake, relax!* I shouted at myself internally. I leant forwards and supported my weight on my hands as Neil pushed up on his knees and began thrusting inside me. *Ok. This is manageable.* It wasn't without pain, but it was more bearable than when we were standing up. At least I wasn't fighting gravity as well as Neil's body.

I couldn't understand why it was so painful. He wasn't particularly well endowed, and he'd put much bigger things up there before. His whole hand and fist had been in there before. *Please just come. Let it be done.* He didn't feel as though he was getting close. His rhythm didn't change. I knew when he was close to coming with my hand because he'd want it faster. *Maybe he's waiting for me? Just fake one and pull away from him.* So, I did. I began to push myself back on him, resisting his thrusts and ignoring the pain around the entrance to my vagina. *The burn. 5. 4. 3. 2....* I groaned and tensed my body as I pushed on to him and rhythmically tensed my pelvic floor so he would feel my entrance pulse and know I was done. I pulled away and caught my breath, not from pleasure, but from the final relief of pain.

I paused for a minute on my hands and knees, my head still spinning, and Neil lay back under the tree. *Thank god.* I knew he hadn't come; *I'll finish him off by hand.* Eventually, after I pulled myself together, I lay back at the side of him with his arm draped around me.

"Was that good for you?" He asked.

"Yes," I lied, forcing a smile.

He paused for a few seconds, and then reached over and guided my hand to his penis. He was still hard. I started masturbating him slowly, my mood entirely gone. He went quiet then I felt the atmosphere change. *Oh no, please don't ask.* But it was too late.

"Will you suck me?"

My blood ran cold as it always did when he asked. He'd been asking me for months to give him oral sex, and I had said no each time. He would sulk a little upon each rejection, but I'd told him of a bad experience before him, and I couldn't get over the mental block. It was a lie. The truth of it was that I just couldn't put his penis near my mouth. He was always slimy, and it was gross. He thought that the "pre-cum" was a turn-on for me. I didn't have the heart to say it made me feel sick, but that was the truth of the matter. I would wretch at the glistening bead of pre-cum on the end of his penis whenever he was horny. I didn't want to hurt his feelings or know that he disgusted me, but it was the furthest thing from a turn-on.

"I can't, I'm sorry," I apologised.

He pushed my hand away and raised both of his arms above his head, resting his head on his locked palms. My head fell off his upper arm and onto the ground. *Oh fuck. Now he's pissed off.* I lay there for a short time. *Get a grip and just do it. What's the worst that can happen? Just do it. Pull yourself together and get on with it.*

I pushed myself up on my elbow and thought about it again for a second. *Just get it over with. You can't put it off forever. Oh fuck it. He wants it, he's disappointed, just do it and stop being such a frigid bitch.* I sighed, a bit harder than I intended to and the volume surprised me. I repositioned myself between his outstretched legs, closed my eyes, and forced myself onto his penis. *Don't be sick, don't be sick.*

"Oh Tan, yes!" He growled as I suppressed a gag.

1... 2... 3... 4... 5... 6...7... 8... 9... 10... Keep counting. Don't get distracted. Just keep counting. I pulled away and edged him further with my hand. *Please just hurry up Neil.* His hand rested on the back of my head and he gently pushed me back down. *Don't think about it, just count. 1... 2... 3... 4... Slimy and salty. Fight it, Tanya, don't wretch.* But it was too late, and I felt myself wretch. *No. 1... 2... 3... 4... 5... 6... 7... 8... 9... 10...* I pulled back up and brought him closer to coming with my hand. I thought it would speed up the process of getting it all over with. Once more. You can do this. I moved my mouth back on his penis. *Don't open your eyes, don't look, don't think about it. 1... 2... 3... 4... 5... 6... No, I'm done.* My gag reflex was too sensitive, I knew if I didn't stop I would be sick. I pulled back but felt resistance in Neil's arms. I forced backwards, a little too hard, but I wanted it known that I'd had enough.

"I'm sorry, I'm done," I said as I rolled off to the side of him.

"You're amazing! You did it!" He joyfully exclaimed. "Don't worry your confidence will come back, at least you've got over your mental block."

I wasn't sure about that, but it felt a triumph to give it a go, even if I hated every second of it. I kissed him, and he said that he'd use that image for the 'wank bank' later. I was pleased I had done it. It felt like I'd stepped over a hurdle, and even though I hated it, it felt like an achievement. He didn't ejaculate but didn't seem disappointed either. He thought he'd made me orgasm, so his ego wasn't bruised, and he was satisfied enough to pull his trousers back up.

We headed back to the car. I got on the back seat again and lay down, my head at the driver's side and my feet on the chair behind the passenger's side. We drove for a short while when he pulled over into a layby on a narrow country road. He turned around and asked me if I was ready to go again. I wasn't, but I couldn't tell him that; *he expects you to be ready*, so I didn't object when he turned around and inserted his middle finger full depth into my vagina. After a couple of minutes, I faked a second orgasm to get it over with, and he wiped his hand on the inside of my skirt before setting off for my village.

He dropped me off at the bus stop, and I waited until he was out of sight before I walked up the hill towards home. I was bursting for a wee by the time I got back. It had been fairly urgent in the layby, but I'd managed to hold it, despite the excess pressure of Neil's fingers. I raced up the stairs to the toilet and sat down on the loo just in time. I let out a sigh of relief about finally being able to relax my pelvic floor.

What the...?

I stared at the tissue that I had just wiped myself with, the white paper entirely claret.

Oh my...

The bowl was lined with crimson stripes, draining off into the pink water, leaving trails of dissipating blood around the water line.

I dropped the tissue in the bowl and frantically wound another handful of toilet paper up in my hand to wipe again. I pulled the paper away to look at it again. Again, dark red dominated my eyes. *Oh shit. What do I do? What do I do?* I wracked my brain for an answer. I leant over and pushed the plug into the bath, turning on the taps to full pressure. I dropped the second wad of tissue into the toilet and wound yet another handful up and pressed it into my genital. I stood up, clamping the tissue to my privates as I looked at the bowl for understanding. *No, no, no!* I flushed the toilet, not wanting to face the consequences of my actions, not wanting to accept the responsibility of that being my fault. *What was I thinking? How am I going to explain this?*

I walked into my bedroom from the ensuite, still clamping the tissue between my legs. I turned around, my skirt hoisted up to my waist to look in my door length mirror. It was everywhere, mahogany and scarlet red pools and streaks all over the backs of my thighs and my bum cheeks. *What the fuck have I done?* I wobbled back to the toilet and dropped the last wad of tissue into the bowl. I pulled my skirt and shirt off, keeping my legs tight together to avoid dripping on the bathmat as I threw the skirt into the sink. *I'll sort that out later.*

I held my hand to my vagina as I lifted the leg over the bath and carefully lowered myself into it.

"Ahh!" I yelped as my bum and genitals made contact with the water.

I held my breath willing the stinging to stop, and I looked down to see the cloud of red liquid disperse through the crystal-clear water. As the water faded to a pale pink and I realised the bleeding had stopped, the panic subsided, and the shame set in. *I hope Neil didn't see.*

CHAPTER 9

Sex continued from that point at every given opportunity, and thankfully, it wasn't as painful anymore. Sometimes we'd be down at the farm and get a sneaky one in; sometimes, we had to wait until school lunchtimes. There would be sexual activity every day, multiple times per day. Penetrative penile sex couldn't happen daily. Penis in vagina sex could sometimes be problematic given Neil's impotence, so this was typically reserved for lunchtimes away from the farm where we wouldn't be disturbed. He only got 4 Viagra per month, so it didn't seem worth using those on the off chance that we got a whole 30 minutes to ourselves at the farm for a dirty romp behind a stable door. That's not saying it was impossible, but it certainly didn't happen on a daily occurrence. He rarely climaxed if we were at the farm, but I would fake one for his ego. Often, he would take too long to ejaculate, and it was unlikely we'd have enough undisturbed time to get one out of him. We would just use the odd ten uninterrupted minutes for fingering, hand jobs or the occasional oral if I was feeling brave enough.

Consequently, it would mean that he would walk around with a semi on for a while, touching me whenever we got a clear couple of seconds. I used to feel guilty when he didn't come because, as far as he thought, I always did. *What if I get him too horny and he goes back home to Anne and gives her one instead?* I preferred it when I knew he had already ejaculated in the day; either knocking one out whilst on the phone or if we'd already met at lunchtime. I knew he could physically go again in a relatively short amount of time after one, especially after Viagra. *But I'm the only one he gets horny for, stop overthinking it.*

We never used condoms or any contraception. Neil had a thing about condoms; he said he wouldn't be able to remain hard enough if we had to pause to put one on. I couldn't go to the doctor for the pill as I worried how much I would have to disclose about our relationship. He only ever came in my mouth, never in my vagina, so I wasn't worried about pregnancy. He preferred to splash his semen all over my back, bum, boobs or face if I wasn't in the position to swallow.

We were sat in the back of his car one lunchtime, smoking and post-coital, before setting off for school again.

"What do you think about anal?" He casually asked.

"I've never really thought about it," I responded "But, yeah, I suppose," shrugging non-committal.

I didn't think anything else of the conversation and we both redressed and headed back to school.

Several weeks passed and opportunity for sex or sexual contact was never neglected. We were at it like rabbits. Marilyn had gone away for a midweek break and had asked me to look after her house whilst off school. It was blistering hot, and after spending a couple of hours in the garden, the familiar sounds of my phone appeared.

Drrr… drrr… drrr… drrr… *Neil's ringtone.*

"Hey" I answered, a smile crept across my face.

"You still at Marilyn's?" He asked.

"Yeah, she's not back until Friday."

"See you in 10!"

I rushed back in the house to straighten up the place after living like a slob all week. I kicked the pile of horse clothes by the kitchen door into the cupboard under the stairs and moved all the dirty crockery into the sink. *Right, that's better. Ok, lounge…. yep, that will do.* I ran upstairs and straightened the bedding back into place, instead of the tangled mess I had left it when I got up that morning. *Done.* I poked my head into the bathroom. *Yep, that's fine.* As I made my way back down the stairs, I caught my reflection in the Welsh Dresser in the dining room. *Hair's a bit wild,* I thought as I ran my hand over the top of my head to smooth out the fly-aways.

I heard the side gate squeak as it opened, and I poked my head around the corner to see Neil walking up the pathway. He squeezed the embers from the cigarette, and they danced their way to the floor, blackening on their decent, as he flicked the stub over the fence into the field that bordered the garden.

"Where do you wanna go?" I asked, but he looked at me as though I didn't know. *Upstairs, obviously Tanya.*

We made our way upstairs and Neil watched me undress. I discarded my vest top to the floor along with my joggers and underwear. Neil started to undress too. *This is a novelty,* I thought. Neil never got undressed unless we were in his house. If we were out in the car, he'd need to be able to jump in the driver's seat if someone slowed down suspiciously, so only I would end up naked. Obviously if we were at the farm, both of us remained fully clothed. He took my direction and kicked his clothes to the side of the room to join mine.

He placed his hands on my hips and turned me around, as he did regularly. I responded and leant forwards onto the bottom of the bed. *This is more comfortable than bracing myself against a wall,* I thought. *Maybe I'll come this way.* Neil slapped my buttocks with his hands, the sting woke my senses and sharpened my mind. *This is going to be a rough one. At least I'm not fighting gravity.* My tiptoes were only grazing the floor, but at least I didn't feel unsteady, with all my weight on my abdomen.

I felt his hands leave my bum cheeks as the thumb of his left hand started stroking around the entrance of my vagina, he slowly but forcefully pushed it inside. I let out a groan. He pushed forward and I could feel the pressure on my pubic bone as he hooked his thumb around. I felt myself getting heavier and relaxed into the pressure, letting my head sink into the cotton duvet, feeling its warmth against my cheek. *This is going to be a good one,* I thought.

In one swift and rapid movement, Neil slammed his penis into my bum. I forced myself to contain the scream that tried to leave my body. There had been no warning. There had been no lubricant, no time taken to allow my body to relax into it. There was nothing to alert me to what was about to happen. My whole body clenched, my knees flexed, my toes curled tightly and no longer anywhere near the carpet. My whole body froze and clamped itself tight against the red-hot poker that had penetrated my bum. Tears streamed down my face and fell into the duvet as I buried my face. I screamed silently, inwardly. My body begged him to stop, but my mouth couldn't find the words. I was face down on the bed fully expecting to bleed to death. Everything stiffened, and I couldn't convince myself to relax and let it happen. The pain ripped through my body uncontrollably and no amount of mental coaching talked my body into relaxing. He pushed my whole body forward as he thrusted into me. There was no friction for him as I clutched on him so tightly, gripped so hard, that he couldn't withdraw an inch to push into me. My whole body was pushed and pulled back across the bed with his rocking motion in a bid to stop him from pulling back and re-entering me. I felt as though I was going to vomit, pass out and have diarrhoea all simultaneously. The pain was indescribable, blisteringly hot and as though a glass shard had been inserted into my bottom and dragged up towards the ceiling. I felt as though I was being sliced open from front to back with a chef's knife.

It went on for what felt like an eternity. Tears of pain streamed down my face for the whole time and he was too wrapped up in the moment to notice. My body was so tense he barely had the capability of pushing and pulling in and out of me, but he was moaning and groaning, gasping and catching his breath. Then he grunted with pleasure, pushed me away and pulled himself out, emptying his load onto my bum cheeks. I was so relieved it was over but couldn't lie face down any longer. Without looking over my shoulder, I peeled my cheeks from the sodden duvet and gingerly walked to the bathroom at the end of the hall, sliding the door closed behind me. I couldn't say a word. My voice had left me. I sat on the toilet, feeling light-headed, my guts twisted inside of me whilst copious volumes of diarrhoea fell into the bowl. It felt like my insides were going to fall out with it. It felt like passing gravel out of my back passage.

Whilst I fought the urge to faint, I tried to pull myself together. *He can't see me like this.* I was so embarrassed. *What is wrong with me?* I thought it was my body letting me down again, unprepared for adult life. Firstly, I couldn't orgasm with Neil, and secondly I experienced the absolute most unbearable pain doing something that women *'do all the time'*. I felt like such a failure, such a let-down, and I felt ashamed that I couldn't enjoy sex in the way I was supposed to. But most of all, I felt hurt that Neil hadn't noticed.

I tidied myself up and washed my face before I headed back into the bedroom. Neil was already dressed and halfway down the stairs when he said he'd meet me outside for a cigarette. I was relieved that he was satisfied for the moment. I couldn't bear the idea of him touching me again. Everything hurt from being so tense; even the muscles in my lower back and hips ached from the continual constriction. I got dressed and made my way outside to share the second half of Neil's cigarette avoiding his gaze as I stared in silent disbelief at the floor.

*

Sex with Neil became frantic, hard and sometimes unbearable. But I never told him no, his silent treatment was too much to bear. More often than not, I'd just flop and let him get on with it. I would say no to a few things, and those generally fell into the realms of oral sex. I never offered oral freely, only ever resorting to it periodically after getting the cold shoulder for saying no. I despised every minute of it. I hated gagging on the semen as it filled up the back of my throat. My eyes watered as I knew what was coming every time. I spent my entire time down there, counting, looking for distraction, hoping that it would be over quickly. Giving him oral sex was the worst. It was worse than the pain of anal rape or the first time he fucked me. It was the only time I can say I felt fearful. I felt degraded, like a tool, not like a person. His penis was slimy and cold. I would wretch as he pushed my head down onto his lap. I'd try to disguise the gagging with noise or movement, *I hope he can't tell that I think this is disgusting?* If he was standing, he would push me down in front of him and hold the back of my hair whilst thrusting into my mouth. I couldn't suppress the panic as my jaw wedged open to make room for his penis. He always pushed so deep inside me, I thought I'd choke to death. The closer he came to ejaculating, the more my body would freeze and just provide a hole for his needs. *He needs this from me*, I would tell myself. *He wants me and nobody else.*

As I moved into 6th form after, surprisingly, positive GCSE results, my days came with a lot more freedom. Technically, we weren't allowed to leave the school grounds during free periods, but we weren't challenged about it if we did. Additionally, they also permitted us to take our phones into school and use them freely within the 6th form block. It made keeping in contact easy as I wasn't limited to break and lunchtimes.

I started 6th form with high hopes. A clean slate having caught a break with top grades at GCSE. Following my love of science and my desire to do medicine *one day*, I chose to do 4 A levels (Maths, Biology, Chemistry, Physics) and AS level in Ethics and Philosophy that I would do over the two years. It was a high achieving school, and I was a high achiever, so I wasn't talked out of it by the teachers. I didn't realise at the time just how much work it would require me to do. My timetable was packed, as much as it had been in compulsory education. The only time I had free was lunch and break times and Wednesday afternoons that had been set aside for voluntary work rather than PE. I had come to a prior agreement with Kelsey that I could claim I was doing voluntary work at the farm. She didn't need the help, as, by the time I got to the farm, the girls would have done most of the jobs, so she covered for me when the school rang to check on me. Instead of using the time to catch up on schoolwork, I used the extra hours for Neil.

On most Wednesdays, except the days that Anne worked earlies, Neil would pick me up from the 6th Form car park, or I'd walk up to the main road, and he'd pick me up on the way through. It was a bold move, as my brother attended the same school, as did Rebekah's sister, Chloe. By that point though, we were nonchalant, bordering on arrogant about our *'affair'*. People's reluctance to confront us had given us the green light to carry on as we pleased. We weren't even discrete about it anymore. We didn't kiss or touch in public, and the conversations were kept vanilla, but hiding a flirt or a private joke had become a thing of the past. It wasn't a secret that we were always together, round at each other's houses or hiding away at the farm. It wasn't much of a secret that we were *'having an affair'*. It was the biggest unkept secret down at the farm. Although people had made remarks or sly comments, we had learned to ignore them rather than succumbing to the panic they would have brought a couple of years before. Talking our way out of being spotted together at my school was probably the most straightforward thing we could have sidestepped.

We had given up on the local nature park down the road from the school, it was too busy, and we had more time to move further afield. We moved further into the moors, about a 20-minute drive along the windy country lanes from my school. It was quiet, especially if it was raining. On the way, we'd pass the odd tractor or milk lorry and occasionally we'd see a white van man taking full opportunity of the open roads and lack of speed cameras. The vast expanse of the moors provided us with the secrecy and seclusion that we needed. There were no houses for miles and most of the roads were unsigned and unmarked. You could see for miles in all directions. Neil drove with purpose. He knew those roads from his days driving lorries and collecting milk from the dairy farms scattered along the country roads. He'd point them out and I would be reminded of the early days when we'd talk about something other than sex. I would sit in the front of the car most of the time as there was no need to hide whilst we were up there. Within a minute of turning off the main road, Neil would unbutton his flies for me to touch him.

"Suck it Tan," he'd say, and I knew what was expected of me.

I'd do it robotically, on autopilot. It was easier than the cold shoulder if I said no. Thankfully, he didn't ejaculate whilst we were moving, so I didn't have to worry too much about being sick. It was only the cold-slimy pre-cum and the handbrake digging into my ribs that I had to deal with, rather than the thick salty fluid clogging my throat.

Sometimes I'd get away without having to suck him if he wanted to be inside me. The logistics of him reaching my vagina were impossible to negotiate if my hair was spread across his lap, so instead I'd masturbate him whilst his fingers were inside me. He'd even leave them in there if he had to change gears, twisting his body to use the other hand to knock the gearstick. I didn't have any fear of crashing. I didn't have any fear of dying.

We frequented a road and the irony of its name caught me off guard; Exhibition Lane. It was an abandoned road, and only raised vehicles would have made their way through it. It was no match for Neil's huge 4x4, but it would have been impossible for most cars. A lower car would have bottomed out on the ridges, that weren't unlike a BMX track. Ditches lined either side of the road, hidden by overgrowth bursting through the stone walls. The derelict road provided an unnecessary shortcut between the two main roads, so it was left neglected by the council, providing a perfect place for the secret rendezvous.

On arriving, Neil would park with the back of his car to a tree, providing a little coverage from the main roads, but it wasn't necessary. Despite being incredibly open, up on the moors, the junction to the road was easily missed if you didn't know where to go. If his car was spotted, it would have taken extreme bravery to try and tackle the road to us. I'd climb through the seats into the back and Neil would exit the driver's seat and walk around the car to the back seat. We'd get straight down to business. There would be no talking or cuddling. His hands would be straight under my clothes before you could whisper "dogging". Two or three hours later, he'd have had his thrill. Penetrative sex would be without orgasm for both of us, so he would be finished off in my hand or mouth and I'd groan and moan for his pleasure. Those shenanigans became par for the course after a few meetups here.

Although mostly predictable, one of the days stands out in my mind. It's slightly diverging from the story's chronology, but it seems fitting to discuss it at this point. It was during Spring 2007. I was taking driving lessons at the time, which I had scheduled for 4 p.m. on Wednesday afternoons. It fitted in nicely with our meetups, giving us a few hours alone before he dropped me off at home. I'd get picked outside my house by my instructor and finish the lesson at the farm, ready for Neil's reappearance. That one afternoon, Neil picked me up from the school, and as I got into the car, he passed me a 37.5cL bottle of Smirnoff.

"Look what I've got," he said as he waved the bottle at me, pointing the neck towards my mouth.

He'd mentioned a few times that he wanted to get me drunk. He'd never seen me steaming drunk, just merry after a couple of cans at a show.

"Drink it then," he said as he placed it into my hands.

I hesitated, but the words of a previous conversation rattled around in my brain. *It will help you loosen up a bit*, he had told me. *Maybe he has got a point, maybe I won't be so stiff and uncomfortable about giving him oral if I'm off my head.* I cracked open the bottle, the red lid cracking from the ring seal. I put the rim to my mouth and tipped it back, knocking a swill into my mouth.

I gasped and coughed. I hadn't had vodka in a long time, as I had stopped going out with Sara and Cleo. Even then, I only every had it with a mixer. I contorted my face as I forcibly swallow, clutching my fist to my chest in response to the burn.

"You can manage more than that, you lightweight," he joked.

"Christ, I forgot how much it burns on the way down."

I took another mouthful, thankfully my response to it was less violent than the first one. I spun the cap back on the bottle.

"No, keep going," he said. *What, all of it?*

I gulped and gulped, which was met with Neil's face of approval. I finally recognised the effects as I reached the last few mouthfuls of the bottle, and the alcohol caught up with my bloodstream. *Woah, fuck.*

That's the last thing I remember from that day. There is a small flashback of lying on the back seat of Neil's car, looking down at my exposed breasts and thighs. And a brief recollection of calling my driving instructor after Neil had dropped me home to tell him I was unwell. I don't remember anything that Neil did to me in those lost hours.

Tanya Pursglove

CHAPTER 10

My first year of 6th form, just after I turned 17, saw me with a terrible bout of the flu. I was almost completely incapacitated with illness for the best part of a week. My joints burned, my throat was as though I had swallowed cacti, and my head felt like it would burst with each relentless cough. I'd spent two days at home, splitting my time between bed and the sofa, not getting out of my PJs. I didn't even have it in me to go down to the farm. The familiar ringtone of my phone awoke me from my stupor.

Drrr… drrr… drrr… drrr…

"Hi," the pain of talking kept my conversation minimal.

"Come on, let me take you out somewhere," Neil said.

"I dunno, I feel shit," I responded.

"The fresh air will do you good!"

He's probably right, getting some fresh air will probably make me feel better.

"Ok," I relented, "I'll see you soon."

Thirty minutes later, Neil reversed onto my driveway, and I let myself in the back door of the car and sat in the middle seat. He drove to a reservoir near my dad's house. He didn't try to touch me up on the way, and I didn't offer anything in conversation. I sat on the back seat, having wrapped myself up tightly in a huge puffer jacket. The cold air burnt my chest as I inhaled. It hurt to talk, it hurt to breathe. My head pounded with every cough and gasp for air. We got to the car park, and he got into the back of the car.

"Will you just cuddle me?" I asked in desperation.

I just wanted to feel safe, *I just want your arms wrapped around me as I fall asleep.* I couldn't bear the thought of sex, the only thing I wanted from Neil was to feel secure and cared for. I wanted to feel the way I felt on the first day he cuddled me, all those years ago in Falmer's Woods. *Protect me, and make this pain go away.* He didn't move but sat at the side of me whilst I rested my head on his warm arm. Comfortable, not quite content, but able to drift into a place of peace. Neil took a drag of his cigarette and offered it in my direction. I shook my head and coughed as the grey smoke entered my nostrils.

"No thanks," I said between coughs.

He finished his cigarette as I shut my eyes and I prayed that my head would stop throbbing. He opened the door and dropped the butt out through the crack, pulling the door closed again. I felt the movement of his hand down the arm I was leaning against. The wave of motion caused my head to slide, so I repositioned myself and hoped he'd take the hint. He didn't. His hand slid between my thighs, and he started rubbing my crotch. *Please, no, I don't feel well.*

"Can we just cuddle; I really feel like shit?" I asked.

"Fine," Neil responded curtly.

He took his hand away from my crotch and placed it across his leg, turning his body to face the window. My head slumped off him and the sudden jarring of the weight on my neck forced me to sit upright. *I want to go home*, I told myself. *I can't believe he still wants sex when I look like and smell like this. I feel disgusting; repulsive. I haven't got the energy. Why can't it just be enough that we are here together? I haven't seen him for two days, surely, can't he just enjoy being in my company?*

Neil sat there in stony cold silence, facing away from me, and made it impossible for me to cuddle him. I didn't care, I didn't have it in me to try and appease him. I just wanted to go home. I too sat in silence. Not stony cold silence like him, I didn't have the energy for that, I just let my brain empty into the vacuum of the car.

When he'd given me the silent treatment before, I'd always make it up to him. I'd always give him the best sex, the dirtiest loudest sex I could muster, even if I was angry with him. I hated the silent treatment; it was more than I could bear. I wished he would just shout at me, argue with me, just air his feelings, and hit me. He never did. He never shouted, he never called me names, he never gave me an inclination that he wanted to hit me. At least I would have received some indication of his feelings towards me. His silence had me dangling; clinging on to life, clinging on to sanity. We had talked and talked for thousands of hours over the years. He knew everything about me, I knew everything about him. No topics were ever out of bounds. There were no boundaries. He could have read a telephone directory and I would have listened intently; he had the ability to turn the most menial conversation into an animated one-man stage show. But his silence was deafening. His silence held me in isolation, a period of suspension; alone and unreachable. It broke me into a thousand pieces and shattered my core. I no longer existed; my fragile soul was decimated to dust. I was nothing. *I am nothing.*

After what felt like hours, Neil broke the silence.

"Did you see Catherine Tate last night? Fuckin' brilliant. *Fuckin' liberty....*" he joked, mimicking the gran's London accent.

"Yeah, it was good," I forced a smile.

He turned back towards me. *Thank God, he's not angry with me.* He slipped his arm over my shoulder and I leaned into him, cradled against his chest. His hand slid down and he held my breast. *Leave me alone.* I knew where it was going. I knew there was no getting away from the fact that Neil was horny. I didn't push him away, and only a half-hearted attempt at saying *not now* escaped my lips, but I didn't fight him. I couldn't have him cut me off again. He started to pull me tight towards him, getting himself more and more excited, moving his hands all over my body. He lifted his arm back over the front of me and slid his hands into my trousers. *It will all be over soon, just let him do what he needs to.* I sat there in silence, unable to muster the energy to even fake a contortion in my face. *I just want to go home.*

I lay back on the seat, my head pointed away from him, whilst he brought himself to a climax whilst his fingers were inside me, emptying his semen onto my groin. He sat there, catching his breath, completely unaware that I had been elsewhere during the entire process. I leant over and reached for the roll of toilet paper kept on the central console and wiped myself. He cleaned himself up and patted my knee.

"I needed that," he sighed as he rearranged his pants, trousers, and t-shirt. "Right, shall we get you back?"

I didn't say anything but pulled my trousers back up from my knees as Neil got out of the car and made his way to the driver's seat. *Yes, I want to go home.*

Neil dropped me off on the drive after a silent journey back. I heard nothing but the steady beating of the Gary Puckett and the Union gap playing Young Girl as he drove. I internally laughed as I did every time he played it. I felt sorry for him. It must have been awful to have sex with someone who wasn't present or showed no enjoyment and was switched off from the whole thing. *Why am I such a bitch, such a letdown? I should have played my part. He doesn't ask for much.* I got out of the car and told him I'd see him soon before making my way back into the house. I lifted my arm in a half-hearted attempt at a wave as he pulled off the drive.

I returned to my PJs and the sofa. I couldn't be bothered to freshen myself up, and I didn't care if I smelled of cigarette smoke and penis. I crawled onto the sofa and wept. The stark contrasts between the sexual encounters in the early days to the most recent ones were at the forefront of my mind. I missed the days where I felt panicked, exhilarated, terrified, longing; at least I felt something. At least I felt worshipped. Instead of feeling overwhelmed and nervous, like in the beginning, I felt nothing but emptiness, a void more powerful than a black hole. I was absent of emotion. I was dead.

*

A few days later, once recovered, I made my way down to the farm for the afternoon. Thankfully, I felt much better by that point, physically if not mentally, so the farm looked appealing- despite the bitterly cold weather. I got down there to find our second horse, Goldie, had a clean stable. I was pleasantly surprised. I thought someone had kindly mucked out before I had got there. Unfortunately, that was not the case, and alarm bells rang out as I realised that Goldie may be developing a life-threatening condition called an impacted colic.

After a discussion with the vet on the phone, I set about the evening trying to get him moving to see if moving it would stimulate his gut to pass faeces. It was a futile attempt, but Goldie didn't seem distressed. I rang the vet back and between us, we decided to wait and see what would happen overnight, with monitoring and regular exercise. He was still eating well, and welcomed the sloppy feeds the vet suggested might help soften his stool and allow for its passing, so the vet wasn't too concerned. Geraldine was working night shifts at the time, and her husband was away, so there would be nobody present who could take over from me and see to Goldie throughout the night. I rang Geraldine at work and asked her if it was OK if I slept on her sofa so that I could keep a close eye on Goldie. Thankfully, she didn't have a problem with it, so after everyone had left for the night, I made myself at home and set my alarm for every 30 minutes.

I was up and down all night, walking Goldie around the yard for 15 minutes at a time, before going back inside to defrost myself. It was sub-zero and the wind rushing through the channel of the valley froze me to the bone. I never got the chance to warm up as I curled into a ball on the lumpy leather sofa, periodically nodding off before being jolted awake by the piercing screams of my alarm. Everything seemed so much louder with the silent backdrop of the farm. It was eerie out in the yard, with nothing but munching horses and the odd scurrying rat that sent my flight response into overdrive. Eventually, after the most unsettled night, having spent ninety percent of it outside in the Baltic conditions, I walked out for one last time at 5 am to be greeted by a large pile of faeces in the middle of the stable. I couldn't feel much in the way of relief as my exhausted and frozen body fought to remain upright, so I went back into the house and turned the remainder of my alarms off as I flicked on the TV to drown out the loneliness.

An hour or so later, I forced myself to get moving and start the jobs I'd have to finish later in the day. It was too cold to sit around, even in the house. After emptying and changing the water buckets, I heard the crunching of the rubbly drive. I looked over the stable door to see Anne's car reversing back against the hedge. I was relieved to see her, a human, someone that would drown out the silence I had endured.

"Morning!" I cheerfully shouted as she walked past my stable.

"Morning! What are you doing down here this early?" She asked, the confusion apparent on her face.

I told her about the night I'd had. How, thankfully Goldie had finally pooed.

"That was lucky!" she exclaimed, sympathetically.

She was right, *it was lucky*, and I finally realised how fortunate he had been. Just after Samantha and Cerys arrived and the yard started buzzing to life, Anne left for work.

Drrr… drrr… drrr… *Neil*.

"Morning you," his warm voice running through my veins.

"Have a guess where I've been all night," I said, feeling more alert. "Only at the bloody farm, trying to get Goldie to shit."

"How are you getting home?" He asked.

"I've got to wait until Dad finishes work this evening, he's working the other side of the Peaks, so he can't nip back, and I haven't got a key."

"Come up here," he said. "I'll put the kettle on."

Yes! I thought, *central heating, a sofa, someone for company!*

"See you later," I called over my shoulder at Cerys, "If you need me, I'll be at Neil's!"

"Ok, bye!" She replied, but I had already closed the gate and was making my way up the drive.

I let myself in when I made it up to his house ten minutes later. He was sitting, waiting for me with a cup of tea on the coffee table and his arms wide open to greet me. I was pleased to see him. I was pleased it was daylight and that the eerie night at the farm was behind me. I sat, shattered, at his side and rested my head on his chest as he wrapped me in his arms. *Warm, you're so warm, so comfortable.* The exhaustion and the loneliness of the night was replaced by Neil's security. I ached, my joints creaking and groaning as they thawed out. *I could stay like this forever, encased in your body; shielded and protected from the elements.* I yearned for his affection. The warmth permeated the black hole that had formed in my soul, shining light on the darkest corners of my mind. *This is what I've wanted all along; you.*

My thoughts were abruptly stopped in their tracks as Neil slid his hands, once again, into my trousers. *Why is it always this? Why can't we just enjoy closeness without resorting to sex? Why can't you just cuddle me?* Neil pulled me tighter and tighter into his body with the arm that he'd wrapped around me. One finger, two fingers, three fingers, pushed their way into my vagina. He began pumping away at my genitals and I felt his body tense with excitement as mine disappeared from underneath me.

"I want to fuck you," he whispered as he pulled his arm away from me, letting me slide back onto the settee.

He started pulling at my trousers, freeing the waistband away from his awkwardly bent wrist. I lifted my bum to allow him access as I had done hundreds of times before. *Just let him have what he wants, make him happy. Do it for him.* I lay there, limp, detached from the reality that I'd found myself in. I was so exhausted that my mind didn't form any thoughts. I lay there like a corpse waiting for him to finish what he wanted to do to me. He pushed my knees apart and went down on me. I didn't feel anything towards it, completely disconnected from my surroundings, like I wasn't even there. *Tanya, the Never Present.* After realising that I had slipped into my wilderness for an excessively long period of time, I recognised that Neil was becoming impatient with me, his forceful fingers ramming me harder and harder. *Oh shit. Sorry, I forgot.* I started my routine moaning and groaning, tipping my pelvis in his direction.

"Come for me, Tan," he urged me on.

I released my inner demon and howled and gyrated at him, pushing him away as I faked my climax. *That'll do*, I thought to myself. He sat backwards, exasperated by his efforts, and reached to light a cigarette, throwing the packet and lighter on my chest as he took his first draw on it. I reached up to my chest and mirrored his actions, not bothering to pull my trousers up. *What's the point? He'll only have them off again in a minute.*

I finished my cigarette indifferent to my environment, stretching my arm periodically to tap the ash in the ashtray on the coffee table, still completely naked from the waist down. As I got to the last drag, the filter burnt my fingers, disappointed that the cigarette break was over, I squashed the butt in the caked tray, drawing the stub through the sandy ash that lay on the surface.

"Let me fuck you on the stairs," he said.

I gave a non-committal shrug, kicking off the trousers from around my ankles and picking them up as I stood up to walk to the hallway. As we had done, numerous times before, we walked up the stairs to the ninety-degree bend at the top, and I lowered myself face down on the top step and dropped my trousers by my head. Neil came up behind me and guided himself into my vagina. I lay on my chest as he applied pressure on my lower back, tipping my pelvis at his desired angle. It didn't take him long, only thirty minutes or so before he pulled out three or four thrusts early and finished himself off on my buttocks. I grabbed my trousers from the side of my head and walked to the bathroom, throwing Neil a handful of toilet paper to clean himself. I turned back to the bathroom and wiped myself down whilst on the toilet, redressing whilst I sat there. I stared blankly at the books on the shelf in front of the loo. A couple of the books that I had lent him were sitting there. *Cute.*

Fucking on the stairs was probably the easiest for me. I didn't have to be significantly involved in the whole process, apart from presenting my rear end for Neil. I warmed up throughout the morning as Neil wanted to go again and again and I took a more active role instead of being a passive receptacle. However, my enthusiasm dampened again as I got progressively sore and increasingly tired from a sleepless night.

As lunchtime approached, we knew Anne would come back, so we stopped the sex. I made my way to the settee as Neil pottered about in the kitchen. As I listened to the distant clinking of cups and crockery, I could feel myself floating in the tranquil realm between conscious and unconscious. My body was heavy and sank into the deep leather cushions of the settee. I heard Neil walking towards the hall, but I didn't open my eyes. I was too comfortable, and I didn't want to go back to reality. Neil's footsteps stopped as he stood in the lounge doorway. I heard a faint rustle of fabric as he shuffled around. After a second or two of silence, he draped a coat over me and stroked it down as he turned and left again. *He really loves me, he really does.* It was a fleeting moment, but it was enough to reawaken my decaying heart. I couldn't sleep, I was too touched by his action, but I didn't want to be awake when Anne got back. I didn't want my bubble popping, so I lay there, motionless for half an hour.

Anne left after lunch. I was still in that flitting between the land of sleep and awake when she left, but as soon as I heard the door click behind her and her car pull off the drive, Neil nudged me alert.

The sex started again and continued for the rest of the afternoon. It was straight down to business. We couldn't be in each other's company without there being sex. It didn't matter if I was on my period or not. If we had time together, there would be sexual activity. If we had time together and alone, it would be sex, sex, and more sex. It was tiresome. The entire time was spent satisfying his ego or providing his sexual pleasure- they were one and the same. We spent the entire afternoon re-enacting various positions from on stairs, the settee, the bed and everywhere in between. At one point, we were even on the kitchen floor. It wasn't like we were passionately romping throughout the house; it was more of a checklist for him. That's how it came across anyway. Plenty of pumping and pounding, awkwardly changing position and repeat. That was the extent of the day. I was sore and unsatisfied.

That evening we walked to the farm at his usual time. It made a nice change to walk down with him, and we knew it would get them all gossiping, but we were beyond caring. The gossip had been around for years, and we were too arrogant to think we'd get caught in the act, so he would push it further and further, taking bigger and bigger risks each time.

*

My mood over the previous months had depleted. I yearned for Neil when I couldn't be with him, but I was starting to notice that the affection was one-sided. I was no longer the goddess he worshipped. I was no longer inundated with flattery and admiration. He was more obsessed with me than ever, or rather he was more obsessed with my body and what he could do to it. He pushed my body to the extremes of its ability, stretching and contorting every inch of me. My once *beautiful blue eyes* and my *big bouncy hair* had been replaced with my *massive tits* and *wet pussy*. I detested that. I detested feeling so degraded, having my body parts lined up and scored; being referred to in the crudest manner. He no longer wanted me for my intelligent conversation, he no longer wanted me for my thoughts, for my mind. For years, he told me that we were soul mates, for years he promised me the world. I'd dreamt and fantasised about having a life with him, away from Anne, away from people who wouldn't understand. I'd never thought about children, but I had imagined us leading an everyday, boring life, somewhere out of the way, just him and me and maybe a couple of dogs.

The talk of us being 'together' was sporadic. It had pretty much stopped by the time I was 16, so by the time I turned 17 in September 2006, it was a thing of the past. Occasionally I'd be offered a nugget of hope that things would change- he'd be dismissive of Anne and angry that she was 'in our way'. He would describe how lonely he felt, and I could empathise. I felt lonely without him. Sometimes I felt lonely with him. My feelings were different, though. He wasn't just good company for me; he was the only thing I had left. We were spending in excess of 18 hours a day together or on the phone. I had lost everything else. I had no friends, no life away from him. My schoolwork had gone out of the window completely. It didn't matter to me, nothing mattered to me. If I couldn't have him, I didn't want to be alive. I was nothing more than a worthless secret, second best, always destined to be a piece on the side. My thoughts and feelings didn't count. It didn't matter how upset I got, how much I tried to step away and find myself again. I was constantly crowded with Neil, he was there at every waking second, and yet I was permanently lonely, permanently isolated.

I would still engage with my friends at school, but I was a shadow of my former self. I had shifted from a bubbly, attention-seeking, vivacious girl to being to someone who was never involved. Neil knew my timetable and would ring me the minute I had a free period or a break. I'd barely have time to pack my books into my bag before I felt my pocket vibrating with his call. If I didn't answer it, I'd get the cold shoulder treatment. His silence was like a knife to the chest. When I did answer it, my ears would be filled with his heavy breathing, his wanting, his voice, deep and gravelly, telling me what he was going to do to me.

I was permanently locked in my head, unable to appreciate life around me. I felt like I was carrying the world on my shoulders, trying to juggle my life around Neil. I wouldn't do anything that would affect the time I spent with him. I wouldn't go out for the night because I knew he'd be upset. I couldn't arrange to see my friends outside of school hours because I'd get the silent treatment. I didn't even want to see them anymore because a minute with them meant that it was one minute less pleasing Neil. My friends had all known about Neil for a while by that point. He was no longer an elusive figure- except to those who had connections with the farm, but those at school had known for a long time. He started to pick me up from the school carpark, so when they'd walk me to the car, he'd charm and flatter them too. He was a 'nice guy'.

I had no life away from Neil. I no longer danced and I barely attended school- often leaving with him halfway through the day. I felt empty when we weren't together. I was tearful through the night and struggled to sleep. I got behind on schoolwork and assignments. I felt like I couldn't devote any time to anything except Neil because he needed me all the time, and he was exhausting. I couldn't bring myself to be anyone else to anybody else because I was giving my all to keep Neil happy, in the hope that one day, it would just be him and me.

The whole situation left me physically and emotionally drained.

CHAPTER 11

Christmas 2006 came and went the same as the years before. For the whole holiday, I spent the days and nights isolated from the only person I had left. Of course, once again, my family took the time off work, but I couldn't be present; I couldn't enjoy their company. My secret was eating me alive, and I didn't trust myself to keep my mouth shut. *They just won't get it*, I told myself. *They'll split us up. They'll hate me for being 'the other woman'. They brought me up to be better than this.*

The end of the Christmas period brought the New Year celebrations and this one was going to be the best one yet, as I was spending it with Anne, Julie, Liam and of course Neil! I was beside myself with excitement. Neil and I would finally be able to celebrate something together. I didn't care that the others would be there as well, as far as I was concerned, I was celebrating NYE with Neil!

Julie was working as a barmaid in a local pub over New Year's Eve. So, we had arranged for the five of us to spend the evening at the pub, seeing in the New Year with copious amounts of alcohol and music. I was somewhat out of practice when it came to going out and drinking, but I didn't care. I meticulously planned my outfit for weeks leading up to the event, down to the make-up look and how I'd wear my hair. I wanted to look spectacular and I did.

My dark long ringlets worked perfectly that evening, coming together along with my sultry make-up. It was rare to have them working together in perfect unison. My bouncy tight curls offered incredible volume and fun, whilst my dark eye makeup glamourised my face, making me appear much older than reality. I looked about 20. I wore the same metallic, backless top that I used to wear out with Sara overlayed with a black pinstripe blazer, and teamed it up with the black Rara skirt with built-in pants that Neil fell in love with many years ago. My matt black stilettoes finished my outfit, I was completely in denial about how much my feet would hurt by the end of the night, but I didn't care, because the length they offered my legs was worth any amount of pain.

Julie worked the late afternoon shift at the pub, so Dad dropped me and Liam off in the car park in the early evening. I teetered over the uneven car park, and we made our way inside. Neil's car wasn't in the carpark, so I had time to squeeze in a couple of drinks to settle my nerves before he got there. *Why am I so nervous? Is it nerves or excitement?* I concluded it was probably a mixture of the two. I felt anxious about the alcohol making me too comfortable around him in front of the others, or rather, that the alcohol would make *him* too comfortable with *me* around the others. There was a part of me that wanted to get absolutely annihilated, so I didn't have to care. At least I'd have a reason to blow our cover, but part of me wanted to remain in complete control. Liam ordered me a double vodka and coke whilst we sat chewing the fat and relaxing. It was still quiet, so we were able to talk without shouting over the ramble of the punters or the music.

I was halfway down my second double vodka when Neil and Anne arrived. I was giggling and relaxed until my eyes met with Neil's. His eyes were dangerous; they spoke words that his mouth couldn't in front of the others. I felt them bore into my soul, penetrate my body. I knew he wanted me. He waited for Anne to lean into me in a 'hello' hug, and as she pulled back, he leaned over the corner of the table and kissed my cheek, perilously close to the corner of my mouth. My heart immediately began to race, and I turned my head quickly to hide the panic that had risen inside me. *Did they see it?*

Neil sat on the stool at the side of me after placing a pint on the coaster and another double vodka in front of me. As he draped his coat on the bench over my shoulder, the smell of the leather wafted under my nose, and a flash of his aftershave caught me off guard, reawakening my senses. He never wore aftershave when we met in secret. We weren't *allowed* to wear perfumed scents around each other in case someone smelt mine on him, or his on me. He didn't take his eyes off me. The tension was palpable, euphoric, electric, unbearable. His leg pressed tight up against mine under the table. I knocked my drink back, the sweet, burning liquid rushed straight into my bloodstream as I swapped out the empty glass for the one Neil had placed in front of me. *Fuck control. Just get hammered.*

As the evening steadily progressed, my ability to remain in the conversation diminished and I lost track of what was being said. The volume of the pub increased, and I got increasingly lost in the atmosphere of the music and cloud of alcohol fumes. My mind drifted like a boat on the open sea, between the current surroundings and the pressure I felt under. The pressure to behave; the pressure to be silent. It would have been so easy to just blurt it all out. To stand there with a lit match and watch all our lives go up in flames like an inferno. *Just tell them Tanya*, I heard the devil in me say. *Do it. Just fucking do it and sit back and watch the chaos. Force his hand, take ownership of this mess.*

Drink after drink, I sat there, being a good girl. Blinking the thoughts away, shutting down my inner monologue with vodka. Neil couldn't see what was happening inside me. His eyes told me he wanted me, told me how desirable I was. He was completely blind, dazzled by my body and his own thoughts about fucking me. He wasn't at all worried that I might suddenly set us all ablaze.

Tiger feet!

"I love this song," I shouted. "I love this!"

I threw myself up out of the cubicle and stood in the middle of the pub, glass in one hand, holding it up in the air as I danced and shouted the lyrics over the beat. I was the only one there and I didn't care one bit. Liam got up and mirrored me, Neil followed a split second after. As the floor started to fill with drunk middle-aged men, the music got louder and louder and the voices in my head silenced. Song after song, I found myself flitting between the men on the packed floor and the table where my drinks were being put one after the other.

Cigarette break. I need a cigarette. I need air.

I slammed my empty glass on the table, and heard the clinking of ice cubes as they bounced from the glass and danced across the wooden tabletop.

Air, I need air.

I could barely stand. I could barely find the door. I knocked into people and tables as I tried to negotiate my way to the exit. I scrambled through my packet of cigarettes and dug down the front of my bra for my lighter. I crashed into the door and I used my weight to push it open. The fresh, cold, crisp air slapped me around the face, and my eyes took a second to adjust to the blackened sky. The door slammed shut behind me and I apologised to it for failing to carefully guide it back into place.

I've.... I've gone too far. Oh shit! I thought as I inhaled my first drag. It flooded my chest, puffing it out into the night sky. As I offered the cigarette up to my mouth for a second drag, the distant pumping of the music from inside became clear and loud. I turned myself to see Neil allowing the door to clap shut behind him. Nausea hit me like a train.

"I'm gonna...." I started to say as I threw my cigarette to the floor.

I stumbled away from him, further towards the car park. *No. Too late.* My hands grasped for the chain linked fence that surrounded the empty beer garden. I allowed my body to hang forward from my arms as I linked my fingers through the fence above my head. I wretched a couple of times before the contents of my stomach made an appearance and splashed between my feet. I used the fence to brace myself on between heaves.

"I've been wanting to do this all night," I heard Neil's voice over my shoulder as he inserted his fingers inside me.

I clutched at the fence, dry retching as my stomach desperately tried to save me from the alcohol I had consumed. I barely acknowledged Neil's presence; too busy trying to avoid spraying my feet with the vomit and saliva that fell out of my mouth. The groaning in my ear as he bent over the back of me didn't register until it was drowned out by the bar music crisping up in the cold air.

Neil quickly pulled his fingers out of me and moved them to hold my hair back as I repeatedly retched.

"Is she alright?" I heard Liam's voice of concern shout from the door.

"Yeah, just gone a bit overboard," Neil replied.

＊

There was a thin atmosphere between Anne and me. It was subtle, but because I had spent so long studying her, I'd become highly attuned to her change in mood. She and Neil had been arguing. He told me that she was annoyed because I was at their house all the time. He said that we'd have to *'cool it off'* in the evenings a little bit. It is worth bearing in mind that I had been at their house every night for the previous few years. We did as he suggested and backed off each other after the farm in the evenings. I'd go to their house two or three times a week instead of all seven, and Neil would stay at the farm with me on the other 4 or 5 days.

Ultimately, nothing changed, but I think Anne was making a point that Neil spent too much time with me. She likely had seen too many things by that point. Too many flirty smiles between Neil and I; too many glances of guilt and shock as it flashed across my face when we were nearly caught. The never-ending gossip at the farm had more than likely got back to her too, which had likely only exacerbated her suspicions. We dutifully did what we interpreted to be an instruction to be discrete. It didn't stop the sex, nor did it stop the rendezvous away from the farm. It didn't even cut down the hours we spent together; all it did was increase the hours Neil spent unsupervised with me. We maintained this for about three weeks before we fell back into old habits.

＊

During Spring 2007, we attended plenty of shows and Neil was always there. Marilyn had voiced how much she hated him hovering around all the time. She'd shared those feelings with me frequently, describing how he was a creep and a dirty old man, her words were like daggers, but I'd always throw them back. Marilyn had spoken to Geraldine numerous times by that point and Geraldine agreed with her. Tensions between Marilyn and I were at an all-time high. I loved her, but I would find myself increasingly frustrated at the barriers she tried to place between Neil and I. *Why can't she just let me be happy? She's jealous because I'd rather be with Neil than her.* She was working increasingly long hours and spending more and more time away from the farm. I didn't complain. I was glad I had the freedom to do what I wanted without having to look over my shoulder for her prying eyes. She covered the farmyard with the stealth of a ninja; able to get around in almost complete silence, waiting to catch us. She was trying to prove it was going on, but we were too experienced at hiding by that point. We would hide in plain sight, making it so normal that it became accepted by everyone. She stood no chance.

As the tensions increased between Marilyn and I, my mood continued to drop. I was stuck in a cycle of depression when alone and euphoria when with Neil. There was no in-between. It didn't help that Neil was starting to blow hot and cold with me by that point. We were either physically having sex or having phone sex. There was no conversation, just straight down to business at every given opportunity. I was tired.

"Can we go out somewhere? The pub, or something? I just want to feel normal for a bit," I asked him. I'd be told that it was too risky; someone might see. *Why is that even a problem at this point?*

It broke me in two. I'd given myself to him in every way I could. There are things that I cannot mention because they are just too painful and humiliating, but for the sake of maintaining some dignity, it's sufficient to say that he had used my body in *every way imaginable.*

The sex wasn't even good, but the attention I got from Neil was addictive. There was not a part of me that he didn't know (except my clitoris, of course), but I had his complete and undivided attention. He would shout my name in the throes of it. It made me feel wanted; it made me believe that it was more than sex. He wanted *me* more than *anyone else* in the world. I was the woman who turned him on, turned on his animal instincts and desires. It made me feel wanted, desired, and attractive; it made me forget the awful hours in between. During sex, I felt like a goddess. His attention was my addiction. Once I knew he had spent his load for the day, the conversation would start again. Then we would talk about the things we used to, and it was like having the 'old' Neil back. The one who would try to woo me, try to impress me; make me laugh, and laud over me in ways that weren't sexual. He reminded me what it was like to flirt and feel loved. If he hadn't finished sex for the day though, we never reached that point. We spent our time alone pumping and jumping, or if we were at the farm, we would be sneaking off to a quiet corner for groping, hand jobs, or oral.

I wasn't the only one addicted. Neil inserted himself into every aspect of my life. He integrated himself into my family and he was a regular feature in our house. He drove us to the airport, took me to my summer ball, invited me out with him and Anne, and came with my family on days out. He was a constant presence in my life. He was as obsessed with me as I was with him. We spent over 18 hours of the day together in person or on the phone. The only time we spent without communication was when we were asleep. He was equally addicted, but our addictions presented differently; I relished in his attention, and he relished in my body.

*

August 2007 was a pivotal point in my relationships with the people closest to me. The strain between Marilyn, Neil, and I was at an all-time high. Marilyn had bitched about Neil to people at the farm and didn't care who heard what she thought about him; openly referring to him as a paedophile and a pervert. One day she caught him walking around to the stable to watch me get undressed and loudly declared, hoping everyone would hear that "Tanya doesn't require an audience". He scurried off in the opposite direction. Marilyn's visits to the farm became sparse, but if she was there, Neil would sit by the school and wait for me to finish my jobs instead of following me around. He was afraid of Marilyn; Marilyn wasn't afraid of speaking her mind to anybody who would listen.

It all blew up one day when we were at a show. We had gone in our lorry, which by then was exhausted and temperamental. A few other people from the farm had also gone to the same show. Marilyn's bitching had got back to Anne, so Anne spent the whole day giving us both the side-eye. Neil didn't come over to us at the show either but spent the day with Anne's friends from the farm. It was awkward; the whole atmosphere was suffocating. I tried to act normal, but inside, my guts were churning. I found that the best way to appease Marilyn was to pretend that everything was normal and that there was no atmosphere. I thought that she'd soon snap out of it and make amends with Anne and Neil. It was necessary to quash the rumours- *quickly.*

As we were preparing to pack up for the day, I loaded the horse, and Marilyn and I sat in the lorry cab waiting to leave the showground. Marilyn turned the lorry's ignition and was greeted with the chugging starter motor but no engine. It was distressing to break down at the best of times, but with a horse in the back, it became even more time-critical. Add in the show's atmosphere with Anne and Neil, and the tension became palpable, unbearable. Neil did nothing to help that situation when he started to walk over to the lorry to help. Anne flew into a rage, and people from the farm had to hold her back; I'm sure if they hadn't, she'd have dragged Marilyn out of the lorry and slit her throat. *Shit!*

*

I was beyond grateful that the farm was empty on our return, so I made a swift exit. I had cried buckets of tears during the journey back. I was furious with Marilyn. I was infuriated that she might have jeopardised my relationship with Anne. I needed to keep Anne onside to maintain my relationship with Neil.

My relationship with Marilyn was hanging on by a thread. Over the next few days, Neil didn't go to the farm. I spent the entire time trying to work around Anne's hours so we didn't have to bump into each other. Obviously, Neil and I were still in communication and would meet up away from the farm, but those extra hours without each other were difficult. My dad intervened in the argument between Marilyn and me. We walked up to her house one evening, and I had it out with her.

"You are being ridiculous!" I screamed at her. "What is your fucking problem with him? He's my friend! You are imagining things, it's all in your head!" (Yes, I really did gaslight her.)

The following day Geraldine intervened and called Anne, Marilyn and I into the house to sort it all out *"for the sake of the farm atmosphere"*. Anne was doing her best to disguise her disgust with the whole idea, but she sat and listened to Marilyn's grovelling apology for the 'misunderstanding'. Anne even defended mine and Neil's friendship at one point, much to my surprise; mostly because she had been telling Neil to distance himself from me for months. Geraldine then suggested that Marilyn should apologise to Neil and make amends. *Ha!* I thought, gleefully, spitefully. *Go on then, apologise!* So, a few minutes later, Marilyn and I found ourselves driving up the road to Neil's house.

She said she was nervous. And the spiteful bitch in me was glad she was nervous. I knew Neil would pick up on it and take back the control he'd lost to her loudmouth. I wanted Marilyn to feel foolish. I wanted all the nonsense to stop. The only way that it would happen was if she swallowed her pride, admitted she was wrong and ate a slice of humble pie. Neil let us in, and I showed Marilyn where to sit. *You're in my territory now.* We waited in the lounge whilst he boiled the kettle. She was paler than the nicotine-stained magnolia walls. Her large frame was swallowed up by the settee and she looked small as she fidgeted nervously. Neil walked in calmly, a cigarette between the fingers of the hand he carried her cup in. *Ha, she'll hate that!* As he set the cups on the coffee table Marilyn blurted an apology. He shrugged his shoulders, nonchalantly. *He is taking the higher ground*, I thought. I think he was relieved to have one over on her. I think he saw the same as me; if we didn't build bridges, we wouldn't have been able to continue. So, he *graciously* accepted her apology, and the tension in the room dissipated in a puff of his smoke.

Although that was quite a significant point in the journey, things settled down quickly, and regular service resumed. It was the summer holidays, so my days were mostly made up of Neil. If we weren't together, we were on the phone. I'd be down at the farm for most of the day as it was easier to be ready if Neil got in touch for meeting up. I had also recently passed my driving test, which gave us so much more freedom. We were meeting away from the farm most weekdays, depending on the hours that Anne was working, of course. The nights were drawing out, so we would spend the evenings talking at the side of the school until Anne left, then we'd sneak off for a grope or sex of some description. I'd be at their house in the evenings, and we'd have dinner together most nights, then I'd drive home at about 10 p.m.

Some of those nights, Anne would fall asleep on the settee opposite the TV. Meanwhile, Neil and I would sit on the two-seater under the window. That allowed Neil to have his fingers in my vagina whilst she slept just a couple of feet away from us. The more risks we took, the bigger the thrill he got from it. It would make him hard enough to for sex, even without needing a blue pill. Obviously, it never got that far; it was easy to quickly remove his fingers from my vagina if she woke up, but he would have struggled to explain what we were doing if I was straddling him on the settee.

With hindsight, I'm not sure if she was ever asleep. Neil seemed to enjoy laughing at her behind her back, but I will admit that I felt uneasy about it, despite how much I had begun to resent her. He would tell me personal things about her when we were alone. I wondered if he told Peter things about me, about what we did, how we fucked, what I had let him do to me. I don't know if he told me the things about Anne to make me feel like I was more important than her or if it was to keep me onside. It had the opposite effect, though. It didn't empower me; it made me feel vulnerable. It made me feel paranoid about what he had said to Peter about me. It wasn't just Peter that knew about me anymore. His ex-wife also knew about me- the wife he'd been married to when he had an affair with Anne. Even at 17, I knew it was weird, but Neil seemed to spin things and make it sound completely normal.

One evening, after he had left the farm, Neil rang me as I finished hanging the night-time hay nets.

"I'm heading out with Helen to fetch some tobacco, fancy a ride?"

Helen was Neil's neighbour. She had known about us for a few months and had been a go-between if I needed to get a message to Neil in the evening when Anne was home. We had texted a handful of times over the months when I needed her to get Neil to ring me. She was really nice; loud and crass, but had a good sense of humour.

Neil picked me up from the road up from the farm, and I jumped into the back seat, whilst he and Helen sat up front.

"Jim has just driven past me, I'm hoping he didn't recognise me in the dark" I said as I clambered across the leather.

"Yeah, we just saw him pulling back into the farm, no doubt going home to drink his Special Brew," Neil said.

I sat in the back and listened to the conversation from the front. I didn't have much to offer, so I just absorbed the menial information that was being exchanged between Neil and Helen. She offered him directions as Neil got closer to the destination, and when we arrived, he pulled into the pitch-black carpark.

"I'll text you as I head back," Helen shouted over the slamming of Neil's door as he made his way on to the back seat.

"Well, hello," he said seductively as he slipped his hands down the front waistband of my jodhpurs.

We got down to business straight away, steaming up the windows of the car in the abandoned carpark. He had just ejaculated and cleaned himself up with tissue when his phone screen lit up in the centre console in response to an incoming text message.

Helen:
Consider this your three-minute warning.

He gathered himself back together and hopped back in the front seat of the car, turning the ignition and fired up the engine. He put the heater on to demist the windows and they had mostly cleared by the time Helen got back to the car.

"Jesus!" She exclaimed. "Crack a window, it stinks of sex in here!"

We all laughed.

*

As my 18th birthday approached, I grew less and less interested in celebrating it. I'd had the offer from my friends that we could celebrate it out in the town, but obviously I declined. I didn't have any desire to mark the day. I was another year older but still had nothing to show for it. My 18th birthday was spent with Anne and Neil at their house. I climbed into Neil's car after I had finished at the farm for the evening, when he passed me a card and a carrier bag. Neil brought me a birthday present from the both of them. I knew it was from Neil, I knew he had picked it out, but the pang of sadness that entered my chest when I saw that he'd signed her name on the card, next to his, hit me like a car. *Neil and Anne. Fuck off, Neil and Anne. She didn't pick this, she didn't contribute anything to the decision. Don't contaminate 'Neil' by putting Anne next to it.*

I sat at the side of him in his car on the driveway of the farm as I unwrapped the present from the carrier bag. *You could have actually wrapped it for God sake.* I turned the box around to look at the picture. It was a necklace holder. A necklace holder in the shape of an elegant dancer. *See, I fucking knew she had nothing to do with this.*

"I love it," I smiled.

CHAPTER 12

Julie and Liam had been living in Shetland for a while by October 2007. They had bought a small hotel on the island with an integrated pub. As the island didn't have much in the way of visitors, the locals used the pub in the evenings, but throughout the seasons, Liam's photography clients used the hotel. It was a delightful little set-up and I loved hearing about it when Julie rang to fill me in on her new adventure.

I had missed them so much since they moved, but they had given me an open invitation to go and visit once I turned 18. They didn't want me to go up before I turned 18 because of Julie's alcohol licence. The island was so quiet the police would regularly drop by and check for underage drinkers or drink drivers. Julie was worried about her licence should she get caught serving someone underage. Neil didn't want me to go. He told me as much, many times during the weeks up to the departure date. He sulked and employed every method he could to get me to change my mind. He stopped taking his bipolar medication. He said he didn't like the way it made him feel. His mood was all over the place for a week or so and I felt overwhelmed and panicked. He hadn't been to the farm for a couple of days, which was most unusual and although we had spoken on the phone, I felt inundated with stress because I hadn't been able to see him in the flesh.

As I finished my jobs on the empty farm, I received a text from him to go up to his house. Dread washed over me, as Anne had been very clear that I had spent too much time up there in recent months, so I felt as though I was stuck between a rock and a hard place. I wanted to see him for myself, instead of him trying to convince me that he was ok, when he clearly wasn't. Anne had left the farm an hour or so before the text, so I knew she'd be home, and I was concerned that it was a trap, so I responded to his message carefully.

OK, do you need me to bring anything? I'll be up shortly, just finishing off down here.

No kisses, no smileys. Just keep it plain and simple in case it was Anne that had text me from his phone. I stayed on the farm for a short while longer. I sat twiddling my thumbs so it didn't look like I was rushing to see him the minute I received *his* text. After 20 minutes or so, I closed the stable door and made my way up the farm. I put the key in the ignition and with a deep breath induced by my anxiety, turned the ignition to hear the engine rumble.

Their house was only 60 seconds from the farm by car, so my anxiety didn't have much time to escalate in the short journey, but that didn't stop it trying. I reversed onto the drive as I had done many times, careful not to back into Anne's car. I turned off the headlights, pulled the handbrake, and cautiously climbed out, slamming the car door so my presence would have been heard.

I'd better not let myself in this time, I thought as I went to reach for the doorhandle out of habit and clenched my fists to knock on the door instead. I heard footsteps approach the door and the click of the sliding bolt as it was disengaged. The door handle depressed and Anne held the door open a few inches, just enough to illuminate my face with the hall light.

"Neil text me," I said as I tried to ignore the shocked look from her face.

"See if you can talk some sense into him because he won't listen to me," she said, obviously exasperated, but a small flash of relief crossed her face that I was there. "He's upstairs"

I made my way up the curved stairs and as I peered into the bedroom, I could see Neil pacing around his side of the bed. He looked in a bad way. He looked manic. His white t-shirt hung from his narrow frame, almost looking two or three sizes too big. He was in navy striped pyjama bottoms, that again, hung from his body.

"Tan!" He exclaimed, "step into my office!"

He wasn't *that* mad, this was just one of the many phrases that he would cycle, quite often in relation to the stable, or the car; his little joke. His eyes were wide, but not in a way I had seen before. He normally looked at me wide eyed, when I'd captivated his attention, but this time, he looked frantic, and behind his eyes looked chaotic, not filled with wanting.

"I take it she didn't know I was coming?" I whispered, pointing to the floor where Anne stood in the kitchen beneath us, aware that noise travelled very easy in his house.

He shook his head. *Thanks for the warning.*

"What's going on?" I asked.

"Nothing much, you?"

But his denial about how bad he was didn't sit well with me. He looked like a grenade just waiting to explode and wipe out everything in his periphery. He continued to pace backwards and forwards, animatedly hitching up his PJ bottoms as they kept slinking from his waist as he marched.

I stood and watched him for a few minutes. He opened his arms to me, but I violently shook my head, repointing at the floor, indicating in the direction of Anne. He mouthed "*go on*" at me, but I restated my hesitancy. Instead, he continued to pace, and I moved to sit on the corner of the bed between him and the door.

"Tell me what's going on. Why have you stopped the pills?"

"I don't need them. I feel great. I feel alive and no longer dull." His voice was as chaotic as the thoughts behind his eyes.

He continued to gesticulate, and I watched, feeling well and truly out of my depth. I carefully thought about how to phrase my next question, but the sound of Anne coming across the laminate floor of the hall, pulled my mind in the direction of the open door of the bedroom.

"Here," she said.

She carefully passed me a mug of tea and placed Neil's on the chest of drawers on the wall of the bottom of the bed. She turned around and left the room, pulling the bedroom door to, so it only remained ajar a few inches.

"Neil, you need to take them," I eventually said, after staring into the brown tea in the mug for a minute or so.

He darted a look at me, but it wasn't a look of audacity at my nerve to suggest such a thing. Instead, it was a look of bewilderment.

"I know you think you're OK, but you're really not. Look at you, you haven't got dressed, your stubble looks like it's housing a family of squirrels and you are going to wear a hole through to the kitchen if you don't stop pacing."

He paused, and flopped onto the bed, sending my tea splashing around my mug. I wiped a small splash from my chest. I stood up and placed my cup on the chest of drawers as I reached forwards to pass him his tea. He looked up at me as I pulled my hands away from his cup, leaving it safely cradled in his hands. *No touching.* His eyes were full of sorrow. The speed at which the chaos left his face had shocked me. I sat on at the side of him, trying to gauge the acceptable distance in case Anne came back in.

"I don't want you to go," he said, painfully quiet so I could only just hear him, "don't leave me."

His hollow eyes welled with tears.

"I've got to. It's all arranged. It's only 5 days and I'll be back. I'm not staying, am I?" I said carefully, gently, as though talking to a child. "You will be fine. It's not for long."

I didn't believe the words as they came out of my mouth, given to his current state, but my hands were tied. I couldn't do anything. I could have cancelled the trip, but at what expense? If I cancelled it then, it would have looked suspicious that I'd have rained off within two days of Neil becoming manic. Anne would have wondered why I had chosen to stay behind to 'nurse' Neil, when he wasn't *supposed* to be my responsibility.

"You'll be fine. We'll be fine. It's five days; not even a week." I looked at him and he blinked heavily in response to the tears forming, pushing them away. "Take them."

I reached across and took the box of tablets at the side of him.

"Take them," I said a little more firmly, and popped a tablet from the blister packet, holding it out in the flat of my hand next to him.

I could see that he was weighing up the choice of reaching for it, or knocking it from my hand. I took the gamble and presented it again. He sighed, having been beaten, and reached for the capsule reluctantly popping it into his mouth and following it with a chase of tea.

"Thank you," he resigned himself.

I sat with him for a couple of hours. Anne had made her way up stairs and sat on top of the covers on her side of the bed and we watched David Attenborough on the small TV on the chest of drawers. Neil had calmed down, seemingly from my reassurance, because I knew his pills wouldn't have worked that quickly. I felt safe to leave and stood from the bed.

"I'll see you tomorrow, then." I sighed.

He nodded, his face relaxed and his body propped up heavily on the pillows. I looked over to Anne,

"I'll let myself out."

The following day Neil returned to the farm, and his mania seemed more under control. Either that or he'd slept for the first time in 4 days. I spent my last few days leading up to my holiday stroking his ego. I knew it was because of his distrust in Liam despite my years of protesting. It didn't matter what I said to Neil; nothing would persuade him to change his opinion of Liam having a thing for me. I don't think that was the extent of his problem. I think he thought that I had a thing for Liam, but I could never call him out on that argument. I could never give him a reason to think that it had even crossed my mind that I could be disloyal to him. So, I let him blame Liam, it was easier than facing the truth that he didn't trust me- despite having been entirely devoted to him for four years.

His appetite for sex had only accelerated by his faltering moods. He'd ring me up in the middle of the night to masturbate down the phone or would turn up unannounced for a quicky. I never argued, *if that's what he needs from me to feel secure, then what right do I have to deny him?*

It was the first time I had been anywhere away from home on my own. I'd always had my family with me before, so I was looking forward to the breathing space and seeing my friends in a world away from home. I was mostly looking forward to a bit of breathing space away from Neil. Especially as in the build-up to my departure, he had exhausted me. Though I think that degree of honesty came retrospectively.

I drove to Glasgow to catch the plane over to Shetland. I couldn't wait to see Julie and Liam, but Neil was never far from my mind. He was unsettled the day before I left, and it was taking a toll. Having bipolar made him unpredictable. Predictably unpredictable. I could see that he was faltering, but I was often left unable to determine which way he would go. Sometimes he would go up and become manic, or sometimes he would sink into a deep dark depression. As I sat on the tiny twelve-man plane in the air space between mainland and Shetland, I imagined how simple things would be if it crashed into the sea and I died.

I arrived in Shetland and Julie picked me up from the airport. It was wonderful to see her. She looked exactly the same, and yet completely different. She seemed so much more relaxed and it made her more vibrant, more animated. We drove back through the exposed country roads, to the hotel where Liam met us in the car park. He gave me a giant squeeze as I got out of the car, and I forced Neil, and his disapproving face, out of my head. I carried my luggage and unloaded them into the spare room in the living quarters of the hotel. From there, Julie took me on a small tour of the buildings and the local area. She introduced me to the horse she had acquired since her arrival, despite claiming that she'd never having another horse again. We pottered about for the next few days, spending the evenings in the bar, and the days in the country. I was the talk of the town. They rarely got visitors on the remote island, so the locals were intrigued by the English girl that had come up for the week.

After a few days and a few heavy drinking sessions that pushed my liver to the limits, we were sat in the bar when the bar phone rang. Liam answered it, and by the tone of his conversation, I knew immediately who was at the other end. Liam and Neil had a weird relationship; they were silly together, and that came out in silly voices and goofy jokes. Neil brought out the silliness in Liam and it was sweet to watch as I'd never witnessed a male friendship before.

"He wants a word," Liam pointed the corded phone in my direction.

"Me?" I mouthed, pointing at my chest and feigning a puzzled look before I stood to accept the phone.

"Hello?" I said, accessing my repertoire of personalities to suit the occasion. This one was 'innocence and confusion'.

I saw Liam leave the room from the corner of my eye and my stomach dropped to the floor. I knew where he was going, so I tried to keep things as normal as possible, but Neil didn't grasp on to my cool tone. I could say little with Julie in the room, but I could hear the other receiver in the hotel reception click and instantly knew that Liam had picked up the phone. I couldn't warn Neil. I don't think there was any malice in what Liam did. I think it was supposed to be a playful prank.

"I miss you," Neil said with a sadness so deep it cut me off at the knees despite my rising panic.

"No. Yeah. I know…. Yeah…. errr." I desperately searched for a way out. "Aww, yeah, miss ya too."

"I love you, Tan."

Oh fuck!

"Yep, love ya, anyway, I've got to go, drinking to do! See ya, bye!" I slammed the phone back on the receiver and looked around, relieved to see Julie still replacing glasses on the shelves.

My heart beat out of my chest. *Oh god! He heard, he heard!* I made my way back to the table I had left and downed the dregs of my lager as Liam re-entered the bar.

"Oh, has he gone already?" Liam feigned innocence too.

I nodded. It was unspoken, but I think we both knew what he had just witnessed.

The rest of the break was uneventful. The signal was so temperamental that I couldn't text Neil. His texts would often come several hours after I knew he had sent them, so I couldn't risk responding as I wasn't sure whether it would be safe at his end. We managed the odd text when I was lying in bed in the evening, the signal was a little bit better there than the rest of the island, but I don't think we exchanged more than 5 or 6 texts during the few days I spent there.

I felt sad to leave Julie and Liam when it was time to go home. Their presence had filled me with nostalgia. It reminded me of the early days when adult friendships were innocent. The fun days where they treated me as a grown up and before there were any obligations. Where there were no dark secrets or sneaking around. The days where I didn't feel like the weight of the world was on my shoulders. I missed the days when we could all enjoy each other's company, laugh, have a few drinks, mess about and gossip. I missed feeling relaxed. I hated looking over my shoulder to make sure someone didn't overhear inappropriate conversations. I missed the days where Neil excited me, the early days and the thrill of the chase, the flirting and the adoration. Instead, over time, it had become dark. The excitement had turned into addiction. The nervous anticipation had been replaced with a grasping, manhandling and the stretching of my most intimate parts. The conversations about music and life switched to phone sex and dirty talk. I didn't feel adored; I felt used. I missed the early days and longed that they would return.

*

I got back from Shetland and life carried on as usual. I told Neil about the incident on the phone, but we soon forgot about it as there wasn't any repercussions. Neil was more determined than ever for sex, though. I don't know if it was because he had missed me or because he needed validation of his masculinity, but he fucked me in every way possible. Nothing had changed. I realised that days that I longed for were firmly behind me.

I had started to acknowledge my depression. My parents had pushed me to go and see the GP because they had seen how flat I had become at home and how little interest I took in my school life.

"You always used to enjoy school, you always worked hard, what's changed?" My mum asked.

"Dunno," I snapped.

"You are lazy. If you think you can sit around here, not making the effort, leaving your bedroom like a shit tip, treating this place like a hotel, you can think again. I'm out working two jobs, your dad's out working two jobs, to keep a roof over your head and you swan in and out of here like you own the place. Well, you don't and it's about time that you started pulling your weight. At least show some enthusiasm in family life. You never do anything unless I erupt. You spend all your time down at the farm with your friends instead of helping here. You are lazy and ungrateful. Everything we do for you, everything we have sacrificed so you can have what you want, and you go and throw it back in our faces. If you don't want to stay on at school, get off your arse and get a job and contribute to this household. Stop moping around like the world owes you a favour, because you don't get anything in life by coasting. Make the effort Tanya, because I've reached the end of my tether!"

I relented in the end, and I booked an appointment at the surgery.

I was so anxious on the morning of my appointment. *What was I going to say? I'm in love with someone four times my age, but he won't leave his wife. Oh, and we've been at it like rabbits since I was fourteen. Yeah, that will go down well.* My name flashed up on the LED board above the door to the GP corridor.

"Hi Tanya, take a seat." Her warm demeanour felt instantly inviting, but I warned myself about giving too much detail because my world would suddenly implode. "What has brought you in today?"

"Ummm…" I wracked my brain looking for a way to answer that would show her I was struggling with life, but that I wasn't being a complete wet lettuce and in need of molly coddling. "I've been really stressed and it's making me feel really down."

"Ok, do you want to tell me more about it?" She gently asked.

"There isn't much to say. I just feel depressed and worthless. Some days I want to die." *Fuck. Too much, you'll be in the loony bin by the end of the day.* "No, not die. Like I don't want to kill myself, but like I just don't want to be alive anymore."

She sat back in the chair and studied me.

"No, it's not that I don't want to be alive. I just feel sad all the time. Well, not all the time. But…. Well… errr… my mum and dad wanted me to come and see you." *Shut up, shut up, shut up. Stop talking Tanya, you are making it worse.*

"What's making you feel this way?" she asked, and I wanted her to stop, because my mouth kept running away from me every time she asked me something.

"I hate being at school. It's stressful, I have too much to do, and I didn't want to do my A-Levels." I blurted, relieved by my ability to think on the spot. *I've got good at this.* I rattled off a list of the mundane things that I might have made someone sad, though obviously, they weren't true to me. *Someone might feel that way, anyway, it won't affect the treatment I get- it's all the same.*

I stared at the tap, counting the seconds between the drips as they fell into the sink, whilst the GP began tapping away at her keyboard. *1… 2… 3… 4… 5… 6… 7… 8… 9… plink. 1… 2… 3… 4… 5… 6… 7… 8… 9… plink. 1… 2… 3… 4…*

"I'd like you to come in with your parents if that's possible, so we can put a plan in place to keep you safe. Are they here?" She interrupted the comfort I was getting from the predictability of the impending *plink.*

"Yes, they are in the waiting room, shall I fetch them?"

I walked from her office and waved sheepishly to my parents from the corridor. My dad slapped his hands to his thighs as he flung himself out of the chair behind my mum. The followed behind me and sat at the side of me.

"Tanya has told me that she's struggling with her mood. I'm a little concerned that she's a risk to herself, so we need to put a plan in place to protect her."

What the fuck, I thought I'd skirted around that effectively?

"I'm going to book her in for next week to come back and talk to me, but in the meantime, I need to discuss with my colleagues how we treat her depression, because it can be a bit tricky with medication whilst she is still so young. I'm going to refer her to counselling, so that we can get things started in the meantime. Do you have any questions?"

"No, that's great thank you," my parents politely responded.

"Ok, Tanya, I've booked you in for next week and we can move forwards with help to stabilise your mood."

I walked out the surgery calmly and sat in the back seat of the car in silence; relieved that I had kept my mouth shut, but appeased my parents' need for me to get treatment.

*

I went back to the GP the following week and was greeted in the same warm and welcoming manner.

"Do you want to tell me a little more how you've been feeling? What worries you have?" She probed.

"Well, it's just school mainly. I didn't want to stay on for my A-Levels, and now I'm here, I hate it even more. I wanted to be a doctor, but now I have no idea what I'm doing with my life.

Everything is just getting on top of me, and I feel under constant pressure to be my absolute best, but it's exhausting."

I felt the start of an upcoming rant, but I didn't hold back.

"I just want to do nothing. I feel tired all the time, and when I don't feel tired, I just want to cry. Everyone seems to look at me as though I'm about to implode, and I'm fed up with trying to pretend I'm ok, when I'm not. Teachers keep throwing work at me, expecting me to do as well as I did in lower school, because I've always been bright, always found it easy, but I'm not there. My heart isn't in it. I'm fed up with school treating me like a child, but *clearly,* I'm not a child anymore. I'm an adult. I want to be treated like an adult. Everything I do is wrong, I can't do anything right, I just want people to leave me alone and just let me sort myself out, but even my parents forced me to come here. Why can't they just let me sort it out on my own, why are people constantly trying to interfere in my life? I'm an adult, but everyone treats me like a child."

I took a huge inhale of breath and continued.

"I get punished like I child, I get told to do things as though I was a child. I constantly feel like I'm letting everyone down. I used to feel like I had everything under control, like everything I did, I was able to do well, but now I feel like second best all the time. I'm in this really complicated relationship with a married man and he blows hot and cold with me all the time."

I stop as the realisation of what has left my mouth bounces back off the wall and hits me square in the face.

"And I'm just really fed up with people putting so much pressure on me to be brilliant, when I just want them all to leave me alone."

Fuck fuck fuck.

"Tell me about this relationship. How long have you known him?"

FUCK

"Umm…. I've known him a while, but nothing happened before I turned 16. Nothing. We just knew each other before I turned 16, but there wasn't any sex or anything."

"Where did you meet?"

What is this, an inquisition?

"Umm… my horse is kept on the same farm as his wife."

She began tap tapping away on the keyboard and I tried to look to see what she was writing, but the privacy screen meant that I could only see into a black abyss where the text should be. She sat in silence as she rattled away at the computer, for what felt like ten minutes. *Please don't put anything about Neil. Did I say his name? No, I don't think I did. I should have kept my mouth shut.*

She looked up and told me that she'd had spoken to her colleagues, and they had agreed that antidepressants were a plausible treatment, but I would need to be closely monitored over the following few weeks. She wrote my prescription out and sent me next door to the pharmacy.

I blew out a sigh as I left the surgery. *Bullet dodged.*

Neil kept blowing hot and cold, in the meantime despite knowing how fragile I had become. He would say the guilt was getting to him and that we couldn't carry on anymore. It left me shattered. I sat crying hysterically down the phone at him, begging him not to stop; we had come so far. I told him that I loved him, that he had broken my heart. That happened a couple of times, and each time it was the same. We would stop having sex for a couple of days, but he would continue to ring me daily. We would make small talk for a couple of hours on the phone, and then the same at the farm. We sat and shared cigarettes, but there would be no sex, no kissing, no sexual talk. On the third day, it would all change. He would ring me whilst he was in the bed or the bath. He would tell me that the sound of my voice was making him horny. He then confessed to masturbating whilst we were talking. He told me that we couldn't be just friends, that he couldn't stop thinking about fucking me, that he missed 'us', and that we were soul mates and destined to be together. By the end of day three, we were back to square one. It was a cycle.

Tanya Pursglove

CHAPTER 13

After returning home from Shetland, my mood flatlined. I had no interest in anything, and my world had become a cycle of sex and sleep intermingled with bouts of insomnia that were crippling. My school life had become sporadic; I barely attended my final year of sixth form. When I did attend, I'd leave at random times throughout the day to meet with Neil. On the days that he couldn't meet with me because Anne was on earlies, I'd drive home and vegetate on the sofa until it was a respectable time to leave for the farm. Then I'd go to the farm, and Neil and I would pick up where we had left off at lunchtime or from the evening before. He was my addiction, my drug. I knew I shouldn't be doing it; I knew he was detrimental to my health; I knew I wasn't enjoying it, but I couldn't stop. I couldn't stop getting high. The highs were less and less powerful than the early days, and I needed more and more of him to make me feel something other than the pain I felt when I wasn't with him. The crashes between hit harder and harder each time. I couldn't breathe, I couldn't think. I had no thoughts.

It was a stark contrast to the early days. The highs in the early days came with breath taking euphoria and a loss of thoughts because I had so many of them that I couldn't line them up to work them out. By the time I turned eighteen, I was breathless because I didn't have the energy to breathe. I didn't have the fight in me to be alive anymore. I didn't have any thoughts because I didn't have a functioning brain anymore. Those thoughts that once flew around my brain at an uncontrolled speed had dissipated into the abyss and all I was left with was a black void. I had no fight to be alive. I longed for death.

I isolated away from both school and farm friends. Neil had long since taken over my lunchtimes and free periods and my dark soul didn't fit in with the buoyancy within my friendship circle. Sara's 18th birthday party approached, and I was reluctant to attend. I didn't want any part of it, but I felt duty bound to go. Despite my continual self-isolation, Sara had forced me to put on a face and dragged me out of the hole I had found myself in, on a daily basis. I'd put on vast amounts of weight over the year. Depression still has that effect on me; I eat to soothe my mind. Sara's party was fancy dress, but I couldn't bring myself to go out and buy anything to wear. I hated the way I looked; I hated the person I had become. There was not one thing about me that I could tolerate. *I wish I was dead. I can't do this anymore. I can't be this shell of a person. I am nothing but a slag; a whore. I deserve to die. They'd get over it. My death would be easy for them all to accept because I'm never here anyway. I'm never anywhere. I'm never with my family, I'm never with my friends. I'm never with Neil. My body appears in all these locations, but I am never there. Tanya has gone.*

In the dead of the night, I'd find myself wide awake. I'd lie in bed and think of the quickest and least painful way to die. I sneaked around the house and pulled open the kitchen drawer, running my thumbs across the knives, wondering how much force it would take to slit my own throat. *Would I hesitate? I wouldn't panic, panic requires energy and I have no energy to panic.* I offered the blade to my throat and felt the coolness of the steel on my neck. It felt comfortable, calming; too calming, too tempting. My brain flashed to the future, and I imagined my dad getting up for work and finding a grey corpse on the kitchen floor, rushing to hold my lifeless body as my blood spread across his chest, his hands, his face. *I can't, it will kill him.* I placed the knife back in the tray and carefully cushioned the drawer as it closed. *Silence.*

*

The week after Sara's birthday, I drove to school at the usual time, in my uniform, but with no intention of arriving at school. I drove past the school to park on the back roads, where I would meet Neil. It was safe up there. I wouldn't see anybody except the odd car flying down the road. I had parked in a lay-by and began chain-smoking until Neil called. I wanted to see him; I wanted my high.

"Hello," I answered his call.

"Talk filthy, I want to come." His voice breathy and horny felt like liquid silk to my ears. He'd clearly been masturbating for a while and struggling to get himself over the hurdle.

"Come and meet me, I'm up on the tops," I said.

Silence

"I can't," he said with a flat tone, clearly having lost the urgency. "She's on earlies, I won't get back in time."

"Come on, come up here and I'll sort you myself," I tried my best to sound flirty and full of promise.

"I can't, she'll want to know where I've been if I'm not here at lunch." He was cold and authoritative.

"For fuck sake Neil, what does it even fucking matter at this point? Who *actually* gives a fuck? I never ever ask for you to come and meet me." I started crying. "Just say you nipped out. Say you went to see Peter. Say you went to fetch something for the car. Say you were bored out of your fucking mind, and you wanted to get out of the house. Say you were out fucking your bit on the side! Does any of it *actually* matter at this point? I need you here, I need you. Can you, just for once, do this for me?"

I sobbed out each phrase of my rant, so desperate to get high off his attention, to be transported to oblivion. To feel the pain of his hands inside me, to hear him calling me by every obscenity he could muster whilst he fucked me. *I just want to feel something, anything other than the emptiness I feel right now.*

"I'm not coming," he cut me off. "She'll be home and I need to be here."

"Fine!" I said as I flung the phone into the footwell. "Fuck you!" I screamed at the phone on the floor, knowing full well I'd cut him off the line, so he wouldn't have heard it anyway.

I don't understand what the fucking deal is. She fucking knows anyway! What does it matter if he is out the house for the thirty minutes she's home for lunch?

I lit up a cigarette from the one that was about to burn out.

I'm there the moment he wants me, I drop everything for him, with a second's notice. I do everything for him, anything he wants, whenever he wants! Is it so much to ask, that one day he just breaks his rule? Haven't I compromised enough for him? Why can't he just do something for me? Just once? Just this one time? Once again, I will never be good enough for him.

I battled with myself as I finished my last cigarette, furious with Neil, furious that I'd run out of cigarettes, furious that I was wasting my time. I turned the ignition and performed a U turn from the layby and sped off down the road. It had been raining at some point, and the roads were damp. Neil was on my mind. I was distracted and disappeared down dark roads in my mind. As I approached a blind bend, the combination of the slippery roads and the debris from the overhanging trees caused my car to screech when I applied the brakes. I heard a loud bang as I realised too late that I had punctured a tyre right on the apex of the bend. The front wheel of the car mounted the verge, and my car flipped. It flipped onto its side and skidded down the road into an oncoming car. I shut my eyes tight and braced myself ready for the impact as I saw the other car coming towards me.

When I opened my eyes, I was disappointed that I was alive. As I sat upside down in the car, looking around at the chaos before me I wondered how I would explain it to my parents; they thought I was still at school. *Oh my god! The other driver! Oh no! Oh no! Are they ok? You need to get out and see if they are ok!*

I was trapped in the car, unable to get out, pinned down to the side of the road. I stared up through the passenger window to the sky. Whilst I had been well within the speed limit, I felt to blame and full of shame that I had allowed my mind to wander whilst driving. The only physical pain I felt was from my face, where the airbag had gone off, but I also felt the deep burning guilt because I hit another car. I had abrasions on my feet where they had slipped under the pedals with my school ballerina pumps, but I could tell I wasn't seriously injured.

The acrid aroma of the car filling up with petrol fumes sent me into a panic. The front window was smashed, but the laminated sheet wouldn't budge from the frame, despite throwing my weight through my arms. *This is how I die.* I thought petrol fumes were going to kill me, but the thought of choking to death didn't fill me with comfort as I thought about my parents having to bury me. I wanted to die, but I needed to live.

I managed to climb up from the seat and stand on the door that was against the floor. The other motorists broke one of the rear passenger windows, and I pulled myself out of the upturned vehicle after searching for my phone. I fumbled clumsily but managed to ring my dad and explain what had happened. I heard the fear in his voice as he told me that he was on his way. I rang Neil, I wanted him there, but he wouldn't come. By that point, the emergency services had arrived. Two ambulances, five fire engines, 8 or 9 police cars filled the damp air with their sirens. I was ushered into the back of the ambulance by a paramedic, where he put me onto the trolley and assessed me. A police sergeant came into the ambulance to ask what had happened. I explained the tyre blow out and that I couldn't get the car back in the instant before it flipped. He did a routine breathalyser which I passed. My last drink had been at Sara's party the week before.

I started getting chest pains from the impact of the seatbelt and the airbag. As a precaution, and because I had been diagnosed with scoliosis at 14, they took me to the hospital. My dad had been at the accident site and followed the ambulance to the hospital, and my mum met us a short while later in the Emergency Department. Thankfully, I was discharged a few hours later with nothing but superficial bruising. I was shaken and deeply ashamed for my betrayal by skipping school and writing off their car. They were annoyed about my truancy, but they didn't scold me over it; they were just grateful that I was OK, especially after my dad had seen the state of the car. I was incredibly relieved to find out the other driver was unhurt.

My dad took me down to the farm straight from the hospital, and I sorted the jobs. Anne and Neil were down there. Neil pretended that he didn't know what had happened until I said it in front of everyone. He was relieved to see me, but with my dad hovering around and helping with the jobs, we couldn't get any time alone. I was heartbroken that he wasn't there when I needed him, that he couldn't ignore the risks and turn up at the hospital to see if I was OK. He could have explained that one away later. It's not as though he was risk-averse.

The lack of support from him confirmed that if I wanted to keep Neil or keep him interested, then all I had to do was keep having sex with him. I needed to be willing to accept that I wouldn't get the same adoration from him as I had gotten at 14-years-old. I realised that the thrill of the chase was over for him, it was all about the risk-taking or him pushing my body as far as it would go. I would do anything to keep filling my void.

I kept trying to convince myself that he loved me in his own way. I'd apportion his bipolar as an explanation. He would tell me he loved me; he would say the right things some of the time. He would say that he loved me the only way he knows how to love. He told me, time and time again, that nobody could love me the way he did. He desired me; that was clear. I boosted his self-esteem. I was reasonably attractive still, despite having put weight on, and I was still 42 years his junior, which appealed to his ego. I was intelligent enough to hold my own in a conversation, so after we finished having sex, we could still converse. My opinions on the world mattered to him. He always showed an interest in what I had to say. However, my opinion about our relationship didn't matter, so I kept quiet. I settled for what I could get. At least I knew that he was thinking about me, even if it was only for what my body could do for him.

It's not how it started. I no longer felt wooed as I had in the beginning, but we were four years in. *All relationships change over time,* I would tell myself. The age of consent had long passed, and I was five months into my first year as an 'adult'. I no longer needed tempting with the sweet words of a future together. He had got me hooked on his drug, and I would continue to go back because I was desperate for a fix. I knew that it had to end somehow. I didn't know how it would end, and it wasn't fizzling out. If anything, I had become more dependent on him; more reliant on the snippets of hope that he offered me. The sex was just as intense- in terms of frequency and style. The phone conversations were still for hours at a time, day or night. We spent every minute at the farm together. I didn't go up to his house in the evenings as Anne had put a stop to it. She argued with Neil that I was there too often. She confronted me about it the following day. She said that it felt like there were three people in her marriage. She explained that she valued my friendship and appreciated the relationship I had with Neil but asked me if I would stop going around in the evening.

I wasn't bothered. It didn't affect me in so much as I had Neil for most of the day whilst she was at work. From the minute she left for work in the morning, Neil was mine until 8 pm. I resented her for the 2 hours that I had 'lost', but as soon as she went to bed at 10 pm, he'd be straight on the phone to me. It didn't stop us from being together at the farm or meeting away from the farm, or the period after she had left the farm when Neil and I sat alone. Given that we couldn't talk about much during the time I spent in her company, it didn't feel like a huge loss.

*

Anne had become my competition; she was, as far as I could see, the only obstacle between Neil and I. As far as I was concerned, I would keep her happy and appease her, so there weren't any more obstacles put in the way, but the overriding feelings of jealousy were hard to bury.

Neil used to get off from risk-taking. The closer we were to being caught, the more turned on he would be. On one occasion I went up to his house in the daytime whilst Anne was at work. We were having sex in the hallway that led from the front door. I knew Anne would be home soon for lunch, so I urged him to stop, not wanting the world to blow up in my face. He wanted to carry on and held on for as long as possible, denying his ejaculation numerous times to stretch it out and increase the turn on from the risk taking. I was bent over, using the wall to brace myself, and Neil was penetrating me from behind. As he was getting close to ejaculation, he pulled out and finished himself off, spraying semen over my bum and the floor. He took a couple of steps backwards into the kitchen to clean himself up as I pulled my trousers back up. I had barely managed to fasten my jeans when Anne walked through the front door. I felt the colour drain from my face, and my heart pounding in my ears. She was startled and as white as a ghost too, but she didn't say a word even as I surreptitiously dragged my sock to mop up the semen from her laminate floor. The air smelled of sex; it had been no longer than 10 seconds since we had finished. I was 16.

Neil told me that she didn't want him. Their sex life had all but dried up, and she'd come home to sit in front of the TV until she fell to sleep. Neil frequently commented on the 'picture no sound' dynamics of their relationship. *She doesn't want you but has you, I want you but can't have you. It's not fucking fair!* I appreciate that this is not how relationships work, now that I'm 32 years old, but at the time, I knew no better. I didn't realise that I was being spun a story, like most other third wheels in a relationship. Neil was telling me what I wanted to hear.

I thought she had suspected something was going on for a long time, there were too many incidences that she couldn't ignore. My inability to hide my surprised face when she appeared part way through an act of sex couldn't have gone amiss. She was a smart woman. I couldn't understand why there was no confrontation. Neil hadn't mentioned whether she had asked him about us outright. She would moan at him that I was spending a lot of time at their house, but she never, as far as I am aware, asked him if anything was going on. She never discussed the day she almost walked in on us, but the smell of sex was undeniable, especially given that she likely knew the smell of his semen. She once found a vibrator box in his car that had fallen out of my bag and threw it at him whilst he was in the bath. Neil never mentioned whether my name came up during that conversation, but I think he'd have told me if it had. I was 16 when we started using the toys. He'd managed to talk his way out of it by saying that it was a joke Christmas present, but even at 16, I wouldn't have believed that if the roles were reversed.

Numerous other incidences would likely have at least raised suspicion if not acted as confirmation. Even when Neil and I weren't secretly having sex on the farm, we were over-familiar with each other, and touchy-feely. We'd always sit on neighbouring chairs, making sure nobody could get between us. We'd sit with our legs comfortably brushing despite there being room to sit further apart. We would share cigarettes from each other's mouths, and share drinks without wiping the rim of the glass or neck of the bottle. We'd do each other's coats up if it was cold or tuck a scarf into the neck. The fact that we'd disappear off together or always come in pairs hadn't escaped the notice of the farm gossipers, so it probably hadn't escaped her. She was sharp as a scalpel. As far as I know, we were never actually seen having sex or kissing, but our intimate body language was undeniable. People are only *that* comfortable with each other if they've been naked together. The countless signs and scenarios had become the new normal; Tanya and Neil were more frequently found colluding together than anyone else.

Even Marilyn had noticed on her infrequent visits to the farm. It was enough to confront Geraldine. Geraldine agreed and even asked Neil to distance himself from the farm until Anne was present. Anne wasn't stupid, these things probably didn't go unnoticed.

*

My final few months of 6th form were disastrous. The head of 6th form called me to his office one afternoon. I had never been called to the office before, in all my years of education. My guilty conscience kicked in as I walked through the school grounds towards the Admin Block of the campus. *Shit. I'm gonna get a bollocking here.* Although I had completely lost the will to be in school, I didn't want to lose the respect I had from my teachers. I was done with the work, I was done with the pressure, but part of me still desperately clung on the need to be liked.

I wanted to be noticed. I wanted to be cared for. I didn't want them to interfere in my life, but I wanted them to *want* to interfere. I knew I was depressed; I knew I was sad and distracted all the time, and although I didn't want them to try and find out the reason why, I wanted them to care enough to notice.

As I crossed the carpark and made my way up the ramp of the department, my stomach churned with the anticipation of knocking on his office door.

I gave two short sharp raps with my knuckles and strained to hear whether he'd acknowledged my presence.

"Come in." Mr Williams called through the wooden fire door.

"I heard you wanted to see me."

"Ah, Tanya, take a seat."

I shuffled to the chair and dropped my bag to the floor. The thud of the textbooks was louder than I had expected as the sound bounced around the cheap office furniture.

"Oops, sorry" I smiled, apologetically and tried to disguise my anxiety.

"I want to talk to you about your plans after 6th form. Your attendance is currently at 34% and concerns have been raised amongst your teachers that you aren't likely to achieve your expected grades."

He pulled a spreadsheet up on his computer and pointed at the row across from my name.

"You did really well in your GCSEs; A* and A completely across the board. You are a very bright and capable student, but in the last 2 years, we have noticed a huge decline in your presence in school, and your grades just aren't where they should be this close to your exams."

He paused and looked at me as though he was expecting an explanation. I remained silent.

"I noticed that you haven't approached your teachers or me for a reference for university. What are your plans for when you leave 6th form?"

"I haven't got any," I mumbled.

"You are incredibly bright, you have so much potential, but you've taken your foot off the gas here, Tanya. I know that you've struggled with your mental health throughout time in 6th form, but that really isn't a good enough of an excuse to let things slide like this."

I felt my eyes tearing up and blinked heavily to swallow them back.

"Have you thought about repeating the year, and applying for university next year?" He looked at me expectantly.

"Sir, I'm done with education. I've had enough. I just haven't got it in me to do another year here and then 5 more years elsewhere. I just need to get out of this now. I'm done." A tear escaped from my waterline, and I rushed to mop it away with the back of my wrist before he noticed.

"Have a think about it," he said gently. "You are intelligent and have so much potential. At some point, you are going to want to go to university, but with the grades you are looking at, you will find it difficult to get into university if you change your mind."

"I'll think about Sir, but I don't think I'll change my mind. I've had enough. I can't face another year of this," I waved my hand dismissively in the air.

He offered me a tissue from the box on his desk. I plucked one out and gently patted it into my eye, inspecting it for mascara, before folding it and offering it back to my eye again.

"Have a think on it and come back to me Tanya, OK?"

I grabbed my bag and slung it over my shoulder.

"Yes, I will. Thank you, Sir," I said as I made my way out of the door.

But it was a lie. I didn't think about it again, and I didn't go back to speak to Mr Williams. Nothing changed, and when the time for my A-levels arrived, I wrote my name on the papers and sat there for 3 hours at a time staring off into the mid-distance, hating myself more and more.

Tanya Pursglove

CHAPTER 14

It all came to a head in June 2008. Neil was in the hospital with abdominal pain. He had been in there for a couple of days but I hadn't visited him because Anne was going up each evening. We had kept in contact by phone as much as possible, but it had its challenges. I kept busy and distracted myself from my missing limb, but it was a struggle. Thankfully, there was a show over the weekend that kept me occupied for most of the time, so I didn't have much opportunity to dwell on it.

On Sunday, whilst at the show, Neil rang me. I made myself scarce for a few minutes so that I could take his call. Although Marilyn wasn't visibly hostile towards Neil anymore, I didn't want to test her by rubbing her nose it. I could tell that she knew what was going on between us, but it remained unspoken. Marilyn knew better than to push me; she knew that I would side with Neil no matter what arguments she had to offer. Rather than cause more friction between us, she chose to keep quiet and that was fine with me. I didn't bring Neil up in conversation, and she didn't offer her opinion of him. We were in a status quo, an equilibrium, and neither of us wanted to tip the balance.

My conversation with Neil had lifted my spirits. Anne wasn't going to be visiting him that evening, so he suggested that I should go instead. I couldn't wait to see him; I'd missed him enormously. It had only been two days, but I felt entirely out of the loop and jumped at the opportunity to visit him once I had finished down at the farm. I felt a wave of relief- as though my high was imminent.

I rushed through my jobs and drove home to get changed before making my way to the hospital. He messaged me as I pulled into the car park to tell me what ward he was on, and I gleefully made my way up to see him. When I arrived, he suggested we go outside for a cigarette, and so we made our way to the seating area just off the car park. Whilst we sat there, smoking and chatting, I flicked through the pictures on my phone and showed Neil my new puppy that I had brought home whilst he was in hospital. We had been there for about twenty minutes when Anne turned up.

She was startled and pissed off that we were together. She sat down at the other side of Neil, and the atmosphere instantly darkened but I tried my best to carry on as normal and actively encouraged her into the conversation to try and lift her mood. I tried to handle her how I would handle Marilyn; pretend everything was normal and nothing out of the ordinary was happening. It was stilted and monosyllabic conversation, but she did force out a few contributary words. I was angry at her presence although I did my best to hide it. Neil had told me that she wouldn't be there; so, I'd get a bit of alone time with him. *Why are you trying to ruin it? Neil wanted to see me; you weren't supposed to be here. Neil had wanted to see me; that's why he rang me that morning to tell me the coast would be clear.*

We walked back up to the ward close to the end of visiting time. Anne walked a few paces ahead, and Neil and I following behind her as had become customary over the years. Neil slumped back into the bed whilst I remained at the foot of it and Anne moved around to his side, keeping a hand on his leg as she did, *marking what was hers.* Visiting time was technically over, but there was a standoff developing between me and Anne; it was clear that neither of us wanted to be the first to leave, and neither of us were willing to be the first one to give in. After what felt like a very long seven or eight minutes, Anne rounded up the stagnant, stilted conversation and leaned over to kiss Neil goodbye. I suggested that I walk out with her and leant in to give Neil a non-committal, friendly peck on the cheek before following behind Anne.

The elevator ride was beyond tense. We only had to move one floor to reach the hospital car park, but it felt like we were trapped in there for an hour together. Just me and Anne. I could feel that she was bubbling over with rage, so I tried to break the silence with small talk, and in true British style, I brought up how pleasant the weather had been. It had been a lovely June day, but now it felt as though a huge black cloud was descending on us both. The atmosphere was palpable and oppressive. After the marathon lift ride to the car park floor, we exited and walked awkwardly, in a similar direction and as we started to part ways to our cars, I cheerfully shouted my byes and climbed in the car. I pursed my lips and let out a sigh in relief and tried to put it out of my mind for the rest of the night. I convinced myself that she'd probably just had a bad day.

*

The following morning, I headed out to my part-time job. As I set off, I plugged my headphones into my phone and ears and turned the radio on for the traffic report. I hadn't got to the end of my road before Neil rang.

"Good morning," I cheerfully answered the phone.

"She knows."

A wave of dread washed over me.

"What do you mean, she knows?" I asked, trying not to be sick. "Knows what?"

"Everything," he continued. "She rang me when she got home last night and said that she needed to come back and talk. She was in a rage. She came back and we went out of the ward into the corridor. She asked me what was going on, and I just told her. I didn't have it in me to try and lie my way out of it. She knew. There was no point in trying."

I listened to what he had to say and although there was an element of panic over a likely confrontation, I was delighted. *This is it! She'll leave him and I won't have to share him anymore. Anne will have decided for him! The door will be left wide open for me!*

"I said it had been going on a year when she asked me," he said.

What? A year? Is that all the recognition I get? A fucking year? 365 days? Am I not worth a bit more than that? Christ, I can see why you didn't tell her I was 14, but I'm nearly 19, it's been legal for 3 years! Couldn't you have said that?

"Just in case she asks you," he finished.

I couldn't see it at the time, but Neil was employing damage limitation tactics. To be a good liar, he knew he had to stay close to the truth, but not so much as to send Anne running for the hills. He needed to look as though he was telling the truth because Anne probably wouldn't have accepted his denial. It needed to be believable so that he could salvage what relationship he still had with her and get himself out of trouble. Neil was always about taking control of the situation, telling Anne what she wanted to hear. She couldn't hear the whole truth, that would have blown up in his face, but likewise, having denied an affair entirely would not have been accepted either.

I'm almost certain that Anne had known much longer; I had been getting the vibes from her for well over two years. I think she knew from near the beginning, but I can't put an exact date on it because it moved quickly between Neil and I. But I suspect that she saw the signs before turning 16. There were too many to ignore:

A 14-year-old girl doesn't typically spark a close and personal friendship with a 56-year-old man. They don't 'hang out' or sit together in quiet areas away from everyone else. They don't choose to be with one another over their peers. They aren't father and daughter, and their relationship doesn't reflect that.

She only had to ask herself:

Why Neil volunteered to travel in the back of a lorry for the entire day, keeping a 15-year-old girl company? Why were they always together? Why did Neil go looking for Tanya instead of her, when she'd been away at work all day? Why did he stay at the farm talking to Tanya long after everyone else had left? What could they be doing down there, on their own in the dark? Why did Neil and Tanya always stay back at the car together when they'd 'come to watch Julie at the show'? Why are they so comfortable around each other? Why does she look so at home on my sofa, her feet tucked up behind Neil? What happened that day I came home for lunch? Why did he invite her up every day?

These are just a small collection of the questions she probably asked herself over the years and are far from all the things she witnessed with her own eyes. These things weren't gossip that she chose to ignore, but the things she saw. Even without the whispers of the farm gossip catching her attention, these things would have raised alarm bells in the majority of people. She'd even made comments about them to Neil to try and stop it. Anne wasn't privy to the other things, such as meeting when she was at work or all the phone calls. Those wouldn't have provided definite confirmation, but short of actually seeing his penis penetrating me, it would have provided tangible proof and certainly removing the need for reasonable doubt. It was not normal. It was not healthy.

*

After Neil dropped the bombshell, I sat in a trance at work all day, it felt so surreal. For the first time in a long time, my head was full of things I couldn't process. It was almost like going back to square one, full of questions and no answers and the euphoria and surrealism temporarily patched the hole in my soul. I had to go to the farm after work and sort the jobs out, but I was concerned about the reception I would get. *Oh god! Will everyone already know?* I didn't want a huge scene, and in all honesty, I thought she'd knock my teeth out. As I drove home from work, I wondered how I could avoid seeing her at the farm. I decided to leave it until as late as possible, in the hope that she'd have left by the time I got there. So, after driving home, I got ready at a snail's pace, even taking time to eat dinner before heading off to the farm.

My anxiety levels were at an all-time high on the way to the farm. *What do I do if she's there?* As I approached a gap in the hedge, I slowed down to look for her car in the car park and breathed a sigh of relief when it wasn't there. I was the only one on the yard and I had never been more grateful for the lack of company. As I had left it so late, there was only time for me to muck out and fill the hay nets; riding had to wait for another day. I just wanted to get away from that place as quickly as I could in case Anne came back down looking for me.

The following morning, Neil rang me the tell me the hospital had discharged him and that he was back at home. I was pleased to hear his voice as I sat in the office at work but part of me felt disappointed that he was out of hospital. I was concerned that being home would make him see what he could lose and that he would sack me off.

The next couple of days played out the same way. Neil and I would be on the phone throughout the day. He would keep me up to date with what was happening at behind the scenes and the arguments with Anne, and then I would visit the farm when I could guarantee that nobody would be there. I timed it perfectly so that the yard was empty and I could get my jobs done without bumping into anyone. I still didn't know how many people knew what had happened, and I didn't want to be thrown to the lions without any warning. I lived on my nerves the whole time. I knew it was only a matter of time before mine and Anne's timetables clashed, but at that time, the coast was clear, and I was grateful.

On the third day, I drove to work that morning. I felt a bit unwell when I set off; I was having abdominal cramps and felt a little warm. I didn't feel unwell enough to avoid work, particularly as the role wasn't exactly demanding so I parked the car and went to open the office. As I sat in my office, my phone started to ring. I knew it would be Neil without even looking down to check the caller number, even the new set of circumstances or our impending doom would not dampen his sexual appetite. So naturally, I performed my best until he achieved satisfaction and was able to move the conversation on to current and more pressing topics. He told me about an argument he'd had with Anne the night before, about me, of course and described how Anne had flown off at him about 'that girl' having fallen in love with him, and he did nothing but encourage it. I felt disappointed that she phrased it that way; that she blamed me for falling in love with him. Especially given that he was the one that had started the whole thing, but I wasn't in the position to make a case.

As the conversation ended, I felt increasingly unwell. The cramps were intensifying, and sweat was starting to bead on my forehead. My clothes stuck to my back and underarms. I ran to the sink in a small side room off the office and vomited. As I looked up and caught sight of my reflection in the mirror and I was shocked to see the person looking back at me. I was grey; my lips blended into my complexion, and my eyes were so dark that I looked dead. My face perspired, so much so that my hair was clung around the edge of my face. I needed to get home.

I got in the car, started my way home and I was less than a mile into my fifteen-mile journey when I found myself doubled over at the wheel and pulling over to vomit with pain. When I finally got home, I just crumpled to the floor like a tower of cards and fell into the foetal position clutching my knees to my chest. Sweat pooled on the laminate floor underneath my fixed body. I lay there and dry retched in silence. I couldn't thrash about like you see in the films. I had frozen to the spot, clenched tightly into a ball, covered in vomit and sweat. *Make it stop, make it stop.*

The sharp stabbing pain in my abdomen intensified and with every cramp my body crumpled. I couldn't move from the floor, even when the paramedics arrived. They tried to pull out my arms from underneath me, but I was too frightened to relax them.

"Tanya, I'm going to need your arm so I can give you some pain relief," a largely built man with masses of ginger facial hair leant down towards me. "Can you tell me what's been happening?"

"My stomach…." I retched again, aiming the vomit into a cardboard bowl that he thrust at my face.

"Can I put a line in your arm to give you something to help the pain?" He asked again, his thick Brummie accent reverberating around the living room.

I didn't say anything, but relaxed my arm as he pulled it from my chest.

"Tanya, have you got any allergies? I'm just going to put this cuff on you so we can have a look at what's happening before I can give you some painkillers. Just try and relax this arm for me," he said as he patted my outstretched arm and I felt the cuff tighten as the machine started up. "Ok, I'm just going to put a cannular in this hand if that's ok?"

I nodded.

"Ok, sharp scratch."

I flinched as I felt the sting in the back of my hand.

"I'm going to give you some morphine and see if we can get you a bit more comfortable before we nip you up to the hospital so they can find out what's going on, ok?"

I let out a primal growl like a wounded animal and nodded before vomiting once more.

"This might make you feel a bit woozy, but don't worry, that just means it's starting to work," he said as he slowly starts squeezing the syringe into the cannular.

The cold sensation of the liquid started to creep up my arm and across my head.

"I'm going to give you something to stop you feeling sick, OK?"

I nodded, screwing my face up as another cramp climaxed.

"Tanya, your blood pressure is a bit low, so I'm going to give you some fluids to see if we can raise it. Is there any chance you could be pregnant?"

I hadn't even given it a thought.

"I don't know," I said.

*

I don't remember much about the ambulance journey. The paramedics had given me morphine whilst at home and had also given me the gas and air for any breakthrough pain. I was as high as a kite by the time I got to the hospital and thankfully, the drug they gave me to stop being sick had taken affect. By the time I arrived in the Emergency Department, the pain had subsided somewhat, and I realised how ill I felt instead. They wheeled me in on the trolley whilst I clutched at the gas and air tubing and the 4th cardboard bowl they had given me to be sick in. I still didn't trust that I wouldn't continue to hurl my guts, even though it had been at least 20 minutes since my last dry retch.

I was taken straight into majors within the department and a nurse came in to take some bloods from my arm and inform me that the doctor would be in to see me soon. I hated needles. I was grateful at the time of the paramedics cannular insertion as I knew it would help with the pain, but I protested at another needle for a blood drawer.

"Can't you just take it from here?" I asked as I pointed to the cannular.

"I'm afraid not because the blood has been mixed with the drugs and fluids the paramedics have given you and the results wouldn't be reliable" she said, in a sweet but slightly exasperated way.

I relented and didn't put up a fight when she reached over me and examined the crook of my arm for a vein. After she took the blood and packaged it up to send it off to the laboratory she came back in to take some information.

"Can you just clarify your name, date of birth and address for me?" She asked and I responded with the information.

"Is your GP still Dr. South?"

"Yes," I answered.

"When was the first day of your last period?"

"I don't know, I can't remember," I responded.

"I'll bring a pan in, could you do me a urine sample so we can test it? The doctor will be in a bit, and we'll be able to get you some more pain relief on board and keep your pain under control." She ended with a condescending smile as she pulled the curtain back around the cubicle and disappeared.

The doctor came a short while later. I'd managed to do a urine sample and the preliminary tests came back. I was just drifting in and out of sleep when he called from around the curtain, checking if it was OK to come in. He'd had a look at the investigations and my observations and said that he thought I had appendicitis. I felt relieved. All the talk about periods and pregnancy had me worried that I'd fallen pregnant and hadn't noticed because I was too wrapped up in the dramas that had unfolded under the previous days. He said that he'd admit me to the surgical ward overnight and that the surgeon would come and talk to me to discuss the plan of action to get me back on my feet again. He prescribed me morphine to keep my pain under control over night as I was eventually moved up onto the ward and off the ED trolley. The surgeon called to see me a few hours later and said that they would take my appendix out the following day as they were concerned that my tests were indicating that it might rupture if they tried a conservative approach.

Neil called me the morning of my surgery. It was the first time I had been able to speak to him to tell him I was in hospital. He said he had to come up to the hospital the following day to review his admission from the Friday before. He said he would call and see me before going home after his appointment and he kept true to his word. The day after my surgery to remove my appendix, Neil came to visit me. I was out of it at the time with morphine and infection. It had only been 24 hours since the surgery, so the staff had drawn the curtains around my bed as I drifted in and out of sleep.

I wasn't even aware that I had fallen asleep until I woke to the feeling of something brushing my lips. As I opened my eyes and my mouth to talk, Neil pushed his penis inside my mouth. I flung myself backward and was startled by the sudden turning on of my gag reflex. He said hello as he tucked himself back into his trousers with a smug smile appearing across his face. I didn't say anything about the way he woke me up, and he never mentioned it. I shrugged it off; *it's just Neil; it's the type of thing he does*. I'd learnt to expect the unexpected with Neil.

He told me that Anne knew that he'd come to see me. He'd told her that he wanted to make sure I was OK. She agreed to it and was apparently OK about it, though I'm not sure how much I believed him. We spoke in hushed tones about everything that had happened over the week, and he told me that he wouldn't be going down to the farm anymore. It didn't bother me. It would have been too hard to try and act normal in each other's presence, so it was probably the best decision. He said that Anne hadn't told anybody what had happened as she didn't want people to know. Part of me thought it was a pride thing. She didn't want all the gossipers saying, *'I told you so'*, but I never found out what her reasons were. I was just glad that there wouldn't be a huge scene.

*

A few days passed, and I was discharged home. I'd had some time away from the farm, so the workers did my jobs for me which suited me perfectly. Apart from the physical discomfort I was in after the surgery, it dramatically reduced the risk of bumping into Anne. Neil and I didn't see much of each other over those few days but instead, we were on the phone for several hours each day. After a few days, I started going back down to the farm again, but still timed it so that I could avoid Anne. Thankfully, I had finished sixth form, my exams having finished in May, and I only worked for a couple of days a week as part of a job share, so I went down during the times I knew she would be at work.

Two weeks after she had confronted Neil, I bit the bullet. I knew I couldn't hold off trying to avoid her forever, so I went to the farm at a time I knew she would be there. It was a risky move, but I knew I couldn't put it off forever. I took my new puppy down with me. I thought it would be a good distraction and possibly help to avoid a confrontation. I knew the yard would be busy, and everyone would crowd around to see the pup, which meant Anne wouldn't have the opportunity to confront me. I had the hope that Anne's desire to keep it quiet would mean that she would try and avoid me as much as I wanted to avoid her.

It wasn't as successful as I had planned, but I don't imagine those things ever stick to a plan. I got to the farm, and Anne's car was already there as I arrived, so I took a deep breath, and walked down with the puppy. Sure enough, people gathered around the cute little bundle, but that was short-lived. As soon as the novelty had worn off and people dispersed, I started mucking out. I took the horse out of the stable and tied him up outside the barn. In doing so, it meant I could shut myself and the puppy in the stable with the wheelbarrow so I wouldn't have to worry about keeping my eye on him. It also meant that the stable door would aid in shielding me from the daggers that Anne had already fired in my direction.

I was a jittery wreck. Anne had seen me and had given me the side-eye as she walked into her stable, so my fight or flight mode had kicked into overdrive. I put my earphones in and played music to try and shut off the noise from the outside world. I tried to keep myself in my own bubble and drown out the people left at the farm. Unfortunately, that meant that I wasn't aware that Anne was stood by my stable door. My response was inappropriate, but the stress got the better of me. She was far from pleased when I let out a scream and then cracked up laughing under the pressure and the shock of seeing her over the stable door. I didn't intend to be disrespectful, far from it. It was purely a stress response to a tense situation.

"I suppose you think this is funny, don't you?" She scoffed at me.

"No, I'm sorry, you made me jump and it was just a reaction," I replied.

"Why? Why did you both do it?" She seethed.

"We didn't mean for it to happen. It just happened. It wasn't intentional. It just happened. I'm sorry. We didn't want to hurt you."

It was a string of clichés that you'd expect written into the script of a soap opera, but it *was* true. Nothing I did, nothing we did, was because we wanted to hurt Anne; she became a victim of collateral damage.

"Just die," she snarled. "Just go away and die you fish-eyed cow."

She stormed off up to the car. *Fish-eyed cow?* Of all the things she could have called me, that was not one I expected to come from her mouth. *I haven't got fish eyes?* I'd have understood if she'd called me a whore, but she came out with the most bizarre insult. I put it down to her being so angry, that she couldn't think fast enough to come up with a smart insult; one that would ring true like a whore or slag.

I rang Neil as I heard her car door shut to warn him that Anne had confronted me. I told him to brace himself because she was seething. Anne never asked me for details or asked me how long it had been going on. I found that strange, but I think she was afraid to catch Neil in a lie. It was easier to believe his version of events because it was less painful than the truth. It was easier to pretend that it hadn't been going on for as long as she had suspected. If she thought about it in its entirety, how long she had been suspicious for, Anne would realise that the *one-year recognition* I earned was in fact a huge lie.

That was the last time we ever spoke.

*

After Anne confronted me, she took a week of work and went to stay with her sister in Somerset. Neil told me it was because she needed some thinking space, but either way, it was most unusual that Anne would act spontaneously. Neil's newfound freedom held no bounds, though. We met up every day that week. We would drive and have sex for hours, from dawn 'til night. It was easier to talk, knowing that we didn't have a schedule to keep to anymore. It made a pleasant change that we could converse naturally, rather than using conversation as punctuation between the sex acts. We drove through the country and stopped for a drink at a remote pub. Having complete freedom was most unusual. Usually, we would have spent our time squeezing as much sex into a session as possible, but now there was no limit on the amount of time we could spend together; we were able to enjoy each other's company again. I asked him what he wanted to do about 'this', about 'us'. He said he wanted to carry on but that we'd just have to be a bit more discrete. So, we did.

Tanya Pursglove

CHAPTER 15

Although I was devastated that we weren't together as a couple and that he and Anne still lived together, I couldn't let him go. He had a hold on me, and I couldn't pull myself away. I couldn't explain it. I knew he was terrible for me. I knew our relationship was toxic. I had resigned myself to the fact that I would never be more than a blow-up doll to him, but I couldn't break away. I was under his control, and I felt it. I wasn't sure what were my thoughts were anymore; they just seemed to be an extension of Neil's thoughts. I'm not saying I was sweet and innocent when I met Neil, but I was naïve, as were most 14-year-olds. I genuinely believed that he was in love with me. I hung on his every word. He charmed me. He convinced me that all his requests were reasonable. I didn't have the power to say no; I didn't realise I had a choice. There was an expectation to do whatever he asked.

I was unable to cut ties even though I knew what that had become. I found myself in the position of the 14-year-old girl again. Instead of my innate insecurities at 14, at 18, Neil created new insecurities for me. He would blow hot and cold, knocking me off my feet, but then within days, he'd be building me back up, telling me that he couldn't give me up. He said he couldn't be without me, that he loved me. He told me that nobody else would ever love me the way that he did. He said it in a way that made it sound special. He had put me back on that pedestal for a while, making it easier for me to ignore the fact I was nothing more than a sex object, that I would be nothing more than a dark secret.

*

My 19th Birthday came and went. I didn't want any fuss. I didn't want anything. My parents had asked me for weeks what I wanted, but I couldn't suggest anything that *they* could have given. In the end, I just asked for money, knowing that I'd spend it on cigarettes or the dog.

Neil rang me to wish me happy birthday in the morning and we talked for a while before he invited himself over. I was home alone all day, so it wasn't a problem because everyone else was out at work.

"Yeah, I'm not going anywhere," I said, noncommittal. "I'll see you after lunch."

I hadn't left the settee all morning. I no longer made the effort when Neil and I were meeting up for sex. When I was younger, I used to shave my legs and tidy up my bikini line, but as time passed, I lost the enthusiasm for it. *I had a bath this morning, that's as good as he's gonna get.*

The dogs barked and I tilted my head up to see Neil. I sat upright as I heard the click of the back door, and could hear the dogs make a fuss of Neil and he pushed his way in.

"I'm through here," I called.

Neil walked into the living room and bent down to kiss me.

"Happy Birthday! Let's go up," he said as he cocked his head in the direction of the stairs.

As he had done many times, he made his way into my bedroom and sat on the edge of my single bed. He kicked off his shoes and began to undo his trousers. He pulled me by my waist and buried his face in my chest. He slid his hands down the back of my waistband and grabbed at my buttocks as he pulled me on top of him.

"How do you want it, birthday girl?" He asked.

"Whatever you want," I replied.

He pushed me up on to my feet and pulled my trousers down.

"Bend over," he said.

I turned around and performed my duty. He fingered me from behind as he warmed himself up with his other hand. I felt the urgency in him develop as he slowed the pumping action of the hand inside me. I felt his arm beating away from behind, but I didn't attempt to stop him. It was up to him whether he chose to finish early. *I hope he does, then maybe we'll actually be able to spend a bit of time together.*

He stopped before he came. *Pity.*

"69?" He suggested as patted the bed and invited me to lie down.

Our height difference always became very apparent during mutual oral. I could barely reach his penis if I was sat on top, and I always felt paranoid as I hovered over him, in case my thighs finished him off entirely. His pat of the bed suggested that he wanted me to lie down on the bottom though, so I had high hopes for a bit of comfort, given that I knew I wouldn't achieve sexual gratification. *At least I'll be comfortable, I suppose.*

I lay down with my head over the edge of the bed as he mounted my face and leaned forward to put his mouth around my vagina. He began thrusting in my mouth as soon as he had got in position, and I knew that I was going to have to place my brain elsewhere if I had any hope of not panicking.

1... 2... 3... 4... 5... 6... 7... 8... 9... 10...

1... 2... 3... 4... 5... 6... 7... 8... 9... 10...

I cocked my head right back and released him from my mouth as I took him in my hand. *Fuck. Nope, can't do it.*

"Suck me, I'm nearly there," he gasped as he lifted his head up away from my genitals.

1... 2... 3... 4... 5... 6... 7... 8... 9... 10...

1... 2... 3... 4... 5... 6... 7...

Neil tensed his body and I felt the familiar pumping of his semen into my mouth, filling my mouth up like salty, toothpaste foam. *Swallow, get rid of it. Don't think about it. Smile, fight the urge. Don't puke.*

He pulled himself upright and removed his penis from my mouth, leaving a dribble of cold semen near my chin. I quickly wiped it away with the back of my hand and sat upright, thinking it would help me to contain my nausea. *Never again. That was horrific.*

Beep... Beep... Beep. Fuck.

"Get dressed, that's my dad's truck. He's early!" I panicked and reached for the trousers that had been dropped to the floor, scrambling myself together as I heard the dogs going berserk. I heard the gate beneath my bedroom window squeak.

"Quick," I whispered as I flapped my arms to get Neil out of my bedroom and shut myself in the ensuite whilst I got dressed.

"Alright, Neil!" I heard my dad say as Neil blocked off the stairs. "How you doing?"

"Yeah, not bad thanks. You got the sack?" Neil poked fun at my dad's early arrival home.

"Nah, just had enough for the day."

I left my bedroom and followed Neil downstairs. As my dad moved to the kitchen.

"Do you two want a brew?" He shouted as I stood in the front room, surveying my face for signs of shock.

"Umm... yeah, that will be good thanks," we both replied.

*

We continued meeting for sex for months after the shit had hit the fan. More often than not, we'd go out in the car, so that on the off chance, someone drove through my street, his car wouldn't be spotted nearby. We always went to one of three places; the ironically named Exhibition Lane, the local reservoir, or up near the National Trust House. We cycled through each on one an irregular basis, so that we didn't draw too much attention from the locals, in Neil's very conspicuous car.

On one occasion, whilst we were on Exhibition Lane, a white van man drove suspiciously slowly as he passed us in the car. Thankfully, because of the terrain of the abandoned road, Neil and I had been able to detach from one another as the man approached in his transit, where we sat side by side on the backseat as I pulled my blouse closed across my chest. Once he'd pulled off again, we carried on, me sat astride Neil as he buried his face in my chest.

"He's fuckin coming back!" Neil exclaimed.

I turned over my shoulder to peer through one eye as I looked up the length of the abandoned road.

"Maybe he's just lost." I shrugged, but I hadn't managed to finish my thought before Neil had pushed me off him and began to do his trousers up.

"Just wait there a minute," he said.

As I sat at the opposite side of the car, Neil elevated his body in the seat to have a good look at the van as he drove back past us, painfully slowing down to look in the back window of Neil's car. I was obscured from view by Neil's body taking up most of the window frame, but instinctively, I slid further down the seat to ensure I hadn't been seen.

"I'm sure it's nothing. He'll just be looking for somewhere to park up on his lunch break," I suggested, but Neil wasn't convinced.

He sat peering in the wing mirror of his 4x4 as the van slowed down to a stop, some hundred feet behind us.

"Nope, he's coming back." Neil was angry. He flung open the rear passenger door and scrambled into the driver's seat and fired up the car. He pulled off and the acceleration flung me back, hard into the back of the seat.

It must be someone who knows us. Shit.

I hadn't been able to get a good look at the driver's face when he passed us, but there would only be one reason why someone would make the effort to drive past us three times. *It's someone from the farm.* My stomach started to churn, and my heartbeat drummed in my ears. My body was thrown around the back seat of the car as Neil hit the mounds of the deserted track. *Fuck.*

As Neil reached the end of the abandoned road he turned left on to the main road. I wedged myself in the seat, pleased that we had finally made it onto smooth tarmac, so the only force I had to work against was the G-forces that aimed to push me into the boot of Neil's car. I strained my vision to focus in the wingmirror of Neil's car, for the white van to come into focus.

He's coming this way too.

Neil made a sharp right onto another country lane, and pushed his foot to the floor, chasing through the gears of the car, smashing his way through the gearbox as his speed increased. I turned to look over my shoulder. The van made the same turn and was a couple of hundred yards behind us.

Shit.

"Who is it?" I asked, adrenalin pumping the words out of me in the same manner that Neil had pumped up and down the gearbox as he made his way through the windy country road.

Neil shook his head, too busy concentrating on the bends ahead to formulate an answer. The van wasn't catching up with us, but maintained the same speed, the skill of the driver unable to match Neil on the roads he knew so well.

Neil made a sudden left turn onto another narrow lane and drove down through the tree-lined country road. Within a few hundred yards, he made another left turn that took us towards a small village. I turned once more to see the van passing the end of the road we had turned off and breathed a sigh of relief.

"What the fuck was all that about?" I asked Neil as I felt his foot ease from the accelerator.

"Just a pervert I think, trying to get off."

*

In May 2009, 10 months after it all came out, at 19 years old, I had my first spinal operation to correct my scoliosis. It kept me in the hospital for a couple of weeks. The first seven days were spent on a High Dependency Unit after a complication during surgery, and the following week was spent recuperating on the spinal ward. Neil and I had remained sexually active up to that point, but when he failed to visit me, I started to slip from his grasp. I began to detach emotionally.

I was hurt. After everything we had been through over the course of five years, it hurt that he didn't come to visit me. He said he couldn't, but I suspected that it was because I was out of action. I'm sure he could have found a way of excusing himself from the house for 2 hours had he wanted to. My eyes were opening to the fact that it was one-sided. The time away from Neil allowed me to think with more clarity. He wasn't clouding my thoughts as much as he once had. Apart from nothing else, I had too many distractions with pain and post-operative healing to overly concern myself with him. We still spoke for hours daily, and I missed him, but he didn't seem to have the same hold over me. I think the operation probably saved my life because it stopped me from falling deeper and deeper into his clutches.

A few weeks after I was discharged, Neil came to visit me at home for the first time. I was lying in my bed when he texted me to tell me he would come around. My dad let him in, and Neil made his way upstairs. He'd been to my house hundreds of times, so had no problem navigating his way into my bedroom. He hadn't been there long before he was leaning over me in bed, with his penis in my mouth. Once that was over and done, we were able to talk. Once he was there, I realised how much I had missed him; he had a way of building me up and then dangling me on the end of my own emotions. We chatted for an hour or so before he left. My parents hadn't realised that the shit had hit the fan at the farm. As far as they knew, nothing had changed between Anne, Neil and I. Marilyn could sense trouble, it was apparent to her that something had happened, but she never brought it up. I think she was just grateful because, from outside appearances, it looked like it had stopped. *Neil didn't come to the farm anymore; therefore, Neil and Tanya weren't a thing any longer.* That was not the reality of it, but at least we weren't rubbing it in peoples' faces. We were much more discrete.

*

My attitude towards sex and Neil began to change over the course of the following few months. There had been a continual decline in my mental health, and my body had been put into autopilot. The monotony of the phone calls and the sex had allowed me to completely disengage from my surroundings.

Neil would ring me up in the mornings as soon as Anne had left for work. He'd be in bed still, or occasionally in the bath, but his location was irrelevant as the conversation would always steer in the same direction.

"Talk dirty to me, Tan!"

I no longer felt uncomfortable by the dirty talk. During the earlier years, I would feel myself blush if he'd asked me to talk filth, but later, I didn't have any feelings for it at all. The words would come out of my mouth before my brain had the ability to analyse them. Half the time, my brain hadn't even had chance to register the things I was saying, so I didn't know whether I was being repetitive or not. Sex had lost all meaning for me. It had once been a way to guarantee having Neil's undivided attention, but Neil's undivided attention no longer brought me joy, just sadness.

As the weeks passed and my 20th birthday came and went in the blink of an eye, the sexual rhythm became predictable, the less and less present I became. He would pull up at the end of the road to pick me up and we'd disappear off in the car for a few hours. He buried himself in me, stretching me, pulling and pushing me across the leather seat of his car. I'd moan and groan in all the right places, but I was empty. I wasn't even running on the reserve; all enthusiasm and wooing had left. I knew Neil and Anne were never going to split, so I stopped showing Neil what he was missing by selecting me as his second. I had no fight in me at all to try and make him want me. Sex was a means to an end. Sex was all that I was good for, and I developed a level of acceptance of that knowledge.

That's not to say that the acceptance of that notion brought about peace in me because it didn't. Guilt came flooding back. I'd obviously felt much guilt in the beginning of the relationship because I was having sex with my friend's husband, but in the beginning, I was full of hope. I thought things would progress and we would be totally committed to each other. That idea had helped me wash away the guilt, because what was happening between Neil and I would all be worth it in the end. But by this point, it had become clear that we would never be together, so why did I keep having sex with him?

The hope I initially felt was replaced with self-loathing. I hated myself for carrying on with it when I knew that I would never be with him. I hated myself for what I had become. I hated myself for all the time I had wasted with him. I hated myself for every tear I had shed, for every fantasy I had created over the years. I hated myself for not being strong enough to say no.

I dreaded him ringing me to tell me he was on his way to pick me up, because I knew it meant that I would have to perform. He wanted me to perform, he *needed* me to perform, but I no longer had the energy to pretend I was enjoying it. I no longer had the fight in me to compete for his affection. I knew there would be no affection, I knew I was running a race that I had no chance of winning. Sex for him was purely an escape, but the sex for me had become a prison. It was in a prison I had locked myself in through years of hopes and promises, and I felt like a fool for ever believing them.

We'd meet up multiple times a week for a few hours whilst he got off, but I was never really there. My absence only increased the guilt and self-loathing, because I had come to accept that I didn't even want to have sex with Neil anymore, but I did it anyway because I was too weak. I wanted out, I wanted an escape. I wanted to die.

Ultimately the sex continued for another two years. We had daily telephone calls stretching for hours at a time, mostly phone sex, but sometimes conversation. It depended on whether we had met up for sex that day or not. We met most weekdays still as I wasn't working. Anne and I would ignore each other at the farm if our paths crossed. Most of the time, I would try and pick a time to avoid her, but I no longer went out of my way to do that. If we crossed paths, we crossed paths. *Fuck it, it doesn't matter anymore; I still have Neil* and, I'm guessing she didn't care anymore either. We didn't speak at all; neither of us muttered a single word after the confrontation. That became the new normal. I had no feelings left to give. I felt nothing.

I thought the amount of sex we had was the norm when I was a young teenager, but age gave me the knowledge to understand that he was oversexed and obscene. I will never divulge in the details of all the things we did because the humiliation is too painful, but I didn't know that *I* had the power to say no. It was expected of me. I didn't realise *I* had a choice. *I* thought it was normal. I also thought it was typical to have sex multiple times a day; not just in the beginning of a relationship, but for the whole seven years. I learnt early on that impotence did not mean reduced libido. The only thing that impotence prevented was penile penetration during sex, easily corrected with Viagra. It did mean that sex with penis in my vagina or anus was limited to once a week, not that it stopped him from putting other things in there. It also didn't stop Neil from achieving orgasm in a variety of other ways. There would be oral sex, hand jobs, and an additional phrase I've come to loathe over the years; 'tit wanks'. Then there would be masturbation, where he would choose which of my various body parts to spray. Being unable to achieve a full erection without medication had forced him to be creative to satisfy his needs. He would try to satisfy me in various ways. I had quite a repertoire of orgasm sounds, just like personalities I'd adopted over the years.

I think Neil got a lot of his sexual desires from porn. Those women seemingly go on for hours, having multiple orgasms, having orgasms from simple pounding. The external organs don't have to be touched at all, she can be on all fours, taking it from behind, yet she still can manage a knee trembler. I think that is where he got his fantasies. I could never say no to anything he asked of me. It was always in the back of my mind that he was more experienced than me, that I was competing with a grown woman for his attention. My self-esteem was so low from always being "second choice", from always being the secret, that I didn't have a choice. If I wanted to keep Neil, keep his attention, keep his love focused on me, then I had to do anything he wanted. In the beginning, I just assumed that he would never want to do anything that would hurt me, so everything would be ok to try. The only thing I initially said no to was giving him oral sex, but *that* was soon guilt tripped out of me. I eventually learnt that saying no meant that I'd get the cold shoulder, a lack of attention, a lack of affection, so I stopped saying no. My need for Neil's attention surpassed my hate for any sexual activity. So, I put up with it.

I put up with the things I hated doing. I put up with pain, I put up with humiliation. It was easier to roll over and let him get on with it than to was to be frozen out; to be cut off. I hated the way I was being gossiped about, I hated feeling like a whore, I hated being a secret, but I had no choice. The years of conditioning had bent my sense of reality into Neil's reality. Neil's every wish was granted. If he wanted to take the risk; to rub it in everyone's face, who was I to say no? My reputation was nothing; counted for nothing. I was his, to do whatever he wanted, and I was a nobody but a dirty secret put on the planet to satisfy him. I hated it, I hated myself, but most of all, I hated the thought of being without him.

My physical and mental health were declining each month as I spent a huge amount of time in and out of the hospital after complications from my back surgeries. The increased dosages of morphine to manage my physical pain and the increased dosages of my antidepressants to manage my mental pain had left me in near stupor as I struggled to manage any daily routine. The decreased awareness of my surroundings had, ironically given me a bit more control on my life, as I found it marginally easier to say no to Neil. He'd ring me up asking to meet, but my high doses of medication had helped me bypass the last fuck I had left to give and it made it easier to decline his request. He persevered initially, almost guilt tripping me into a yes, but as time progressed, he found me less and less engaged, and the number of sexual contact hours decreased each week.

*

I reached a point in 2010, just before turning 21, almost seven years in, where I didn't want to have sex with Neil anymore. I told him as such during one of our lengthy, daily phone calls. He was disappointed and asked if we could still have phone sex. I said no to phone sex too. I didn't want any form of sex with Neil anymore. My body, heart or mind couldn't take it. I was broken.

I wasn't mean about it. I wasn't cruel. I just explained that I thought we had outgrown each other in a sexual capacity. We were sexually incompatible, and it was too complicated. I thought it would be better for us that we just remained friends. He asked if we could still talk on the phone, and I agreed, but I made it clear that I didn't want to meet with him anymore. I knew that he would be able to talk me into it if we met. I was tired of the secrets and the lies and all the sneaking around. I was emotionally exhausted. Apart from having completely lost any libido I once had, I hated feeling used. I was done, broken and I felt like he had shattered me into a thousand pieces. I couldn't take it any longer. My depression had reached an all-time low and I was giving it everything I had to keep myself alive.

We'd talk the day away together. He'd ring me as soon as Anne left for work in the morning, and we'd talk for a few hours until lunchtime. He'd ring me back after lunchtime, and we'd talk for a few more hours. Occasionally he'd try to engage me in phone sex, but I wasn't receptive. I didn't want to. I never shot him down, but I stood my ground. He'd try his luck every couple of weeks initially, but as time progressed, our relationship became purely platonic with no discussion of sex.

It was during one of those platonic phone calls that Neil told me Anne's father had died and left some inheritance to Anne.

"Oh, that will be handy then," I casually commented in response to the news. "At least some of the financials pressures will ease."

The conversation continued lightly and easily moved between topics, but we eventually found ourselves moving back to the discussion of the inheritance.

"I'm going to spend some money on the car, tart her up a bit."

"That will be nice," I responded, "she's a nice car, so it would be good to show her a bit of love."

"Yeah, I'm going to go and get her sprayed."

"Ooooh, nice, are you sticking with white?" I asked.

"No, thinking of steel grey, it's a bit less conspicuous than white," he finished.

I immediately thought that his comment was weird, given that there was no longer the need for his car to blend in, now that we weren't trying to slip through the countryside unnoticed. Given how many hours we were still spending on the phone, I didn't think that there was anyone else regularly spread over his leather seats, so I brushed the comment aside. After we ended the conversation, some hours later, I thought back to the comment and smiled at how poetic it was. For all the years we spent in that car together, getting up to no ends of mischief, it's after we stop that he decides to have it spray painted a more inconspicuous colour. *Well, it would have been handier to blend in at the time, but hey ho.* The ironic smile crossed my face when I thought of it even more. Anne would be the one paying for it.

Over the course of 18 months, my feelings for him all but dissipated. I began to feel the same for him as I did for my female friends. The relationship had gone for me. I valued Neil's company in the daytime as I was still unable to work, but I no longer felt a flutter when the phone would ring. It became a routine in which we had both found ourselves on the phone for the whole morning and then again after lunchtime until early evening. My mental health was all over the place. I didn't know if I was coming or going half the time. I grew increasingly distant and more isolated as my freedom had diminished. I frequently ended up in the hospital for pain management or due to complications. Life was grim and I was barely holding on. Thankfully on the occasions where I lost my grip on life, I was unsuccessful in my attempts, destined to live regardless of my actions.

*

In the summer of 2012, a few months before my 23rd birthday, I had my third and final spinal operation. Neil and I were still talking for hours on the phone each day. The friendship suited me more. I didn't pine for him. I no longer wished to be in a relationship with him. It was company for the both of us. He was home alone all day, and I was home alone all day. It seemed to be a happy medium where we would both have human contact without the added complications that sex or relationships would create.

During those last two years, I felt like I developed more into myself. I felt like I was no longer an extension of Neil, but I had become my own person. I developed some of my own opinions, my own personality. I could admit to what I liked and didn't like. I became mentally stronger. The medical complications had put a pause on my life and had given me time for self-reflection. My parents' influence had more of a profound impact on me and our relationships improved. Once Neil had become a smaller part of my life, I felt like I could breathe again. My mood became more stable and there were no longer attempts on my life. My cloud never disappeared, and remained with me for many years, but it felt more manageable.

I lost my sense of entitlement, which made me so much happier in myself. I gained self-confidence without arrogance. I was happy being "single". I was happy that I didn't have to justify meeting up with my friends and that I could have my own life without guilt of upsetting Neil. I didn't go "out-out", but I would go out for lunch with my friends from school or the local pub for a few drinks. Our friendships grew stronger once I was no longer attached at the hip with Neil. I was no longer staring at my phone, urging it to ring. If he rang whilst I was out with my girlfriends, I would cut the call short and explain that it wasn't a good time, and he could get back in touch with me later if he wanted. I am so incredibly grateful that my friends persevered with me because I'd been a really bad friend up until then.

My final surgery had given me a bit more of my life back. I was no longer confined to a wheelchair but was able to walk short distances using elbow crutches and furniture for stability. I was enjoying the freedom that bettering physical and mental health offered me. I had developed a new lease for life and saw myself taking more steps to recreate the lost teenage years, I'd started to meet with friends again, I went to a couple of weddings over the summer and into autumn and I had started taking trips to the pub to socialise. Life was turning a corner and I no longer found myself guarded and solitary.

As with all good journeys, there were ups and downs along the way, and this journey from the black hole was no different. In the Autumn of 2012, my newfound freedom saw me meeting with friends for a birthday party at a pub a considerable distance from home. As it was so far away, I had planned to stay out overnight in the accommodation adjoining the pub. Although I knew that I would be meeting a lot of people who I hadn't met before, I didn't have any kind of anxiety about going. I was looking forward to spending a night away from home, and doing what normal 23-year-olds did.

I had stopped drinking alcohol during that period of my life as I didn't like the feelings of loss of control. I can't say as I was aware of any reason why I chose not to drink, other than the feelings of being out of control of my own mind made me feel vulnerable, so I chose to abstain. As the evening progressed, I flitted between tables in the privately hired room and acquainted myself with the other party goers as they got more and more drunk. I found myself talking to a tall slim man called Adam. He was in his mid-forties and we hit it off straight away. Although I wasn't attracted to him, I felt safe in his company, as he offered to walk me outside for cigarettes. I was self-conscious about my crutches as I felt as though people pitied me when they saw me walking with them, so I didn't hesitate when he offered his arm for me to link as we made our way outside.

"I didn't realise how much of a live-wire Emily was once she's had a drink," he said as we sat out in the pub gardens.

"I've heard some stories about her time at Uni that would make your hair curl!" I joked.

"Oooh, don't! There are something's that an uncle shouldn't hear," he chortled.

We spent the next couple of hours sharing sordid gossip about the Birthday Girl as we moved between the seating inside and the gardens outside. Adam drank quite a bit and he had moved from pints of beer to shorts as the evening progressed. By the time we went out for what we had planned would be the last cigarette of the evening before parting our ways, we walked the perimeter of the large gardens and ended up at a small private pergola nestled within large shrubbery.

I heard the thumping of the music and saw the flashing of the disco lights through the windows of the pub. Their flickering in time with the beat seemed as though it was miles away and I strained to hear what song was playing but couldn't work it out. The stars were out, twinkling in the blackened sky, and the crisp air moved over my skin and gave me goosebumps. It wasn't like going out as a teenager, being outside at that time of night usually meant that I had consumed a lot of alcohol, and the coldness of the air would have gone unnoticed. I wished I was drunk, as I was ready to get back in and warm up, but we were too far away from the door, and my slow, supported amble would have taken me a few minutes to get back. Adam was still finishing the last few puffs of the cigarette, so I didn't want to be rude, after he had been so kind to me.

"I think you are really sexy," he slurred his words and my stomach fell to my feet.

"Ok… umm… thanks," I muttered, as I looked behind me to the door.

I no longer felt safe. I no longer felt secure, and I weighed up the options of getting back inside and making myself scarce. He pushed himself towards me with such force that it knocked me into the wall of the pergola and I hit the back of my head on one of the exterior beams. The shock waves travelled the back of my head around to my eyes and I felt unsteady. I didn't have time to regather myself before Adam shoved his tongue into my mouth and pushed me hard against the wooden wall, pushing into my body and pulling me up the wall.

I put my hands on his chest, and he pulled his head back, but his body remained firmly fixed against mine. He pushed against me with his torso and supported my weight, suspending my feet inches off the block paving.

"No, let's go inside," I said, hoping that he would take the hint.

"I won't take long," he said, and my body immediately became lead beneath his weight.

His hands hitched up my skirt. *He's going to do this, isn't he? He's going to have sex with me.* My legs dangled beneath me, unable to move as he reached behind me and grabbed the crotch of my knickers from between my bum cheeks and dragged them to the side, pulling the hem tight across my right groin. I felt it cutting into me.

"I won't take long," he said once more, and I felt his hands fumble around the fly of his trousers as he freed his penis.

He pushed inside me, and my lifeless body hung beneath me as my mind left. I watched myself from above. My body and soul disconnected. It wasn't happening to *me*, I wasn't there anymore. That wasn't Tanya, she was no longer inside that body, but floating in the blackened sky, amongst the twinkling stars. He's raping that corpse, that shell of a being. His face was buried in her neck as she looked blankly into the distance, unable to fathom what was happening. She felt no pain, she felt no disgust, she felt nothing. She was no one.

When he had finished, he held himself inside her for a minute as he got his breath back and her soul returned to her body as I began to flatten my dress down. I didn't rearrange my underwear but left them as he had, as he put himself away and offered me his arm as we walked back to the party. My knickers chafed along my right groin every time I stepped forwards with that leg, but I turned off to it when I felt his semen running down the inside of my thighs.

Once we got inside, we made our way to the bar and Adam ordered himself another drink and I asked the bar tender for my crutches back. I don't think Adam even noticed that I had left.

Upon entering the suite, I ripped off my dress and pants and stomped them onto the floor before getting in the shower and turning it as hot as it would go. *Wash him off, wash it all off.* I pulled the shower hose off the fitting and held it between my legs, the boiling hot water scalding my vagina as I pumped handfuls of shower gel from the wall into my hand and scrubbed and scrubbed. *Get him off me, get him off.* I felt soiled, tainted, worthless, and yet so utterly deserving.

*

In October 2012, I attended a neurological ward at a specialist centre in London. I had been waiting for admission for over a year. It was going to help me walk properly again. I'd already made dramatic improvements after my final operation, but this was a specialised rehabilitation facility that was going to give me the extra push. I didn't want to go but it wasn't that I didn't want the recovery because I desperately wanted to get better; my reluctance to go was because I knew I would be in there for at least a month, miles away from home and my protectors.

I turned up at the hospital on crutches on a cold Monday morning. After being shown to my bed in a room with three other patients, I hugged my parents and planned to see them at the weekend. My relationship with them had improved in the time since I'd stopped obsessing over Neil. We were able to enjoy each other's company without me disappearing off into my own world. They had been separated for six months by that point, so we were still in a slightly awkward phase of readjustment, but overall, the family dynamic seemed to be more stable.

I felt a little tearful as they left, so as I unpacked all my things, I decided to go out for a cigarette to gather myself mentally for the coming weeks. As I was heading out, I bumped into another patient heading out for a cigarette too. The ward only housed 12 beds; it was quiet and relaxed. Trevor had been the only smoker on the ward until my arrival, so he was grateful for the company as we rode the lift five floors down and made our way out to the square to smoke. Trevor and I got talking. He was lovely. Warm and friendly. We bonded instantly.

Neil continued to ring me for the first few days that I was in the hospital. I explained that I had physical therapy sessions for 3 hours a day during the weekdays, but the rest of my time was my own, to come and go as I pleased. My parents were coming down at the weekend, so I advised him that it was probably best that he didn't ring until Monday. Ward life was an unusual set-up compared to the countless other hospitals I had been inside. We had a timetable of our week printed off by the nursing staff, including the hours blocked off for therapy, but for the rest of time, we could be off the ward, travelling through the streets of London if we wished.

By Wednesday, Trevor and I had spent 21 hours each day together, isolated in the bubble of the hospital. There was definite chemistry between us. Whether it was because we were forced into each other's company or not, I don't know. Over the following three weeks, Trevor and I spent the days together. We went out a few times in the evenings to the cinema or for something to eat. We had kissed a few times, but it had gone no further. Neither of us wanted to, it would have just made things too complicated. It was the first time in my life I genuinely felt in control of my own body and feelings, and really understood the impact of my actions. The day before he was due to go home, we were sat outside on the square having a cigarette when he asked me what I wanted to do. I didn't know. He suggested that we spent 6 months trying to figure out what we wanted. The logistics of it were complicated, we lived almost 200 miles apart. I was 23 at the time and his eldest son was about to turn 18 and although separated from his wife, they were still living under the same roof to raise the children together.

I wasn't in the position to move closer to him, I had just got my health back, I had just got the ability to walk back. I was safe and felt safe in the comfort of my family home. Trevor wasn't in a position to move closer to me, he had two sons to think about. His finances were tied up in the family home in the south and his health just threw in an additional obstacle. I had strong feelings for Trevor, but I was also aware that I'd had history and lots of baggage. I didn't know if I would still feel the same way once we'd left the hospital to travel in different directions. *Had we only grown so close because we were isolated in a bubble away from the real world? Would we even still like each other in the real world when the complications of life got in the way?* It was almost like we'd had a holiday romance, but I knew that wouldn't necessarily translate into a real-life romance.

Trevor's idea of a 6-month break was a good idea and I told him as much. It would give us the time to work out what we wanted. It allowed us plenty of time to get back to a state of normality and to decide if the feelings we had were real or if they were as a result of being cooped up in the hospital together, the following day he went home. We hugged goodbye.

Trevor and I were in touch by phone, and I travelled down to see him a couple of times. Over the next few months, my feelings for him developed. I was in love with him. It felt pure and clean, and it was like a breath of fresh air. There was no sex between us. There was no pressure to have sex; we didn't even talk dirty. We had different opinions, and that was ok; I no longer felt the need to try and appease someone else. I didn't feel the need to stroke his ego or apologise for having a voice or opinion. We talked on the phone, and he encouraged me to do my own thing, be my own person, be with my friends. It was then that I realised that I could be in love with someone; be completely head over heels, madly in love, without losing my own identity. That love for someone else meant *not* having to change who you are, *not* having to pretend to be interested in all the same things. That it was ok if we had different ideas, different tastes. We could discuss things openly and frankly, and if I thought Trevor was wrong about something, I'd speak up and say so, and he wouldn't shoot me down for daring to have disagreed with him. I felt like my own person.

Meeting Trevor had opened my eyes to how it could be with someone. It opened my eyes to how awful I felt for a great proportion of the time that I had spent with Neil. I didn't feel under any obligations with Trevor, he was kind and sweet. I felt a stability in me when I was around Trevor, that I hadn't even realised just how unstable Neil had made me feel. I looked back on my time with Neil, and I came to the realisation how toxic the relationship had been on me. I never felt relaxed, I felt permanently on edge. I had spent so many years looking over my shoulder for the next surprise, that I had forgotten how it had felt to switch off. My constant need for reassurance from Neil was because he had made me feel as though I was freefalling for the whole time.

My feelings for him had altered in light of meeting Trevor. I looked at the past relationship with Neil and came to understand that it had never been about me. The flattery had never been about me. The constant love bombing had never been because Neil really loved me, but it was so Neil could get his end away. The thoughts of being used for sex had become increasingly apparent over the years, but it was the first time I could see that Neil had a level of control over me, far beyond the need for sexual gratification. The wool was starting to slip from over my eyes, and I was slowly starting to see Neil with an adult set of eyes.

I told Neil that I'd met someone, when I came out of hospital. We were *'friends'* so we could discuss that like grown-ups. I told him about Trevor and that we had formed a bond. I knew what Neil's reaction would be, but part of me wanted to hurt him. I wanted it to sting when he realised that I didn't love him anymore. I wanted him to want me, so I could dismiss him, and he would understand how it felt to be discarded like yesterday's news.

"I feel jealous," he said after I told him I'd met someone. "I knew it would happen one day, but I wasn't prepared for how I'd feel about it."

"Well, it's understandable, we've been part of each other's lives for a long time, it's bound to feel weird that I've found someone" I tried to be empathetic, but I knew *that* conversation would happen eventually and part of me felt smug that I'd seen it coming from a mile away.

I had to fight the urge to smirk, in case he could hear it in my voice, but the satisfaction of the realisation that I didn't feel anything towards him made me happy. I felt as though there had been a powershift between us. For so many years I had begged and pleaded to be the first choice, and he had made his excuses as to why that would never be the case. Now, he felt like second choice. What he didn't realise was that he wasn't even second choice anymore. He wasn't a choice at all. Interacting with Trevor had opened my eyes to how much Neil had hurt me with his constant controlling behaviours, and I was all but ready to cut him off completely.

"I miss you, I love you. I've always loved you. I can't lose you. I can't Tan, I love you."

"I know," I said, gently.

But I was done, I told him that I didn't feel that way about him anymore and that I hadn't felt that way for a long time. It didn't stop him trying though, and for the next few weeks he cycled between emotional blackmail, sexual discussions and trying to woo me with flattery and love bombing. It didn't work, I was no longer receptive, and I pushed the conversations on or made my excuses to get off the phone.

Neil continued to ring me, but as time progressed, our conversations dropped from multiple times per day to once a day, then every couple of days. It felt like he was trying to make me want him. He repeatedly told me that he missed me. He told me he loved me and tried to reignite the spark that had long been gone for me. It had been two years since I last felt that way about Neil. I don't think it would have made a difference whether I'd met Trevor or not; I don't think that spark would have ever returned. I was happy without the pressure of Neil but glad of the company. I'd respond to his *'I love you'* with an *'I know'*. I didn't want to hurt him, but I hadn't loved him for years.

CHAPTER 16

Four more months had passed, and it was February 2013. Trevor had just moved up to my area, and we had moved into our first rental house together. Neil was still ringing me, and I would reluctantly answer his call because I knew he was hurting. He knew that Trevor and I had started living together. I'd look at my vibrating phone and see Neil's name and feel irritated. I would try to keep the conversations light-hearted and brief. I didn't want to hurt him, and I was hoping he'd get the message from the cool tone of my conversation. I wasn't in the habit of being intentionally sharp, but I hoped he'd pick up on the stilted conversation and back off. Trevor knew about Neil, but because he is a gentleman, he kept his opinions to himself. He was secure and knew I didn't feel anything for Neil. Secretly, Trevor hated Neil, but I didn't find this out until many years later.

Trevor could see what I couldn't. I just saw Neil as a lonely old man that missed his friend. I couldn't see that he was trying to keep control of me; that he didn't want to let me get on with my own life. It had escaped my notice for all those years that Neil saw me as his object. That he could make me do whatever he wanted. Whatever Neil wanted; Neil got. Was he a narcissist? I don't know. That word is banded about without taking full consideration of the actual diagnosis it provides, but it was clear that he had plenty of the traits. Trevor kept quiet, of course. He saw that I needed to come to my own conclusions about Neil, that if he had tried to influence my opinion, he would have also been one to control me.

In June 2013, Trevor and I had decided we wanted to try for a baby. I was only hearing from Neil every 2 or 3 weeks. I think he had slowly realised that he had a minimal grip on me. I was extraordinarily happy with Trevor. It must have been apparent because Neil stopped trying to keep me on the phone for long periods.

Trevor and I were sat watching back-to-back runs of Judge Judy one afternoon when my phone started to vibrate on the arm of the settee.

drrr… drrr… drrr… drrr…

"Oh, for god sake, it's Neil again," I said as I waved my phone in Trevor's face. "I'll get rid of him as quick as I can."

drrr… drrr…

"Hello," I said *oops, that was a bit blunt.*

"Hey you,"

He is trying to charm me.

"How's things?" I asked as I got up and walked into the kitchen, placing my coffee cup in the sink.

"Not bad, what's happening with you?"

"Not been up to much, just the usual." I said, noting the awkwardness of trying to attempt small talk with Neil.

The stilted conversation carried on for another fifteen minutes or so, but every time I mentioned Trevor, he'd get a little curt with me and divert me off the topic. *Right, it's now or never Tanya, just tell him and maybe he'll get the message that you're trying to move on and there isn't space for him anymore.*

"Trevor and I are starting to try for a baby," I said, cheerily, knowing the news would hurt him, but pretending that I was oblivious to the fact that I'd just stabbed him in the middle of his chest.

Don't make a big deal out of it. Remember Tanya, he's just a friend. Friends don't get jealous when other friends share big news. Maybe he'll just be happy for me.

"Oh, ok," his voice cracked.

Shit, he is hurt.

"Anyway, I should get going and leave you to it. It's been nice catching up," he said.

"Yeah, it has, don't be a stranger."

Fuck, why did I just say that?

"Bye," he ended.

"Yeah, see ya!"

And that was that. Nine years had drawn to a close and that was the last time we ever spoke.

*

My 24th birthday was due to arrive, and I was in the first trimester of pregnancy with our first baby. Trevor wanted to celebrate my birthday, but I had got so used to trying to avoid milestones like birthdays, that I forgot that it was normal to mark the occasion. The last birthday I remember really looking forward to, had been my 16th, every other birthday had been a milestone to mark another year passed, another year without anything to look back on and say I'd succeeded at something. Trevor booked tickets for the West End and a night in a five-star hotel in the middle of London. I'd never been to the West End before, and I couldn't wait to soak up the experience, even though the first few weeks of pregnancy had completely drained me of all energy.

We arrived in London, back in the birth town of our relationship, and drove to the hotel where we were met by the parking valet attendants. *How posh!* As we checked into the hotel, our luggage had been carried up to our room by the concierge. Unfortunately, we didn't have any cash on us, so Trevor and I felt very red faced at our apparent lack of class and failure to offer a tip. I sneaked a peak of his name badge and made a note of his name in my phone, so I could draw some cash out and leave it for him at the desk.

We took a cab to the West End a few hours before Les Misérables was due to start and picked a nice, quiet Italian to start the night off in style. Obviously, I couldn't drink, but I hadn't really drunk much in the way of alcohol for a few years. The feeling of complete loss of control had not sat well with me for some time, so very rarely would I drink more than the odd glass of wine on special occasions. Given my pregnancy, I washed down my margarita pizza with a large glass of sparkling water.

The show was fantastic, and I was completely captivated throughout. I couldn't stop talking about it as Trevor and I enjoyed a stroll along the Thames on the way back to the hotel. The night was crisp, and the evening had crept in at the back end of summer, but the fresh air and the warmly lit city scape made for the most perfect romantic birthday.

*

Pregnancy had not been an easy ride, but Trevor and I welcomed our first son in April 2014. Life had its ups and downs, but overall, I was the happiest I'd ever been. I was relaxed and enjoying our family life and we had moved back to the town where I had grown up to be closer to my family. I had never experienced a love so deep until I met my first son. It was true what people said, the love that a mother has for a child is incomparable to any love that you'll feel for anyone else. I found the movement into motherhood fairly easy aside from the sleepless nights and the sudden removal of freedom and spontaneity. Throughout pregnancy, I had made aware to the midwives and health care providers, that I'd had a long history of depression and low mood, so precautions were put in place for additional support, if necessary, but thankfully, I had never had to call on their services.

I seamlessly went through the transition of being accountable to nobody, to being responsible for this new little life. I relished when strangers would peak into the pram to look at our sleeping little prince, with complete adoration visible on their faces. But, one day, whilst pushing the pram through our local Boots, one elderly couple stopped to have a look and I flinched as the old man reached into the carrycot to stroke the baby's cheek.

"No, don't touch him," I barked. Completely taken aback by the harshness of my tone. "Sorry, he's just gone off to sleep and it took ages to get him down."

It was a lie, but I didn't want them to take offence. The way the man snapped his hand back when I shouted made me feel guilty, so I had fuddled around in my brain for a reason as to why I didn't want a stranger touching my son. I didn't know why I didn't want anyone to touch him. I couldn't explain it, but my instinct had taken over and I was in full tiger mum mode.

"Sorry, I need to go and pay for these," I said as I waved a packet of wipes at the couple and made a swift, red-faced U-turn and joined the back of the queue. *What is wrong with me?*

I told my grandmother about it the following day and she scolded me for being overdramatic. I tried to fight my corner, to justify why I didn't want a stranger to touch my child, but I couldn't think of a legitimate reason. I just didn't want him to be touched. *It feels as though they will taint him because he's so new and clean.*

"It's just what people do, you're from a different generation, but we all did it when I was your age," she said.

"I know, but it just felt weird."

We dropped the conversation as we knew we would never see eye to eye on it, but it did leave me questioning why I had been so over the top about a simple, friendly gesture.

*

Having a child reignited a spark in me that I had lost many years before. I had ambition again. I wanted more. I wanted to be a better person for my child, I wanted to be a better person for myself.

Even though I had enjoyed the process of becoming a parent, and on the whole, my mood had been the best it had for five years, there was a part of me that kept being dragged down with fluctuations in my mental health.

"What's the matter?" Trevor would ask me when I'd look forlorn.

"I dunno," I responded "I just feel 'off', but I can't explain it. Something just feels weird."

My mood would jump between buoyant to dark in the space of a few hours and I could never pinpoint why I felt so unstable. I'd do well for a few weeks or months at a time, but then I'd get really low for a few days and completely detach from my environment.

"I feel like I don't know who I am, what I'm doing with my life," I said one day. "I feel like the only purpose I have is to be a mother, but other than that, I don't have an identity. I don't know who Tanya is."

Trevor looked concerned; like he didn't know where my thoughts were going, or what he could say that would help lift me out of my lethargy.

"It's not that I'm ungrateful for what I have, from what we have together, as a family," I continued. "But I feel like something is missing, like I'm not fulfilling my potential."

I missed learning, I missed education. I missed a competitive environment. I'd been showing dogs over the previous few years but trying to do that with a baby had been difficult because of the long days and the nights away from home and the added financial strain. I also didn't find it challenging enough, as when all said and done, it's the dog that performs and the handlers don't really need to do as much when compared to showing horses.

I felt unfulfilled, and like I needed to do something with my brain. I felt disappointed that I had never pushed myself at the end of my compulsory schooling. I had so much promise in early secondary school, but my mood had plummeted so dramatically that holding on to life was difficult, never mind getting an education. I felt a bitter about how I had given up on schooling because Neil had taken over my life. I was annoyed with him, and annoyed that I had lost out on finding my own path. I had been too wrapped up in his world, to see what I could have become in my own. *I'd have been a doctor by now*, I thought as my brain moved through the argument I was having with myself. *Why don't I start that again now?*

I signed up as a part-time university student to work through a Bachelors of Science with Honours in Biology. I had thought about going straight into a medicine degree, but I knew we were planning on having another baby, and I thought that the sleepless nights and the difficulties I had experienced in my first pregnancy, would have made it too taxing. So, in October 2015, I started my degree with one baby in tow and another baby well on the way.

I excelled. I was focussed and driven. Our second baby arrived at the end of November after another complicated pregnancy, but I didn't let the complications get in the way of achieving a distinction at the end of the academic year. We were two babies in, the first year of my degree completed and life seemed to be going in the right direction. I was feeling satisfied with the work I was getting through, and the achievements I was making, but still, there was an uncomfortable gnarly darkness in the pit of my stomach that I just couldn't shake off. That dark cloud had followed me around for years, and it didn't seem to matter what I did to try and combat it, nothing would stop the cycle of mood instability.

On and off throughout that time, I would go to my GP and tell her about my low periods.

"Hi Tanya, come in and take a seat," she said.

"Thank you," I said as I made my way to the chair at the end of her desk.

"What brings you in today?"

"My mood, again." I didn't skip a beat. We'd had these conversations many times. "I just don't understand it. I can go for weeks feeling good, feeling upbeat, and then I just crash."

"What happens when you crash?" She asked carefully.

"I don't feel anything."

"Can you explain that?" She probed again.

"I don't feel happy, I don't feel sad. I feel nothing. I completely detach all emotion from the world around me and just spend the days on autopilot. I don't cry, I don't laugh. It takes everything I have to just try and get on with life and do the things that need doing, but I feel nothing towards it. I just do it because it needs doing. When I feel good, everything feels good. Everything will bring me joy, and I spend a lot of time appreciating that joy, because I feel so much happiness. I think I appreciate the joy, because I know when I go down, I'm going down hard, and it will be a while before I feel anything again."

"Do you feel sad on your down periods, or angry, or...."

"I don't feel sadness, I don't feel anything, except a short burst of anger and then frustration when I get angry, because is often unnecessary."

"What do you do when you get angry, what gets you angry?" She asked.

"I storm off. I normally just get in the car and chew on my anger until it disappears. I get frustrated because I feel a pent-up rage over nothing. It will be over something stupid, minor and my brain just feels like it's going to explode." I rant. "Normally, I feel it coming on before it happens, and tell Trevor I'm going out to clear my head, and then I'll come back half an hour to a couple of hours later, and I'll feel like a new person.

He's really understanding about it. He knows it's just one of those quirks that I have and that I just need to go and get a change of scenery. But then I feel bad, because he doesn't deserve my snappiness, because he does nothing wrong, and my anger is never aimed at him, but he has to put up with it."

"What do you do when you drive off? Do you ever want to hurt yourself?"

"No, nothing like that. I'll just sit in a layby for a bit. I'll start by running through whatever minor grievance has triggered it, then I just unplug my brain for a bit." I said.

"What do you mean when you say 'unplug your brain'? I don't understand," she said.

"I just turn it off and completely zone out. It's like I'm not there, but I am there, if that makes sense? I'll just sit there, and my brain will empty and I'll completely detach."

"Do you mean that you sleep?"

"No, I stay conscious. Like, I'll know if something needs my attention, like if someone walks towards the car, or if my phone rings, but it's like my inner monologue just turns off. I won't have any thoughts, any feelings. I won't take in any of my surroundings, I won't focus on anything. It's not like I sit there and look at the fields, or the flowers, or watch the cars as they drive past me. I see them, but I don't really see them, if that makes sense? I just, sort of, stare off into the distance and my brain goes black. I stop processing things, I stop thinking about things, I stop my inner monologue conversing with me. I stop hearing music. It's almost as though, everything that makes me, me, leaves, and I just become a shell."

"And what about the periods between these low periods?"

"I feel fine. Normal. I feel like I should feel, how *normal* people feel. I feel upbeat, capable, energised. I feel as though I can meet with friends, engage in social situations, have fun. I can laugh. I feel like me again. I don't understand what brings me down. There doesn't seem to be a trigger, but I feel myself falling and I know what's coming. It doesn't happen all the time. I can go weeks and weeks without any drop. And, when the drops do happen, I never want to die, or anything like that. I don't go anywhere near as low as I did as a teenager. I was sad all the time then. Now, I don't go sad, I just go to nothing. I can't even describe how nothing feels because it just feels absent."

"Ok, so you've obviously done a fair bit of counselling and talking therapies over the years, but if I remember rightly, you didn't find it very helpful. Let's see if increasing your antidepressants help, or we could look at changing them. We'll increase them for now, and I'll book you back in for a couple of weeks' time, and we can have another chat about it."

I'd go back a couple of weeks later and I would be back to my usual self- happy, buoyant, and expressive. My GP was brilliant, and she really did make a difference, as much as was in her power to do so. When all said and done, she didn't know why those things kept cycling. I didn't know why those things kept cycling. All she could do was treat the symptoms as they appeared because neither of us knew the root cause of the 'illness'. I didn't flag up as having a psychiatric illness, as had been determined by a couple of different psychiatrists, I just had a generalised depressive disorder, that didn't seem to have any root cause.

Over the years from 23 to 29, I had developed numerous character quirks along the way. One of the obvious ones was my ability to detach at a moment's notice and completely dissociate from my environment, but interestingly, I had developed some from the polar opposite end of the spectrum too. Trevor and I would be sat in the lounge or the car, and something would change.

"What's the matter?" I would ask.

"Nothing, why?" he would say.

"Your breathing has changed."

"You say that a lot, why?" He asked.

"Because I notice it and it always means one of two things, something physically has changed, like you aren't very well. Or," I'd pause, "or, it means that you're thinking about something and it's stressing you out."

"Well, yes, I'm just thinking about waking up to the pup having pooed in the dining room again this morning."

"See, I told you. I knew something was on your mind."

"Nobody has ever noticed that before. I've never noticed that before."

Trevor's breathing patterns weren't the only thing I was hyper attuned to. It extended amongst a range of different scenarios or people. I had developed the ability to know what was happening in my surroundings all the time. Even when I detached emotionally, I could sense when things were about to take a turn. My hypervigilance had become almost a superpower. It told me when things were changing and allowed me to adapt immediately. People always used to tell me that I had good interpersonal skills and that they could talk to me about anything, and I could see that. I developed the ability to read a situation from a mile away. It became a crutch, a supportive mechanism that allowed me to always stay on the good side of people. I was very good at diffusing tension towards me, I became brilliant at knowing whether someone was interested in what I had to say, or whether they had switched off and wished they were elsewhere.

Hypervigilance made me a people pleaser. I knew what would make people happy, so I always bent over backwards to spread as much happiness as I could. It felt good to spread a bit of joy, walk that extra mile to relieve some of the pressure on other people- quite often at my own detriment. I didn't have much in the way of boundaries and found it very difficult to say no to people. I just wanted to make people feel good. I wanted them to like me. There was a part of me that constantly sought approval from other people because it kept me from slipping down into that shadow. Naturally, it became exhausting, as that level of 'helpfulness' can only be maintained for so long before it starts to take a toll on your own wellbeing, so I'd find myself in a stupor anyway.

I'd also developed an unhealthy relationship with sex. Sex, for me, became the currency of affection, and I couldn't understand why Trevor and I weren't at it like Neil and I had been. Trevor never instigated sex; it was always me. We had countless arguments in the beginning over his lack of urgency because I thought that his desire for sex once or twice a week, was a reflection on me. I thought he didn't want me, or that I'd done something wrong, or wasn't attractive.

I took his lack of sexual appetite personally, and it hurt my feelings. *Why doesn't he want me?* I thought blokes would jump at the chance of sex at any time of day. It wasn't that I was horny, or anything like that, I just thought that it was supposed to be that way, I didn't realise that my expectations were unrealistic in a long term and loving relationship. *I'm turning into Neil. I'm becoming a sexual tyrant.* I felt awful as the realisation hit me like a tonne of bricks. That we weren't supposed to be jumping each other at every given opportunity.

I also couldn't understand why Trevor didn't want to hit me during sex. He didn't want to slap my arse until it was raw, he didn't want to shove things inside me until I winced. He didn't need me to be loud and vocal, or like a porn star. He just wanted simplicity, being able to enjoy each other without putting on a huge show. I realised that simple sex was the best sex. No song and dance, pounding or stretching of my vagina, just two people enjoying the moment. Lazy Sunday morning sex became my favourite sex of all, just carefree, relaxed and without any pain. It also turns out that a partner induced orgasm was better than any of the shenanigans I had experienced before.

My sexual wanting decreased over the time together, and we fell into a nice comfortable rhythm, but my unhealthy attitude to sex didn't just limit itself to the quantity that we engaged in, but it stretched itself across other aspects of our relationship.

One evening Trevor and I were having a heated discussion about an upcoming hospital appointment that he had booked but was reluctant to go.

"I'm going to cancel it, I don't want to go," he chuffed at me.

"You need to go, it's important," I pleaded.

"I'm not going."

We went round and round for hours, both of us getting more and more animated as the evening progressed. I argued, he argued, and I became completely hysterical and screamed like something possessed. Trevor shut off and gave me the silent treatment and I bottomed out.

"Talk to me!" I screamed at him.

"Not until you calm down, you're being unreasonable," he didn't look at me, he completely froze me out.

I grabbed my coat and the car keys and stormed out. I dramatically slammed the door behind me. I drove a couple of miles away from home and sat in a layby off the main road. I had stopped smoking, so all I had was a playlist of music to act as a mood calmer. *Maybe I am being unreasonable? I mean, it is his choice, and I did go pretty nuts at him.* I sat there feeling foolish at erupting over something that could easily have been a calm conversation. *Why do I blow things out of proportion? Why do I feel like I need to try and control everything?*

Over the course of the previous few years, I had become somewhat of a control freak. Not in the sense that I tried to dictate to everyone around me, except for the above argument, but I had developed a need to feel in control. If I wasn't in control, I became anxious and jittery; my heart would race, and my palms would perspire. I couldn't even bear it if I was a passenger in the car, I needed to be the one driving, it's the only time I felt safe in the car.

It translated across all areas of my life. If I was in control of a situation, I was happy and relaxed, if someone else took over the reins, I felt as though I was spiralling towards insanity. Even when it came to organising things with my friends, I would be the one that arranged the schedule, where we would go, what time we would meet. I'd arrange the whole agenda. I couldn't delegate or let anyone else arrange anything as I had an overwhelming fear that something bad would happen. I needed to be in total control of my own environment. If something out of my control happened, or if an unexpected bill or appointment came up and I hadn't had time to plan for it, I'd have a complete meltdown. I was completely irrational and borderline terrifying to those around me. I couldn't trust that anything would be OK unless I was in control of the situation, and it was exhausting.

I sat for a couple of hours and realised what an absolute bitch I had been to Trevor. He was well within his rights to not attend an appointment. It wasn't even a life-or-death appointment, it was only a check up to make sure a new medicine was working well enough- and it was. The problem I had faced, was handing over responsibility to him, for taking control of his own wellbeing. I felt awful, I had been awful, and he didn't deserve it at all.

I made my way home sheepishly and feeling like an irrational idiot. Trevor had gone up to bed when I got in and I made my way up the stairs to get undressed. I crawled into bed, he was awake, watching a film on the TV, but his back was towards me.

"I'm sorry," I apologised, "I didn't mean to be such a bitch."

"It's fine," he said curtly, "it's done now, but you didn't have to go off at me like that."

I put my arm over him, and he gently patted my hand, wrapping his fingers up in mine for a brief moment. The argument was over and the tension in the room eased.

"You should get some sleep," he said, "we've got an early start in the morning as the health visitor is coming to weigh the little one first thing."

He released my fingers, and I patted his arm as I turned over, pulling the duvet up to my neck.

"I love you," I said as I reached to check the time on my phone.

"I love you too," he replied, but he still sounded a bit frosty.

I lay there for a while, with my back towards Trevor, but I couldn't sleep. *I need to show him I'm sorry. I need for him not to be angry with me.* The fear of abandonment creeped in, and an overwhelming panic washed over me. *He's still angry with me. I can feel it.* I knew what I had to do. I turned to face Trevor's back and put my arm over him, pushing my body into his. I breathed him in as I pulled his body towards me, submerging myself in the smell of his skin. I moved my hand down his body and towards his groin.

"What are you doing?" He stopped me dead in my tracks.

"What do you think?" I flirted.

"I'm not interested Tan, it's not that I don't love you, I'm still angry with you."

"I'm trying to make it up to you, I'm showing you I'm sorry," I responded.

"That's not how you show you're sorry."

It isn't? What? It's how I've always said sorry. I turned over, reeling from the revelation that you don't say sorry with sexual favours. *I thought everyone apologised this way.*

*

I had a complete and utter breakdown over the week of my 29th Birthday. *My twenties were supposed to be the best years of my life and now I'm in my final year and I still haven't got my shit together.* I felt so panicked at the thought of becoming a 'proper grown-up'. When I was 15, 30-year-olds were so old, they were literally a lifetime away from 15. I wasn't ready to be 30. I hadn't anything to show for being 30. Yes, I was married and had two children and responsibilities around my home life, but I hadn't anything to show from a career perspective.

Social media was the worst for highlighting my insecurities. I looked at all the people I went to school with and most of them had families and has successful careers on the side. I didn't have that. I still hadn't finished my degree, yet my newsfeed was full of friends who had become doctors, barristers, investors. My school had successfully churned out middle class and elite professionals, and there I was, barely holding myself together whilst comparing myself to who were once my peers.

In one breath, I didn't feel old enough to be turning 30, and when I looked back at my 15-year-old self, I felt more mature and more ready for life then, than I did at 29. But in the other breath, getting ready for 30 filled me with a sense of failure, like I hadn't done enough, like I hadn't achieved enough. I felt as though I had let everyone down, I felt as though I had let myself down. 30 had once been so far away, and now, it was less than 365 days away. *It's true, time really does go quicker as you start chipping away the years.*

I couldn't understand why I felt so low about time ticking by. I did have a lot to show for it. Trevor and I were happily married and had our 2 children. I had accomplished my part in the recreation of life. I had literally served my purpose as an animal on earth by reproducing. My children and husband filled me with so much love and joy, but the guilt of letting them down was overwhelming.

*

Year after year, two babies and a wedding later, we were carrying on with our lives. Unfortunately, after years of smoking,

Trevor had developed COPD. The toll of smoking had made Trevor susceptible to chest infections and pneumonia, resulting in his hospitalisation several times a year. In winter 2018, although we had not smoked for five years, Trevor developed a severe chest infection and, whilst in the hospital, he was referred for outpatient rehabilitation at a local community hospital. The rehabilitation consisted of 4 hours a week spread over two days for six weeks. It was a group system and ran like a conveyer belt, so as one person would finish, another person would start their 6-week programme.

Neil was far from my mind. We hadn't spoken to each other for over 5 years since the conversation where I told him that Terry and I were trying for a baby. We hadn't seen each other in the flesh for at least 2 years longer, but as we made our way to the rehab, he came up in conversation. Trevor brought up a conversation about feeling violated, in relation to someone stealing from him many years before.

"Have you ever felt really violated like that?" He asked.

"Yeah, I suppose I have, to some degree, but it's probably not what you're thinking I would feel violated about." I started. "Interestingly, you know the birthday party thing years ago, just before we met? Well, I don't feel as though that was a violation, I think that was just someone who got too drunk and took things too far. I don't blame him for that, I should have made myself clearer. You know what has left me feeling strangely violated…. the whole Neil thing."

I flicked up the indicator stick in the car and pulled the car out of gear as I coasted towards the traffic lights.

"Yeah, I mean, he betrayed my trust. I trusted him implicitly and he just used me for S.E.X." I was aware that our youngest child was nodding in the back of the car and didn't want him repeating the word. "That feels like a violation, you know, he used my body exactly the way he wanted, but I never got anything in return."

I knocked the car back into gear and started pulling away through the junction.

"What Neil did, feels more like a violation than the whole birthday party guy- because birthday party man didn't know me at all. I hadn't put any trust in him, it was just a case of using a stranger for kicks, rather than using someone who loved you for kicks." I said, matter-of-factly.

"I can understand that," he paused, "hmmmm…"

I could feel he was brewing up to say something, but I completely cut him off.

"I don't fucking believe it!" I stuttered.

As I pulled into the car park at the end of our conversation, my stomach fell to my feet.

Trevor looked over at me, his face aghast.

"What's the matter? Tan, what's wrong?"

"That's Neil's car!" I managed to spit out before pulling the car to a stop in the middle of the car park.

I trembled like a leaf. My knees didn't belong to me. If it wasn't for sitting, I'm confident that my legs would have buckled underneath me, sending me crashing to the floor. My whole world fell out of the bottom of me. I couldn't breathe. I couldn't formulate anything remotely coherent. Everything I knew about myself vanished into the atmosphere. My arms couldn't work, my whole body was numb. I completely detached from reality. Neil had been a something that happened a lifetime ago. I hadn't seen him for years and his presence had been a thing of the past. It was almost like he hadn't been a real person, but just a drawing; a piece of history, that no longer existed anymore. Like he had died. But he wasn't dead, he was there. He was in the building where Trevor was about to go. The reality that Neil was a real person and not a piece of history hit me like a train.

He had lived too. Our lives had continued in parallel. I had not considered that he would still exist. It felt as though Neil had just stopped existing the instant he left my life. I hardly ever thought about him. I never wondered what he'd have been doing, because as soon as I washed him out of my life, he disappeared down a plug and ceased to remain on the earth. Neil had almost become a weird dream, and I never really knew if he was real or not. It's almost as though Neil summed up an idea or an era, rather than remembering that he was an actual person walking on earth. It hadn't occurred to me that he had gone on living a life and doing the normal things whilst I had been developing my own normality. For years, he'd been a shadow lurking around in my history, but it was hard to picture him as being anything other than the mythical being that I had formed him into.

I didn't want Trevor to go inside. I didn't want those two worlds that I had created to collide and merge into one. My present had been so light, so buoyant, so free aside from the wobbles, and I didn't want that merging with the dark and secretive world that I once inhabited. My present world crumbled from around my ears and all I could see was my black hole. I finally pieced together what had happened. I finally identified the years of hidden trauma, the years of self-loathing, the manipulation. I finally realised that Neil wasn't some sort of historical being, he was very much present, and he was my abuser. I had been the victim of a paedophile.

Trevor had known about Neil, obviously. He'd known about the history and he detested Neil, I could feel it on the odd occasion where his name popped up, but I could never understand why. He hated Neil and what he had done to me during our time together. I was worried about a confrontation. I was worried that Trevor would hit Neil. Trevor knew who Neil was, but, Neil had never seen Trevor. I thought Trevor would kill Neil. Neil must have been frail; he would have been 70. Trevor sat in the car with me until I'd calmed down, giving me the chance to gather my thoughts. I didn't know what to do. I sat there cowering like a rabbit in a vast open plain, waiting for the fox to spot her. I completely froze with fear, detached from my surroundings, just waiting to be picked off by the predator.

After about half an hour, my brain caught up with my body.

"You need to go in," I whispered to Trevor.

"Are you going to be OK?" He asked me with his kind and expressive eyes.

"Promise me, promise that you won't engage with him."

"If that's what you want, I won't even look at him," Trevor reassured me.

"Please, promise."

"I promise."

Trevor reached for the door handle and climbed out of the car. I sat in the car park for about an hour before I could drive again. I was shaking with the adrenalin coursing through my system. My thoughts were muddled and confused. I didn't know what I would come back to if I drove away, but I needed to get away from there, so I drove around aimlessly for the next hour until I could pick Trevor up.

Thankfully, nothing had happened in my absence. I collected Trevor at the usual time and asked what had happened. He said he just avoided being near Neil, that he kept his promise and hadn't engaged with him. Neil had already left by the time I got there, so I didn't need to try and conceal who I was. My appearance had changed considerably since the last time we had seen each other. My long dark ringlets had been replaced by a short blonde bob. I'd developed fine lines under my eyes and around my mouth. My once sky-blue eyes had gone and grey discs encased my pupils, but I knew that if Neil looked at me, he would know who I was. I was still identifiable to the man who had been intimate with me daily for years.

Neil was now at the forefront of my mind. I was peaking in anxiety when he turned up in my thoughts. Everything reminded me of him. I couldn't listen to the music I enjoyed because it would keep his face etched in my head. I felt repulsed at the thought of his existence. I could smell him, and it turned my stomach. I could feel his touch, and it would make me shudder. He'd haunt me in my dreams, and it would take me back to the years that plagued me. The years I had spent so long trying to bury. I would wake in a sweat, my heart pounding as though it would burst from my ribs. I stopped sleeping because I knew I'd see his face.

At Trevor's final rehab, I dropped him off at the door and leant over to kiss him goodbye. As I sat back up, I was aware of Neil walking from his car towards rehab's front door. I locked eyes with him for a split second, but I felt him recognise me instantly. There was an immediate pang in my chest, but it wasn't like the way he used to make my chest feel. Instead, adrenalin coursed throughout my body and I had the sudden urge to run. I wanted to run like a fox being chased by a pack of hounds. I wanted to run for my life I drove away and continued to drive for the 2 hours it would take for Trevor to finish. I didn't want to go home in the interim. I didn't want to sit at home alone. The act of driving allowed me to process my thoughts better than if I had sat at home, staring at a wall. I picked up Trevor after a final and uneventful rehab.

*

I hardly slept at all over the next few weeks. It left me short-tempered and irritable. I became stuck in an endless cycle of anxiety and depression. I decided that I needed to speak to someone. I'd spoken to friends and Trevor, but I needed an impartial ear. Luckily, we have access to seek counselling as part of the local health service without waiting for a GP appointment. I made a self-referral and attended my initial appointment within a few weeks.

When the therapist asked me why I had sought out their service, I explained that I wanted to talk to them about what had happened to me as a child. I was aware that the Local Health Authority had an obligation to report any incidences of child abuse. I explained that I didn't want it to be escalated things, but I felt like I needed a counsellor's support. The kind lady listened and advised me that if I used any identifying features, such as his name, or a location, she was duty-bound to escalate it with senior management and possibly the police. I didn't want to report it. I didn't want it escalating. I just wanted help to stop feeling the way I did. The counsellor and I came to the agreement that the service would likely not benefit me. I needed to speak freely to address my problems without being guarded about the information I chose to share. Thankfully, the counsellor gave me details of a local sexual violence group who would suit my needs.

Months passed, and I awaited the news that a therapist had been appointed to me. It was a 6-month waiting list, but I persevered and carried on with life until I got the phone call for my first appointment. The charity offered six months of weekly therapy sessions with a trained practitioner, far beyond the 6-week programme on offer by the NHS. It was an organisation that dealt with a vast range of sexual violence, from rape to childhood abuse and everything in between. It contracted out to therapists from the private sector trained in sexual violence counselling so that the appointments would take place at the therapist's base rather than in a clinical building. I received my first appointment for June 2019 with a counsellor called Katriona. My thoughts were erratic as I drove to my first appointment. I didn't know what to expect, but I knew I wanted to engage fully. I wanted the demons that I had been carrying around with me for 15 years to leave.

Katriona greeted me on the driveway, her flowing skirt gently danced in the breeze and mirrored her long and free blonde waves. *She looks too innocent, carefree and calm. I'm not sure this will work*, I thought to myself. She guided me down the length of her country garden to a summerhouse nestled in the bottom corner and opened the door, welcoming me inside. It was a stark contrast to the NHS clinical buildings, with their harsh fluorescent lighting and posters that covered the holes in the plaster of the walls. It was cosy and calmly decorated with pale grey and neutral tones. It felt too clean to be soiling it with the dark matter that encircled my head. I didn't want to taint it.

A two-seater sofa lay along the wall and an armchair sat in the corner, both were draped with pale grey throws and scatter cushions. *Won't be needing those*, I mentally scoffed at the box of tissues sat on the arm of the sofa. The eight months that had passed since bumping into Neil had made me hard, detached and completely emotionless. Katriona introduced herself, and she talked me through some formalities.

She folded the binder closed and placed it across her slim legs.

I hesitated for a second and then the words flooded from my mouth. I gave her the highlights of the teenage years, from meeting Neil, how it started, how it progressed and then bumping into him years later. I'm not sure if I came up for breath during those 45 minutes. I touched on a few of the sexual experiences I'd had with him, like the first time he touched me, the first time we had sex. I couldn't stop. It felt liberating to talk so freely, without having to filter what I had wanted to say out loud for such a long time. Yes, of course, I had spoken to friends and Trevor a lot over the years, but it's a different kind of engagement when you sit in front of someone who holds no judgement and can remain completely impartial.

Katriona had a perfect poker face and sat there without judgement whilst I spilled my thoughts.

As the session rounded off, I felt euphoric and drained simultaneously. It was a weird set of emotions that I hadn't experienced before. It felt liberating. We arranged to keep the same time for the following week, and as I walked out, I remember feeling as though my legs didn't belong to me. I hadn't noticed that when I was sat in the summerhouse. My knees were jittery as I walked to the car. I was all fingers and thumbs as I tried to open the car and connect my phone up to the car speaker system.

I rang Trevor on the way home. I knew Trevor would have been sitting at home, wondering if I was ok. I told him I felt great. I felt free from the burden. I didn't think I need the entire six months of counselling. I told him that I thought I'd be ok after a few more sessions, probably no more than a month. I thought I'd covered all the bases with Katriona that day. I'd told her the story, and I thought the freedom to speak had fixed me.

*

The following week came quickly, and before I knew it, I was driving back to Katriona's for my second session. That time I needed her to ask questions to prompt my thoughts, rather than the free flow verbal diarrhoea that I'd experienced the previous week. She asked me what I thought my biggest problem was, but I didn't know how to answer it. I felt torn in two. My instincts had told me that I needed to report what had happened between Neil and I, but I couldn't shake the feeling that I was to blame too. I felt torn up to that point, especially since it dawned on me what happened between Neil and I was wrong and shouldn't have happened.

"I know what I should be doing, as a human being, I should be protecting other people," I started to say. "But I don't know if I can. I can see the black and white line here. I can see that the line is at 16, and if you touch someone before they are 16, you have broken the law. That age is the boundary, and it's completely unacceptable to cross that line. But I wasn't a normal 14-year-old. I wanted him to do it. I chased after him. I encouraged him."

"Why do you think the law is in place," she cut me off.

"Well, because people under the age boundary aren't capable of making those decisions. But I wasn't like other 14-year-olds. I was an exception to that rule. And I know what you are going to say *but you've said yourself that 14-year-olds can't give informed consent bla bla bla,*" I gently mocked her. "But I was not the same as the others. I've always been older than my years, I've always hung out with people much older than myself. I chose to be around Neil. I wasn't frightened of him. He didn't creep me out. I wanted it. I could have walked away at any moment and told someone, but I didn't. Instead, I flirted with him, I kept going back for more and more. It was my decision. At any point, I could have said no. I could have said stop. I could have said to him, right back in the beginning, that the feelings he had were not reciprocated. But I didn't. I made the choice to say, I feel the same way too."

"Why do you think you didn't say no?"

"Because I didn't want to say no!" I exclaimed.

"Why do you think you didn't want to say no?"

"Because I needed him. I didn't want him to leave me alone, that's why I told him that I felt the same way, because I had become so dependent on his attention, on his thirst for me. He made me feel good. He listened to everything I had to say. He worshipped the ground that I walked on. I was a goddess. He's the first person that paid me attention and I was hooked on it. I didn't want it to stop, I made that choice to allow things to develop between us. I didn't say no. I needed him." I paused for air.

"Do you think he made you need him?" She probed.

"Umm…" I paused to think. "I don't know, I've never really thought about it."

We sat there in silence for a couple of minutes. It wasn't an uncomfortable silence, but it was heavy. My brain warped under the strain of the question Katriona had put to me. *Did Neil make me need him?*

In the same way as I sat at 14, with a million routes opening for me to explore. I felt just as frightened as the first time, and my mind approached them tentatively, not knowing what would be lurking at each of the paths. Would they all take me to the same destination? Would they all take me on the same journey? I doubted it. I doubted that there would be a nice easy journey from point A, where I sat, to point B, where I understood everything that happened.

I wasn't sure whether I wanted to understand it, but I knew that I would never be able to understand me, if I didn't reach point B. Not only was point B the endpoint in which I would finally be able to comprehend my longstanding mood disorder but point B would also be the acceptance of knowing what happened between Neil and me was darker than I originally thought. Point B would be the making or breaking of me.

"I really don't know," I restated several minutes after the question was posed. "How can one person make another person need them? I didn't need him for money. It was never like the cases of domestic abuse you hear about. I wasn't reliant on him for a roof over my head, I wasn't reliant on him for shelter. There was nothing that he provided that was necessary for me to live, but yet, I needed him so unreservedly, that I was willing to put up with all of the bits I hated about him."

I paused again.

"Surely, that's what love is though, right? Loving someone so unconditionally that you love them for all their faults," I asked.

"That's not what you said," Katriona interrupted. "You didn't say *faults*."

"No, I said the bits I hated about him. There were bits I hated about him. I hated his constant need for sex, for degrading me. I hated him constantly pawing at me, I hated the way he wanted to take my body and make it his. I hated how every conversation we had would become dirty. I hated the way it made me feel, the way he made me feel when it was done. I hated how he would gasp dirty obscenities at me in the middle of sex. I hated how much I loved him because it made me weak."

"Does that sound like love?" Katriona asked.

"I hated all of those things, and yet, I loved him so much that I chose to turn a blind eye to them."

"Why?" She pushed.

"Because I didn't know any better."

"There you go," she ended.

*

I drove home, confused. Katriona had asked some probing questions, something that nobody had done before. I had never told anybody about the guilt I felt, nor the shame of being a whore. That's how I saw myself. I saw myself as an accomplice in the acts, not the person being dragged along for the ride.

Between each session, I would think about it all. I had thought about contacting Neil; I wanted to know what had happened between us. Had he pursued me, or was it an actual relationship? I decided not to contact him. I knew he would tell me that it was a two-way thing. He was never going to admit that he pursued me because I was a child or that I turned him on because I was a child. He would brush over it and tell me that we'd had an affair together; 50:50. He would tell me that it wasn't my imagination; that we had been a couple. I believed that he believed that. I think Neil really did see what we experienced *was* a relationship, though an unconventional one.

It made me wonder if a lot of paedophiles really realise they are paedophiles. Obviously, they will know they have an attraction to people of a certain age, but do they really consider themselves to be attracted to children, or do they convince themselves, after years of denial, that each 'child' they are attracted to is just a 'special' child? That they are in a *relationship* with a 'special child'. I suspect, if this is the case, it's almost like a psychological protection, because admitting the truth, would be admitting being the worst possible version of themselves; the worst version of society.

I knew if I ever spoke to Neil about what we had been through, he'd fill my head with the romance of it all. I think that is how he had sold it to me, but more likely, how he had sold it to himself because being labelled a 'nonce' as he called it, would be the death of him. What he wouldn't have realised, if we'd ever had this conversation, is that he would have had the same effect on me at 29 as it did at 14. I wouldn't have fallen back in love with him, that much I knew, but it would have held me back in that period of suspension between two worlds. This time, however, those worlds weren't the suspension between childhood and becoming an adult, but instead between truth and fantasy.

I think there was also a part of me that didn't want to hear the truth come from his mouth, much like I imagine Anne had felt all those years before. Part of me didn't want to feel the full force of the lie I had lived, hit me like a tonne of bricks. As much as I had been desperate to understand myself, desperate to be acquainted with the reason why my brain was so chaotic, part of me didn't want to accept the shattering realisation that I had been taken for a mug.

It was hard to admit to myself, that I wanted to remain in the dark, especially given that the feelings I had carried around for so many years, were largely because I felt in the wrong. It was harder to admit that I wanted to be kept in the dark, given that I had sought help to seek the truth from a therapist, the very nature of which suggested that I wanted to accept the truth. I had so much baggage of guilt and shame. I'm not sure that the knowledge that it wasn't my fault would have helped release me from my torment. It felt as though admitting that I didn't want to know the way Neil had played me like a fiddle, was admitting that I wanted to keep hold of the self-blame. I didn't want that either. I wanted to know that I wasn't a whore, a home-wrecker, that those names didn't belong to me, but also, they had formed such a large part of my identity over the years, letting go of them would leave me without a name.

Katriona asked me at the next session why I had apportioned so much blame onto myself for so many years. I revisited the idea of making the choice to flirt, that maybe I had been the one who flirted first.

"How many people did you flirt with as a teenager?" She asked.

"I can't even begin to count. It was my natural state. Maybe I am just a whore who liked to flirt and tart around with anyone. Maybe this is my fault, because flirting made me feel good, so I did it for fun. I'd flirt with anything that moved. Men, women, boys, girls. I'm not sure it was because I was attracted to women and girls, because I don't think I've ever fancied them. But, yeah, I flirted with most men and boys."

"How many of those touched you, told you they loved you, kissed you?"

"Oh! Ummm… just Neil" I paused to check, though needn't have. "Just Neil. He was the only one."

"So, if you flirted with everyone, but only one person overstepped that mark, who do you think is likely the one at fault here?" Katriona asked.

I paused. Open-mouthed and searched for an answer.

"It wasn't my fault, was it? It *was* him."

That was my first lightbulb moment. The realisation that my behaviour hadn't changed at all, but that someone else had acted on it. It helped me to see that I wasn't the problem, that my behaviour hadn't caused me to experience what I had with Neil, because if my flirting had been the issue, I'd have had hundreds of inappropriate relationships, and I hadn't. Neil was the only one who had ever stepped across that line, that invisible boundary that dictates whether it is sexual abuse or not.

Try as I might, though, I couldn't keep that lightbulb lit. Although Katriona had given me a helping hand to see that my actions didn't provoke Neil, the feelings I still had, couldn't be silenced. I still felt I was to blame, and even though I accepted that Neil had broken the law by sliding his hand across that threshold, I still felt accountable.

My thoughts didn't marry to what I knew to be the truth. I mentally went through the checklist to prove to myself that Katriona was right. I pulled apart at the law, or what I understood of the law, anyway. Neil touched me sexually. *Check*. I was under the age of 16. *Check*. Neil broke the law. *Check*. The ticks all lined up neatly, in front of my eyes. Neil had broken the law, Neil was in the wrong, not me. *Then why do I feel like I am to blame for this?*

"I'm a scientist," I said to Katriona in my next therapy session. "I deal with facts and figures. I look at the evidence and use that to way up the probability of the hypothesis being true. This is what I have felt has happened with my experience with Neil. If I were to take the evidence put forward that Neil is a paedophile, the probability of that is true. Neil struck up a relationship with me when I was 14, that, according to the law is illegal, and the nature of that crime, makes him a paedophile. It should be that easy. I should be able to accept that his actions make him entirely in the wrong, but I can't feel absolved that my actions didn't cause this too."

Katriona looked at me, remaining completely poker-faced, but I could tell she was disapproving of where my thoughts were going to go.

"It's like we were two people, each completely harmless, until we came together. It's like Neil was a can of petrol and I was the spark. Each of us completely benign on our own. Petrol is only dangerous when it's near a spark, a spark is only dangerous when it's near petrol. Something; fate, bad luck, whatever you want to call it, brought us together and the results were devastating, a complete inferno- that I'm still trying to recover from now."

*

When I went to my fourth session with Katriona, I battled between these feelings. She'd say things like *'the law is the law, it's there for a reason'* and *'you were not of legal age to consent to those things, so you cannot hold any of the blame'*. Part of me believed her, the evidence suggested that this was correct. Neil was a paedophile, but despite knowing it to be true, I couldn't get what I knew to be logical to meet with the feelings I had carried around for so many years.

It's the first time anyone had allowed me to challenge my feelings. Nothing helped me understand why I was feeling the way

I did. I knew what had happened was so incredibly wrong, I knew he shouldn't have laid a finger on me. That was crystal clear. The law was in place for a reason, and children do not have the capacity to provide informed consent, because, well, they aren't informed. They do not have the life experience to deal with the consequences of sexual relationships. They are vulnerable, easily led and manipulated or coerced into behaviours they do not fully understand. I found this hard to accept. I found it hard to accept that I didn't know my mind as well back then, as I do now. I found it hard to distinguish between my 29 year old brain and my 14 year old brain.

I was sitting in the hairdressers one day when the cloud started to clear and I developed a little more clarity. My hairdresser had finished putting the foils in my hair and I was sat under the lamp, waiting for the timer to go off, so the bleach could be washed out. In due course, the playful jingle sang its little tune, and one of the trainees came over to unplug the giant alien hat and escorted me to the sink. As was usually the case with large city hairdressers, the salon trainees were recent school leavers, completing their apprenticeship in hairdressing which normally involved keeping the salon tidy and getting the boring job of washing the hair of the customers. I lay back on the chair and felt the gentle tug of the foils being pulled by the very young trainee. To avoid feeling the awkward silence, I struck up a conversation with her. I couldn't remember the topic of conversation; it was menial hairdresser chitchat that seemed par for the course. What I do remember though, is the realisation that this young trainee was three or four years older than I was when it started with Neil. I remember feeling captivated by her youth and innocence. I listened to her rabbiting on about something or nothing and the awareness of how young she was dawned on me. We had *nothing* in common, her innocence and naivety kept the comments she passed superficial without any depth of thought. I had to do everything I could to suppress a laugh at how naïve she appeared. I don't remember what we spoke about, because for the most of it, I lay there thinking *was I ever this young?* The reality of this experience hit me like a train because I was once that young. I was once younger than her, and by the time I had reached her age, I had been sexually active with a man four times my age for many years.

Coming to accept that I had a different brain, and a different outlook at 29 than that of my 14-year-old self had not been easy. It had been a hard lesson to learn in the hairdressers that day. I struggled to acknowledge that I had not been the person that I thought I had been- that Neil had not seen me as a goddess, but rather as someone who was young and naïve and was susceptible to his charm.

I bounced backwards and forwards about whether I should report Neil or not. I was on the fence. I knew what I *should* do because I knew what Neil had done was wrong. Although the blaming and shaming of myself hadn't even begun to disappear, I was getting a more vivid picture of that black and white line, and the acceptance of having forgotten what it was like to be a child. There was only one thing holding me back, and that was the notion of all those people finding out.

I spoke to Katriona about it, I explained that I was really worried about everyone finding out. Naturally, I still felt incredibly guilty about it all, but the largest part of my guilt was because I knew my parents would be devastated to know I had lied to them for so many years. She asked me if I had thought about reporting it anonymously. I hadn't even realised that was an option. She explained that I could report it anonymously, and that way a police file would be generated. She said, although they couldn't use it as evidence, it might be that if anyone else has ever been in my position with Neil, that it could be used to support their case. Her words stung me, as the thought of not being Neil's only girl blistered my inner ears.

The idea of reporting Neil anonymously seemed to fit with what I needed. I needed to put the matter to bed, and I thought the act of making it official, would do that. I had long battled with reporting him in the lead-up to starting therapy, but the thoughts of my parents finding out had kept me from picking up the phone. If I could report him anonymously, nobody would know it was me and it would be the best of all worlds. My conscience would be clear, and my reputation intact.

I didn't sleep a wink that night. I had a million things whirling around my brain. I came to decide that I would report Neil anonymously. It seemed like the best option. *Yes, that is the most sensible decision. I can release myself from these chains and nobody will know it was me.*

But what if Anne realised it was me and came looking for me at Dad's? I don't want him to find out that way. That would be the worst way to find out. There was only one thing for it, and the conclusion I came to at 4 am was that he would have to know before I reported it.

Tanya Pursglove

CHAPTER 17

I had been awake all night. I didn't even toss and turn. Instead, I just lay there, motionless, flat on my back, staring at the ceiling as I mapped out the choices I needed to make. The fan in the room was the only sound in the house and its rhythmic clicking kept me company.

1... 2... 3... 4... 5... 6... 7... 8... 9... 10...

1... 2... 3... 4... 5... 6... 7... 8... 9... 10...

Counting the clicks helped to draw my mind back to me when my adrenalin started to soar. As my mind played out the scenarios that could unfold, the clicking and the whirring of the blades snapped me back to reality and helped to soothe my intrusive thoughts.

Thankfully it was a Wednesday, which meant both children would be at school and nursery; I needed some breathing space. I lay there and thought about the possible consequences of reporting Neil. I wasn't bothered about the consequences for him, but I had gone through a hundred scenarios of what could happen to me if I opened the gates of hell, even if it was anonymously.

I had an overwhelming urge to tell my parents. I didn't want them to find out accidentally, but I felt ashamed that I had lied to them whilst it was happening. The shame from that was something I had been discussing with Katriona. I didn't want to carry the shame and guilt around with me forever; it felt as though it was eating me alive, but I worried about their reaction.

I needed to collect dog food, it was a 3-hour round trip, so there was plenty of opportunity to process my thoughts whilst in the car. Talking to my parents was at the forefront of my mind. I knew what I needed to do, but I played out every possible scenario of how it could turn out. I had planned how I would say it, almost having a script in my head for the words I would use. My mind was like a notebook, with scratches, scribbles and notes in the margins. I had constructed a mental flow chart of phrases that I could say, ensuring I was clear about what happened, but without being too descriptive. I spent the day with the jitters. I felt sick to my stomach and shook with anxiety. As I hadn't slept the night before, I was overtired and clumsy. I was devoid of all emotion except for an overwhelming sense of impending doom. As I collected the children from school and took them home, the clarity struck me like a bolt of lightning. *I just need to do it. I need to do it right now.* I had worked myself up by stewing on it. I dropped the kids off at home and told Trevor what I was about to do. He was worried but supportive. He knew that I needed to free myself from the burden and, with that, I drove to my dad's house.

*

I prayed during the 10-minute journey to my dad's, that he would be home from work. I didn't want to back out once I'd found the courage to tell him. As I approached the end of his road, I could see his work's vehicle parked on the drive; I felt half relieved, half crippled with nerves. I pulled up on the drive and my legs barely carried me in. He was home alone which was good. It meant that I'd only have to concentrate my mental flow chart on one person, rather than adapting it to suit two people.

"Alright?!" He cheerfully asked as the dogs calmed down enough to be heard.

"Hi," I said. There was an awkward pause. "I need to talk to you about something, and I don't want you to react, or have an opinion. You can't freak out at me; I just need you to hear what I have to say."

"OK," he replied tentatively.

"I was groomed and sexually abused as a teenager." The words were true, even if the feelings still hadn't landed.

His eyes were wide, but his furrowed brow made it look like he was about to commit a murder.

"It's fine, I'm fine, but I needed to tell you because I'm thinking of reporting it and I didn't want you to find out accidentally," I continued.

"Who was it?"

It was written all over his face that he knew what I was talking about, *who* I was talking about.

He needs me to say it out loud.

"It was Neil," I said.

He clenched his fists and put them into the front of his work pockets. I looked away.

"Please don't go anywhere near him. Don't engage with him, stay away from him. I can't have you react, because then it will be my fault if you end up killing him."

The rest of the conversation is a bit of a blur, but overall, the conversation was calm. I was there for about an hour or so. He said he'd had suspicions at the time, but his hands were tied as I'd denied it to him previously, several times in fact. It was at a time in the pre-Saville era, when you felt powerless to do anything without proof, and my denial had stone-walled him. He thought he was protecting me, my friendships, and my reputation by keeping quiet. He thought that I would be labelled. I think he was more surprised that I had chosen to have the conversation with him than he was that any of the events had taken place. I didn't go into any details with him; I was just relieved that he was calm about the whole thing, plus it would be weird to talk to my dad about stuff like that. Neil was old and frail, and my dad was fit and looked after himself. Neil knew exactly how to push buttons, and I didn't want my dad to be compromised in any way. By far my biggest fear was that my dad would overreact and would ultimately pay the price.

The conversation rounded off and I told my dad that I needed to go and discuss it with mum. She'd be home too, and I didn't want her to think that she was the last to know, but I didn't want to arrange for them to be together for this chat as it would have been harder for me to gauge the room. I made my dad promise, one last time, that he wouldn't engage with Neil in any way, and this was something I needed to do my own way without any external pressures. Then I made my way over to mum.

I wasn't as nervous. The fact that my dad hadn't erupted had kept me grounded and feeling more in control. The conversation with my mum was easier but I censored it just the same as it felt weird to talk to my parents about sex and body parts. I had given her enough detail for her to process, and the nuances allowed her to interpret some of the events. She told me that she thought I was brave, and I immediately felt awkward and uncomfortable. I didn't feel like this confession warranted the title of bravery. I wasn't brave, I didn't feel brave. I felt relieved that I had finally spoke my truth, but I felt like I had also drawn attention to the fact that I had lied to them for so many years. *Brave? I feel like a fraud! Bravery is earned by those who run into burning buildings. Brave is someone who stands up to people who have beaten them into a corner. This isn't brave, this was just putting off the inevitable. You aren't awarded the title 'brave' for procrastinating all these years. You can't be called brave for being a liar. Brave? What, for agreeing to shag a married man?* Calling me brave felt like an insult to people who really did deserve the title. This wasn't something that required bravery, this was something that I should have done a long time ago, which made me feel like a coward.

On the way home I had to drive past Marilyn's house, so I thought it would be a good time to get all of it off my chest to her. As I had predicted, she was not surprised at all. She had seen it happening at the time but try as she might, she couldn't put up enough obstacles to stop it. This time the conversation was akin to a big fat *'I told you so'*. It wasn't patronising or rubbing it in my face, but it was a case of *'I knew it'*. So many things fell into place for her. All the things I thought Neil and I had got away with; we hadn't. I provided her with the missing pieces to her jigsaw though, and cleared a lot of the grey areas up, putting dates and events into reality. She too was supportive of me reporting it. Well, in fact, she actively encouraged me to do it!

My family didn't make me feel ashamed. They didn't blame me. All the fears that I had before telling them were just my mind playing tricks on me. The scenarios I played were nothing like the response I received. They were angry *for* me, but they weren't angry *with* me. I was supported and understood. I felt on a high for finally saying it. I felt such a rush of relief as though speaking out had taken a massive weight off my chest. A weight I hadn't realised I had been carrying around with me for all those years. I couldn't sleep. I was on a high.

✳

Thursday arrived, and I tried to carry on with my day as much as possible. Once I had put the children to bed, my brain caught up with my body and I finally realised how desperate for sleep I had become. I was exhausted, but I couldn't switch off. The stress from the previous few days had accumulated in the worst tension headache and my head pounded as I lay in bed. I drifted in and out of sleep for the next couple hours, but by the time 10 pm approached, I was restless. Trevor was asleep at the side of me and with his back towards me, gently snored, as I lay staring at the ceiling. I couldn't keep still. I felt fidgety, agitated. Like I might burst. I leapt out of bed and ran downstairs. I sat in the front room, grabbed hold of the house phone, and rang 101.

"You are through to the non-emergency line, 101, can I start by taking the number you are calling from?" Said the call handler. I gave her my details.

"Could you tell me the nature of the call today please," she said in a calm and welcoming voice.

"I need to report a historical case of sexual abuse," I responded before clearing my throat.

My heartbeat thumped inside of my ears, and I could feel my throat closing, my voice became hoarse as I relayed the outline of my teenage years at Neil's hands. I spent the next 40 minutes on the phone to the police and I couldn't stop shaking the whole time. I gave her my details and brief descriptions of some of the offences and the years in which it had taken place. She asked me to provide Neil's name and last known address and age, along with any identifying features. I probably went a bit into too much detail, as I was even able to recall his car registration, but I didn't want to leave any detail out. *I have been silent for too long.* The adrenalin was surging through my veins. *This is it. I am making it official. I am taking the bull by the horns and wrestling it to the ground.* The lady on the phone told me that a detective would ring me back the following day to arrange a time to take a complete statement. She stressed that the next few days would be a quick process because they didn't know if Neil was a threat to the wider public. I hadn't given much thought to that before. I hadn't thought that he could be doing it to someone else right now. *Would he even be capable of doing that now? He looks so frail*, I thought. But when I reflected on it more, the worst part of what I experienced was the controlling behaviours. *Sex is just sex, but the control ran deep to the core.*

I felt like my opinions weren't my own. That on some subconscious level, Neil had sculpted me into the choices I made. *Am I the person I would have been if Neil hadn't been in my life?* I had questioned my sense of self for so long.

The people we meet in life will affect us somehow, whether it's for the better or not. Our experiences help shape who we are; whether we choose to act or not is defined by previous encounters. Are mine and Neil's opposing opinions on things, my choice in spite of him, or despite him. The truth was, I didn't know who I was. I doubted every choice I had made, every path I had taken up to that point. When I caught myself thinking in a specific way, I questioned whether I had listened to Neil's voice inside my head. I had recycled phrases Neil had used for my entire life; were they phrases I would have chosen had I not been tied up with him? I saw myself mirroring his behaviours, saying his words. *Are they mine or his? Is this opinion mine or his? Does he do that with things I have said?* In a short amount of time, my life had flipped on its head. Nothing made sense anymore. I didn't know who I was or what I was doing. I felt sure a few years before, but I realised that he had influenced my entire life in one way or another.

After the phone call to the police, I woke Trevor, and we talked for the following few hours. I couldn't sleep, so I spent the night going through my social media accounts and deleting all friends from the farm who had connections with Neil- occasionally nodding off for 10 minutes before jolting awake again as though startled. I didn't want anyone from the farm or other mutual contacts to look for me. *They will call me a whore and a bitch and defend Neil; Anne is still down at the farm.* I made sure my accounts were strictly private. Those people wouldn't be able to message me or add me as a friend. I culled my friends lists right down to the few people I wanted to keep in touch with, who had no connection to Neil.

I changed all my visible profile pictures to black, so 'non-friends' were unlikely to locate my profiles. I hid my friends lists; I hid all my details. All that remained in place was my name, of which there were multiples of accounts sharing my name. The morning light broke through, and I listened to the sounds of the birds waking. Time stood still, I thought an hour had passed, but when I looked at my phone, it had only jumped five minutes. I just wanted the day to come. I wanted to get it moving. I needed to keep out of my own head and get everything out in the open. I wanted to tell the world.

I was on edge all day. I didn't let my phone out of my sight in case the police rang. Nothing had happened by the time I did the school run, so I collected the eldest and took him home before fetching our youngest. As I pulled up into the car park, my phone beeped with a voicemail. I listened to it, hoping it would be the police. I yanked open the glovebox for a pen to take down a phone number and returned the call immediately.

"Hello, this is Tanya returning a call for Joseph," I said as soon as the receiver on the other end clicked.

"Hi Tanya, this is Joseph speaking. Sorry for the delay in calling, I have just received the paperwork from the 101 service and wanted to make contact and arrange for you to come in and do an evidential statement. When is a good time for you?" Joseph asked.

"Anytime. As soon as possible. I just want to get it over and done with." My voice cracked and I coughed to clear my throat.

"Are you available Monday afternoon? I can do any time after 3pm," he said.

"Yes, that's fine."

"I'll book you in for 4.15 p.m. Do you know where the sexual violence hub is?" He asked.

I flinched. *Sexual Violence? That feels so abrupt. Is that really what it was?* Joseph gave me the address and told me to get some rest over the weekend and ended the call after explaining what would happen over the course of the following weeks. He filled me with confidence. He was very self-assured and professional. I was a little worried about him being male as I didn't know how I would feel about discussing all the details with a man, but I tried to convince myself that he had heard it all before, to dampen my concerns.

On Monday morning, I arranged to pick the eldest up from school a few minutes early to make sure I wouldn't hit traffic on the way. I did a dummy run in the car the day before to ensure I knew where I was going and how long it would take me to get there. It wasn't a long journey, but there was a potential for traffic to cause congestion on the way. I was jittery all day; fingers and thumbs, dropping everything I had tried to pick up. I collected my eldest and dropped him at home as I drove towards the interview, but I hadn't got more than a mile from home when my phone rang. It was Trevor. Joseph had rung the house phone and cancelled our appointment.

My heart plummeted to my feet; I was gutted. I had spent the previous four days building up the interview, not sleeping, not eating. I rang Joseph after seeing the voicemail from him. He was very apologetic, but unforeseen circumstances had taken it out of his hands.

We rearranged it for Wednesday. I drove the 5 minutes home on autopilot, frustrated but expressionless.

*

Wednesday came, and I drove to the interview. I arrived a few minutes early but decided to sit and wait in the car outside the building, having convinced myself that if I was there early it would mean less chance of a cancellation. It was a strange building in the middle of an old council estate. It didn't look like a police building, but like a house, an old, run-down house. The only thing that made it stand out from the other houses was its purpose-built car park.

As I walked up the concrete path, the old council house morphed into an official and highly protected building as the reinforced door and intercom system focussed into view. It reminded me of an old probation house. *Do the locals think I'm the criminal coming for probation? Or do they know this is where people come when they've been raped? Are they judging me or are they twitching their curtains pitying me?* I wasn't sure which thought was worse- *a criminal or a rape victim?* I approached the door and hovered my finger at the multiple buttons wondering which one to push as I glanced up to see suit laden men with leather-bound clipboards crossing the car park. I finally located the intercom button and pressed it.

"Hi, I'm Tanya, I have an appointment with you at 4.15."

"Ok, I'll be right with you," a voice said as the intercom clicked off.

Within a few seconds, I heard the clicking of several locks and the heavy metal door opened in front of me.

"Hello, Tanya," said the short stout woman as she opened her hand to gesture me inside. She told me her name, but I instantly forgot it. She showed me into one of the rooms immediately inside the doorway and told me to grab a seat.

"The detectives will be with you shortly," she said as she walked off.

I sat on the small sofa inside and felt myself get swallowed into the cushions. I fought the urge to pace by picking at the skin around my nails and checking my phone twenty times to make sure it was on silent.

It felt as though I had been sat hours when I heard the masculine voices muttering in the neighbouring room. I strained to hear, but then panicked when I heard my name being mentioned. *No, no. I don't want to hear you talking about me.* I stood up and walked into the hallway, coughing loudly, so they would come to enquire who was present. A tall, dark-haired, slim built man introduced himself as Joseph as he thrust his hand in my direction to shake mine.

"Hi Tanya, I'm Joseph."

"Hi," I muttered, "nice to meet you."

"So, Gareth, my colleague will be the one to interview you today. I am new to the unit and haven't been interview trained yet, so I'll be sat in the room next door watching on the cameras. Gareth is just setting up the room and the recording now and then we'll have a look inside so you can see what's what. Is that ok?" His voice was warm and felt familiar.

He seems nice, it will be fine, I tried to convince myself.

Gareth came back and introduced himself before showing me the rooms that would be involved. He pointed to where I would sit and where he would sit. He was trying to be kind and approachable, but I had closed down and completely detached from the conversation when I glanced into the room. My warmth was overridden by tension. The room was designed to look like a living room. It looked like my sister-in-law's lounge, and I couldn't pull myself away from the thought. I understood that it was supposed to make me feel more relaxed, but it had the opposite effect. *It's too normal. Can't we do this in an interview room?* I could smell the horror stories that people had told in that room burnt into the sofa and curtains. I could only imagine the tears that they had shed in that room. I knew I wouldn't be like that. I had developed a barrier between myself and the things that I had been through with Neil. I had no emotion- years of depression had taken care of that- I couldn't feel anything. I explained my detachment to the detectives at the time of the interview. I explained that the only way I could talk about that *stuff* was clinically, as though recounting an embarrassing medical condition to a doctor.

After seeing the neighbouring camera room and where Joseph would sit, I was taken back to the faux living room. There were two intrusive cameras in the room. One of them was in the corner facing me, and the other one was behind me in the opposite corner. Gareth noticed my eyes being drawn to both as we walked in to sit down.

"That camera will record what we say," he said as I looked at the one pointing directly as my seat, "and this one will record the room, so that the court can see that I haven't prompted you."

I nodded, pretending I had already worked that out. I sat fidgeting. I fought the urge to flee for the door. My mouth was so dry that I couldn't stop sipping the water that I had been given. The tape started rolling, and Gareth introduced the interview.

Gareth asked me why I was there and what had prompted the interview. I didn't stop for breath for 2 hours. I had been asked to do it with as much chronology as possible, so as I approached my 16th birthday, I asked them if they wanted to hear anything else. They told me it was only relevant if it wasn't consensual. I thought about it for a few seconds. *Well, I didn't say no to anything, so that's consensual right? I didn't tell Neil no to the anal, the alcohol, and I eventually consented to oral, so that's all consent. He never pinned me down and did it after I told him no, so that's consent, right?*

I hadn't stopped talking for 2 hours, and I was exhausted, my brain was incapable of forming any argument against stopping the interview, so I agreed to Neil never having forced himself on me. The tape could only record for 2 hours before it stopped and uploaded to the police cloud. If there was much more to say, they would start a second tape, but as I only had questions to answer, Joseph and Gareth conducted these in person without the camera. I wasn't questioned like an interrogation; they asked me to clarify what I meant by specific phrases.

"When you say the farm, can you tell me where you mean by that? Likewise, can you tell me where you mean by the stables? Who is your aunty, can you give us her full name? When you say the girls at the farm, can you tell us who you mean by them?" They asked.

I explained that the terms that I used to describe the location where names that I interchangeably used for River Farm. I gave them the details for the people I had mentioned within my statement.

"You mentioned that Neil gave you oral sex in the back of the lorry, can you explain what you mean by oral sex?" Gareth asked.

I felt my face flush.

"He used his mouth and tongue to stimulate my clitoris and vagina" I recalled as though consulting a dictionary- almost completely detached from the words as they came from my mouth.

"Sorry to ask that," Joseph said, "it's just that we need to make sure that you know what it is, in case you have a different idea in mind. I know it's intrusive, but if you use a term thinking that it means one thing, and we interpret it as something else, it can cause huge legal problems later down the line."

I nodded.

It didn't feel as though they had interrogated me. Both detectives were sensitive and had excellent poker faces. I found that to be helpful. *Let's keep emotion out of it.*

After discussing the details for Neil, so that they could search for his current location, I explained to the police that he had told me about his suicide attempts and bipolar disorder. They said that they would speak to the detective up the chain of command. It would likely mean that Neil would be arrested, rather than invited to interview so that safeguarding measures could be put in place to protect him from himself. They said, if they caught him in a surprise arrest, Neil wouldn't have time to hurt himself before a risk assessment had taken place.

I had awful diarrhoea after the interview, but I had been able to eat and sleep for the first time in a week. It felt like the most challenging part was over. It wasn't, but at the time, it felt like that.

*

"So much has happened since I saw you last week!" I flumped down into the small sofa at Katriona's, forgetting how far it allowed me to sink into the cushions. "I reported Neil."

"Wow, this is a big step Tanya, well done! Tell me what happened," she said.

I recounted the events from the previous week. I told her about telling my parents, about telling Marilyn. I told her that I couldn't sleep and that my mind wouldn't stop screaming at me to *just get it done*. I explained how weird it felt to talk to the police about Neil, and how uncomfortable the room had made me feel.

"A bit of me is worried that they think I'm lying because I didn't cry," I confessed to Katriona.

"Why would they think you're lying because you didn't cry?" She asked.

"Well, because I'm supposed to be upset, aren't I? I am supposed to feel distraught and terrified, but I don't, and I'm worried that makes me look like a fraud."

"There are a hundred different ways that people deal with traumatic events. When I look at the things you've told me over the last few weeks, I think that you've been traumatised, but you have dealt with it by detaching yourself."

"I don't know what you mean, you can't detach yourself from trauma," I argued.

"Think back to the first time you mentioned that Neil forced you into anal sex. How did you tell me about it?" Katriona asked.

I sat there puzzled, trying to flick through my brain for the conversation we had in the last appointment.

"You threw it in to conversation as though you were telling me what you had planned for dinner that evening. You even laughed about it as though it was completely nothing; almost like you were apologising for it having happened. The words you said meant nothing to you." She paused to let my thoughts catch up. "If one of your friend's recounted that event to you, how would you feel? If I sat here and told you how I was raped, how would you feel?"

"I'd be devastated for them, for you," I answered.

"Then why don't you feel that for you?"

I sat in silence, I had no answer.

"Ok, different approach needed. What did you do at the time? When he was raping you, what did you do?" She continued to delve.

I flinched in horror at the word *rape*.

"I froze."

"Why did you freeze?" She prodded for my thoughts to be said aloud.

"Because I was frightened it would hurt more if I moved."

"Exactly, you protected yourself in the only way you knew how; you detached yourself from trauma." she sat back and looked triumphant at making her point.

It was starting to become clearer in my mind. I had detached from the things I had experienced. I had shut down emotionally, physically, spiritually. I had taken on a whole new body, a whole new mind. I had distanced myself in the only way I had known how. That's why I'd spent a huge period in complete numbness. Katriona had a way of helping me understand my own behaviour, my own responses to uncomfortable situations. I looked back on other situations I had found myself in with Neil. I thought about the first time he touched me, kissed me, penetrated me. I froze in all of them. I thought about all the sex that I didn't want; I froze, flopped and just waited for it to be over with. *Maybe I have detached. Maybe I have been detached from this the whole time.*

CHAPTER 18

Over the following few weeks Joseph approached 'my' witnesses. They weren't 'my' witnesses per se, but they were the people that no longer had any ties with Neil. Joseph and his Sergeant would only approach the witnesses from the farm, or Neil's friends after he had been interviewed, so that the news of the investigation didn't get back to him.

'My' witnesses included my friends from school, such as Sara and a few other girls who had seen Neil picking me up, and my GP who I had spoken to about 'dating an older man' many years before.

For the month following the evidential statement I could not settle. Every time I had to leave the house, I found myself looking over my shoulder, expecting to bump into Neil or Anne. *I don't know why I feel so paranoid, Joseph told me he would be in touch before he goes to arrest Neil.* I even informed both children's schools to keep an eye out for someone asking for me, fearing that Anne would come looking for me and create a huge scene. I asked my neighbours to pretend not to know anyone called Tanya if someone turned up on the street and asked them if they wouldn't mind keeping their security cameras pointed in the direction of my house, so I'd have evidence if I needed it. Everybody was supportive and swore that they'd ring the police if anything untoward happened. I tried to carry on with life as much as normal, but the paranoia started to eat me alive.

I turned 30 in September 2019, but I didn't have it in me to celebrate. There was too much happening around me, and the thought of feigning excitement over a milestone I wasn't ready to reach, was too much.

＊

I felt as though I was going round and around in circles when I visited Katriona. I found it useful, as she continually challenged my perspective.

"How do you feel now it's all in the open?" She asked part way through a session.

"Partly relieved I suppose. I knew that reporting him was the right thing to do because, no matter what angle you look at it, the law is in place to stop adults having sex with children. I mean, when all said and done, children are not capable of taking on the lifelong implications of having sex. Apart from the emotional side of sex, 14, 15, 16-year-olds are not equipped to deal with pregnancy or raising children. Even if they went for a termination, they aren't emotionally equipped for dealing with all the feelings that will follow them around after that; every due date anniversary, every termination date anniversary, every time they see pictures of people sending their children off to school for the first time. That kind of thing will obviously impact that child for the rest of their lives, all because they had sex. Can you even imagine how someone at 14 would ever cope with knowing they've contracted a serious STI? It doesn't bear thinking about.

The law is clear, and I suppose that is why the law is in place; to protect children. Children should not be having sex. Neil broke the law, and he broke it intentionally, so he should be held accountable for that. It's just purely luck that I didn't catch anything or end up a teenage mother."

"So why are you only *partly* relieved?" Katriona emphasised on the part of my sentence that I thought I had been smart enough to gloss over.

"Because I still feel so guilty that I made him do that. I made him want me." I looked at the floor, equally ashamed of how I felt, and frustrated because I knew that's not how I *should* have felt.

"You were 14. He groomed you! How are you at fault?"

Is she exasperated with me?

"I know that I *shouldn't* feel at fault, but I *do*, and now he's the one that will pay the price for how I chased after him."

*

Throughout the previous few months, I received regular calls from Joseph informing me of progression within the investigation. As he had planned to keep the knowledge of the investigation concealed from Neil, Joseph had decided to interview the witnesses that were not likely to be in contact with Anne or Neil, such as those from school or those in my family. One morning, in October 2019, I received the phone call I had been equally expecting and dreading.

"Hi Tanya, it's just a quick call to let you know that we have put plans in place to arrest Neil today," he said. "I'm just about to head over there now."

My ears pounded with the sound of my pulse beating rapidly.

"What if he's not there? What will happen then?" I fired at him.

"I'll ring you and let you know when we've got him, don't worry, I'll be in touch shortly, ok?"

My stomach immediately started to growl and groan with nausea and an imminent feeling of explosive diarrhoea. I hung up the phone after thanking Joseph for keeping me informed and began to pace backwards and forwards across the dining room. My head was spinning with a thousand possible outcomes of the day. *What if Neil isn't there and his neighbour tells him the police were looking for him? What if he kills himself before Joseph manages to catch up with him? What if he tells them all I'm a liar? What if Joseph believes him? What if he manages to manipulate everyone into thinking that he's a nice guy, and I'm just a vengeful little bitch? What if Anne comes looking for me? What if she's there when he's arrested?*

My head didn't belong to me, I could no longer control the direction of my thoughts. It felt exactly the way it did all those years ago when I would circle around and around, completely overwhelmed and without any answers. I marched backwards and forwards, having the conversation with myself out loud as I wildly threw my arms around, gesturing to the ether as I tried to make sense of my feelings. Every few minutes I'd rush upstairs to the toilet as I could no longer ignore the noises from my abdomen. I felt panicked, sweaty, nauseous, and as though my heart would burst through my ribcage.

After Joseph's call I was a shaky wreck. I couldn't think clearly, I had a complete case of brain fog all afternoon. My mind kept wandering to what Neil would be saying. *Is he laying all the blame on me? Is he calling me a vengeful a whore, or a woman scorned? Am I being labelled a liar and fantasist?* I was so worried that Neil was working his magic on Joseph. He was an artful manipulator, almost brilliant in his ability to control people without feeling any kind of remorse or regret. I knew Joseph's role was to remain impartial. That was his duty. However, I also think police have an intuition they can't shut off. Before I got the news of Neil's arrest, I felt reassured that Joseph had heard me, that he'd believed me. He was sensitive and I felt like he knew I was genuine. Once I knew he was being interviewed, my mind was full of doubts. I saw Neil charming Joseph and the other officers with his witty one-liners. I saw them joking at my expense, shaking hands as they parted ways; *don't worry Sir, I'm sure we'll tidy this up nicely, and you don't have anything to worry about.* I'm not sure why I envisioned this, but this is the way I saw Neil. Whenever I thought of Neil, I would be transported back to my 14-year-old self. Not the confident 14-year-old self, but the part of me that became oppressed by him. The part of me that felt insecure, the part of me that he saw as my weakness and used this to his advantage.

*

It was hours before I heard from Joseph again. He rang me later that evening and his tone of voice as I answered the phone suggested to me that something had changed.

"Hi Tanya. Well, we managed to arrest Neil from home earlier today, but it's not exactly gone to plan," he said.

I held my breath.

"We weren't able to interview him," he continued.

"What do you mean? Why?" I panicked.

"We were able to surprise him, and once we were inside the house and told him why we were there he started to be unwell," he said, with emphasis on *unwell*. "He put on quite a performance. We got him back to the station and into the room and the custody nurse said he was unfit to interview. One of my colleagues even commented that he deserved an Oscar for his performance! This never happens."

"What happens now?" I felt sick.

"He's been bailed for 28 days, in which time we will pass things on to his appointed solicitor. Then he'll come back and report for bail and be interviewed."

"But he knows what he's being interviewed for, yes?" I said, as the realisation that the can of worms had well and truly been opened.

"Yes, we told him when he was arrested," Joseph replied. "He's not allowed to contact you directly or indirectly, and he's prohibited from being on your street. Does he know your address? I'll redact it from the paperwork, but he obviously knows your street as his bail conditions ban him from entering the road."

I thanked Joseph for keeping me in the loop and ended the call robotically.

I was gutted. Neil had got 28 days to work out what he was going to say in his interview. He had got 28 days to spin his story, to turn my words against me. *Neil only needs a few minutes to spin a web of lies but now he'll have a whole month to prepare.* I panicked throughout the evening.

What if he's still unfit to interview in a month's time? What if they decide he'll never be fit to interview? Does that mean they will drop the whole thing? Surely, they can't continue with the investigation if he can't be questioned? Has all this been for nothing? Has a month of stressing, insomnia, paranoia been for nothing? Is this the beginning of the end? Has this just proven what happened to me wasn't bad enough to do anything about?

I didn't know the answers to those questions, and I couldn't settle. I emailed Joseph to ask him what would come of it, and he rang me back later that night. He put my mind at rest and assured me that they had ways and means to make sure Neil would be interviewed one way or the other. He explained, if the worst came to the worst, and a trip to the police station was *too stressful for Neil*, they would interview him at his house with a camera set up to record the interview. Joseph reassured me that he would be interviewed in 28 days' time regardless of the barriers that Neil put in the way.

The following day, as I circled the Tesco carpark with my children in the back, I saw Anne for the first time in over 10 years. She was just heading from the car into the store. *Seriously, what the fuck? The world is conspiring against me.* Part of me had the overwhelming urge to carry on as normal, park up and walk into the shop with my head held high. I had nothing to be ashamed of, and if she started anything publicly, I could easily shoot her down with one sentence: *well, at least I haven't been sleeping next to a paedophile for the last 30 years!* That would have sent her running for the hills. There would have been nothing she could have shamed me for that would have remotely affected the people around us more than that sentence. *I should go in. Why should I be making the effort to avoid her? If anything, she should be trying to avoid me!*

Is she looking for me? In the last 10 years of living in this very small town, I haven't once bumped into her. She always used to shop at the Sainsbury's in the neighbouring town, I come in this Tesco nearly every day, at random times throughout the day, why is this the first time I've seen her here. She is looking for me, isn't she? Anne was always regimental in her routine; Sainsbury's on Wednesday afternoon, after work but before the farm. If she was on lates, she'd swap it for Thursday. Then, Saturday afternoon she'd go back to Sainsbury's after she had finished the farm, so she could take stuff around to her elderly father before the night routine at the farm. She never, in the nine years that Neil and I were getting it on, strayed from that routine. It doesn't make sense that she would casually use Tesco now, the day after he was bloody arrested, unless she was hoping to bump into me.

Part of Neil's bail conditions meant that he wasn't allowed to contact me directly, or indirectly. So naturally, if Anne had wanted to look for me, she would have had to do it in a very public manner, so it could look accidental. It's not like she could have gone to my dad's house looking for me, because there was no way that she could claim it wasn't premeditated. *Am I losing it? Am I going mad? I'm going mad, aren't I? What am I doing? This whole thing is going to kill me!*

"Mummy, why aren't we going inside?" My eldest son asked, snapping me from my thoughts.

"We are just going to wait here for a few minutes, Sweetpea," I said as I turned the car off.

I had parked in a bay two rows behind Anne, so I could watch and wait for her to get back in the car and leave. *I can't let the kids see some deranged bitch kicking off at me in Tesco. They'll be scarred for life.* I turned the ignition back on and put Paw Patrol on the in-car DVD players.

"Let's just watch this for a minute and we'll go and do the shopping in a minute," I said, as the theme tune played through the speakers.

I bloody hate these tiny hero dogs, but it will keep them entertained for a minute, whilst I watch for my own entertainment. Oh no! Am I a stalker now? This feels like stalking! I am going mad. I'm going to end up one of those crazy women that stalk her ex's wife. Wait! No, he's not my ex. This is not the same, is it? No, don't be stupid Tanya, you are protecting yourself, not stalking. Stalkers don't do it to avoid bumping into someone, they do it to intentionally bump into someone. But I do want to go inside to give her the chance to rage at me. What is wrong with me? Why doesn't anything I feel make sense? Part of me wants her to shout and scream and cause a scene, so I can have the smug satisfaction of shooting her down. That makes me the vengeful bitch, doesn't it? Is that what this is? Have I done this for revenge? What if I have? Does being vengeful take away what he did, or is he still the villain in all of this? Am I now the bad guy? Was it even revenge? No, it wasn't revenge, it was for vindication, validation for all the self-hatred and confusion. I did it to stop feeling guilty. I reported him to relieve the slow burning ache I've felt for all these years. I reported him because it was the right thing to do, right? Why does none of this make sense anymore? The more I think about it, the more confused I get. Oh shit, that's her!

Anne was walking back to the car carrying a couple of carrier bags and 8 pints of milk. Her sunglasses flashed a reflection of the late autumn sun as she turned her head in my direction, and slammed her boot shut. She proceeded around to her driver's door and climbed in. The brake lights flicked on as she started the engine and began to pull off down the carpark. I breathed a sigh of relief.

"Right kids, let's go!"

*

I went back to Katriona and told her how Neil had been released on bail.

"What do you mean he's too unwell to interview?" She asked, astounded at Neil's ability to dodge the bullet.

"Joseph couldn't tell me much, but I got the impression that it was all a bit of a farce. Not that Neil wasn't unwell, because I'm sure that the police see people feigning illness all the time when arrested. I just think that his long list of ailments have finally caught up with him, and once the custody nurse saw them, and a touch of high blood pressure, she decided it would be too risky. I don't know about you, but I imagine my blood pressure would shoot through the roof if I'd just been arrested for paedophilia, regardless of the rest of my health."

"Ha, yeah, I can imagine."

"Anyway, who did I bump into the following day? Only bloody Anne, for fuck's sake."

"No! What happened?" Katriona's open mouthed expression didn't go unnoticed.

I told her about what had happened at Tesco and how I felt at the time.

"I think if I'd been there alone, I'd have gone in and thrown caution to the wind. What's the worst she could have done? Stabbed me with a frozen leg of lamb, knocked me over with a trolley?" I laughed which became the norm when discussing anything remotely traumatic. "I think if I hadn't had the kids with me, curiosity would have got the better of me. Yes, OK, I did feel anxious, but in reality, what kind of a fool would cause a scene in the middle of Tesco if her husband had just been arrested for having sex with children? You just wouldn't, would you? She's not stupid. She knows that all it would have taken would be for me to ask her, in front of a crowd of shoppers *what's it like sleeping next to a paedophile?* She wouldn't have any come back from that. Paedophiles are probably the only people in society that everyone hates. There is no defending that."

"What do you think she'd have done?" Katriona asked.

"What could she have done, it's indefensible isn't it? Even if she really didn't know at the time it was happening, she still took him back into the house after he was arrested."

"How do you know he's back there?"

"Joseph told me. Because Neil couldn't be interviewed on the grounds of ill health, when he was returned home, he had to be left in the company of a guardian. Well, apparently, Anne wasn't at home when they tried to drop Neil off, so they drove down to the farm to look for her. Neil was in the back of the police car at the time, and Joseph had to go walking through the farm looking for Anne, so Neil could be released into her care. I can only imagine how mortified that she would have been; everyone on the farm knowing her business. She was so private, she didn't even tell them that we'd been at it when the shit hit the fan."

"Why do you think that was?" Katriona asked.

"Because she was afraid of a big fat, *I told you so.*"

"How do you feel about Anne?" Katriona asked yet another question that I hadn't given much thought to.

"Feel about Anne? I don't really know. I suppose part of me is still stuck back in the old days, and there is an element of frustration there, but it's not jealousy, like it was back then. I suppose it's frustration because I don't understand her. I had been painted this picture of her over the years. Of course, it's only Neil that painted it, so I'm not sure how much of it was true. He always told me how she was *picture no sound*; completely uninterested in the relationship, but I think truth of the matter is, she was a hard worker. She worked full time and then went to the farm. Once finished at the farm, she would go home, clean, sort out the dogs and cook dinner. She was a skivvy to Neil, so it's no wonder that she was exhausted and unable to function well enough to communicate by the time she had finished her day. Her only day off was Sunday, as she spent Saturdays working at the farm. On Sunday, quite often in the Summer, we would be at shows, or I'd be at their house. Looking at it through my eyes now, I wonder why she put up with me and him. I don't know whether she knew about our secret meetings, but she knew we'd be off cavorting at the farm or shows. She knew he would bend over backwards to help me with my horse jobs but rarely offered her help, unless I was in the stable too. She knew that he'd wait behind for a while so he could spend time with me on an empty farm, after spending the whole day away from her- he still put me first. She also knew that I'd go up to their house occasionally whilst she was at work."

"How much do you think she knew?" Katriona asked.

"Well, that's the sixty-four-million-dollar question, isn't it? I thought she'd known for a long time before the shit hit the fan. I'd been getting vibes for months, possibly even years before it all blew up. But then I wonder how someone can have sex with someone when they suspected that his penis had been inside a child? It makes me shudder, just to think about it. If I came home from work and found a fourteen-year-old on my sofa, I'd feel uncomfortable. The first time, I'd probably be able to excuse it, thinking that my husband had been charitable, but if it happened a second time, even if I trusted my husband implicitly, I'd be having words. Even if it was only to warn him that it only takes one small miscommunication for horrific accusations to be made. I couldn't see it happening again and again. I'd probably ring the police and report it myself."

"So, who would you have blamed?" Katriona asked.

"Oh god, my husband. He knew that the accountability fell on him, particularly as I'd have said something the first time I saw something a bit weird. You don't come home to an unrelated child sat on your sofa."

"So, you didn't blame the 14-year-old?"

"No! Why would I?" I exclaimed.

"Exactly!" She exclaimed.

Well played Katriona, well played.

*

Katriona's point rattled through my brain over the following weeks. She did have a point. If I could see how I'd have reacted, had the shoe been on the other foot, then why was I being so hard on myself?

Why was I blaming myself for what happened between Neil and I? *Because I wanted him, I chased him, I threw myself at him.* My intrusive thoughts were still there and would resurface every time I asked myself the question. *I wanted him. I didn't stop him. I didn't say no.* But the more and more I revisited it, the more I started to argue with myself. *But I didn't know I could say no.* Neil had never offered me the chance to say no. The way Neil framed my direction for me had been what had forced my response. *He didn't ask if he could touch me the first time. He just did it. He caught me off guard, unaware. It wasn't a choice I made; it was one that he made. Who would I have told? He was my friend's husband, and I didn't want to lose my friend. I didn't want to tarnish my reputation by being labelled a whore.*

I got bursts of clarity that would fracture through my thought patterns, and I'd see Neil for what he did, but they were short-lived. My brain continually moved backward and forwards, and for every argument, I could find as to why Neil deserved to be punished, I would find three arguments for why I was in the wrong. *Small steps Tanya, it's still progress.*

As 28 days approached, I got a phone call from Joseph saying that they had interviewed Neil that day. It came as a complete surprise as I had marked it off in my calendar for after the weekend, so I hadn't expected to hear anything for a few more days. Apparently, Neil had a medical appointment coincide with the day he was supposed to report for bail, so Joseph had requested that he attend a few days before to *get it out of the way.*

"What did he say?" I asked with bated breath.

"Not much I'm afraid, Tanya."

"So, he gave a no-comment interview?" I said, almost triumphantly at my expectations having been met, almost disappointed that he hadn't thought of a way to spin it.

"Yes, pretty much. He offered a couple of bits, but his solicitor cut him off and reminded him of his advice to remain silent."

I was fuming, seething. *How dare he? He had 28 days' notice to sort out answers for the questions he was going to be asked. How dare he? He was sat in an interview room, full of males, all younger than him, with a solicitor holding his hand for the entire time, and he had the audacity to use 'no comment' on repeat for the entire process.* I was livid. For the first time in a long time, I experienced a burning hate. It was directed at that coward. Just a few months prior to that I sat alone, in a room with an older male police detective, being asked to recount whole passages about what had happened to me. Being asked to describe what I meant when I used the phrase 'oral sex', 'vagina', 'fingering', being asked to describe the details of Neil inserting various items into my vagina; having to explain that at the time I wanted him to do it. I was humiliated all over again in attempt to get justice and vindication for what happened to me. *He had the nerve to say 'no comment'.*

I had always been liberal-minded, a little left-wing, perhaps a bit 'soft'. I don't know. I'd consider myself forgiving, I suppose. Willing to offer the benefit of the doubt; innocent until proven guilty. I had not considered how victims would feel during this process. If the *accused* is 'innocent until proven guilty', then victims are 'liars until proven truthful'. It's a horrific, gut-churning realisation, that in the eyes of the justice system, the victim has to prove the crime was committed. I understand the need to protect the accused against people who are out for vengeance, but I didn't think how this would make me feel, as a *'complainant'*. It felt like Neil had more rights than me- the right to silence, innocent until proven guilty. I couldn't have sat in my witness interview and said nothing, or 'no comment' to avoid the humiliation of being asked to describe the things Neil did to me. Once again, I was made to feel vulnerable; made to feel inferior to him. He didn't have to prove his innocence, it was *my job* to prove his guilt.

It felt unfair that his right is to say nothing at all:

"You do not have to say anything. But, it may harm your defence if you do not mention when questioned something you may later rely on in court. Anything you do say may be given in evidence."

Those are the police rights read to the accused in the UK. I'll break them down according to how I interpret them, as a layperson:

'You do not have to say anything'- *you need not supply yourself with a defence as you are innocent until proven guilty.*

'It may harm your defence...bla bla bla... in court'- *what I have learnt from the judicial system is that huge proportions of accusations made, particularly in sex crimes, do not even make it to court.*

My sole evidence was my statement. I didn't have any forensic proof those things happened. I had things that helped to add credibility to my case, but I didn't have anything concrete to show they took place. I didn't have pictorial evidence; there were no videos of sexual activity. Phone records from 15 years before were unlikely to exist, and if they had, the man hours required to sift through them would be an unjustified cost for the police. That meant that his defence was only harmed *if* the case made it to court. *Why couldn't he be forced to answer questions in the interview?* If he was innocent, he wouldn't have been able to trip himself up by accidentally supplying evidence in the favour of the complainant. Instead, the burden was all on me. It was my word against his.

We are told time and time again that police are trained to believe that victims of sexual violence; but how can this be true when the police also must treat the perpetrators as innocent until proven guilty? It's impossible that both statements can be true, and that is the battle I felt I was up against from the beginning. If he was to be believed, then there were more questions surrounding my credibility. It's up to the victim to prove the act happened. I don't know what solution there is to this, I don't think there is a solution, which probably explains why so few of these cases even make it as far as an initial reporting, never mind to the courtroom.

I did have the advantage in that I had confided in several witnesses at the time of the events. I had spoken to friends about Neil (who were called as witnesses), I had also spoken to the GP about an "older man" that I was seeing, and where we'd met etc. I didn't know what they had included in their statements, as I had made the conscious effort to avoid asking or sharing what I had included. Although I hadn't been told that I couldn't discuss it with them, I was too afraid that it would make me look like I was trying to get my story straight if it ever made it to trial. I had experienced flashforwards of standing in the witness box and breaking down because I had to admit that I'd spoke in great detail comparing our accounts. There was also a part of me that wanted to make it a 'fair trial', because I knew Neil had committed the offences, and I wanted to make sure I could come out of the other side of it knowing that I had 'won' purely because the evidence proved it, and not because I had 'cheated the evidence' by swapping stories and details. I thought that if Neil was found guilty in a trial, it would relieve me of the blame and shame that I had carried around with me. I thought it would release me of the burden that was chained to me.

*

I returned to Katriona week in, week out, and after Neil's interview, I turned up to our session, still seething from his *no comment* interview.

"Why are you so angry though, what did you expect?" She asked me.

"I don't know. I think I wanted him to tell his version of events. I wanted answers. I wanted to see it from his perspective. I wanted to know whether he's spent the last 15 years feeling terrible. I wanted to know if he'd felt guilty. I dunno, I suppose part of me wants to know if the guilt from all of this has been eating at him too. Do you think it has?"

"No" Katriona replied, very matter of fact.

"Why?" I asked.

"Because I think you are giving him too much credit. I think you are trying to relate to him because you still see him as though you are that little girl, and he is still that same person to you. But you see him through the eyes of the child that you were, not the adult you have become. I think, if you'd met Neil when you were older, you'd have developed a sense of self and you wouldn't have fallen victim to his words or attention. He singled you out when you were still trying to find your place in the world. I don't doubt that he didn't think he loved you, but from what you've told me, he saw you as a possession. You don't feel guilty about how you treat possessions."

Her words hurt to hear. *Singled me out? His possession? No, that's not true. He loved me. I was special; I was brilliant. He only wanted me; I was different from anyone he'd ever met. I was unique, intelligent, beautiful, and funny. I was the only one for him.* Then I heard my thoughts for exactly what they were; a script. They were the script from every soap opera, every film, every drama. They were words that had been repeated so many times by so many third wheels in a relationship. They were words that once held so much power over me, had once persuaded me to do anything that he wanted. They were a script that had worked on so many other women that I had shouted at through my TV screen over the years. I felt so foolish.

"He made me need him. He moulded me into everything he wanted," I said, but the realisation of what I had endured crushed me. "He really did groom me, didn't he? I didn't really believe it when I said it last time, but I think I see it now."

I sat there for a few minutes as the words bounced around the summer house. *He groomed me. He groomed me. He trained me like a dog. The whole time. The whole time he trained me to do exactly what he wanted me to do.*

"Oh my god! He did it with everything!" My brain was on fire, and pulled apart the scenarios and applied the logic of training a dog. "He put me in positions where I felt uncomfortable, but he used the same reward-based training! When he touched me, I felt uncomfortable, but then when I responded the way he wanted me to; by not telling anyone, he rewarded me! Like when you train a puppy to sit, you press on its bottom and it feels uncomfortable to the pup, but the minute that puppy puts its bum on the floor, you release the pressure and reward it with a treat. Eventually that puppy doesn't need a treat every time you want it to sit, it chooses to sit as an expectation of reward. That's what he did, isn't it? He trained me by making me feel a bit uncomfortable, but then rewarded me with something I valued so highly, when I conformed in the way he wanted me to!"

"That is exactly what grooming is," Katriona said, satisfied that I'd managed to find my own way there. "You were conditioned to expect reward when he asked you to do something, so eventually, he didn't need to ask anymore, you offered those behaviours knowing that you would be rewarded for them."

"I feel so stupid," I sighed.

"Why? You were 14!"

*

Over the next few weeks, more witnesses were interviewed. Julie and Liam were the first ones on the list, as Joseph hoped that if he got their interviews done quickly, Neil wouldn't have time to talk to warn them. Julie and Liam played the *oblivious card*. I didn't know if they were genuinely oblivious or not. I'm confident that Liam had heard conversations between Neil and I, but whether he'd remembered them or thought they were irrelevant, I don't know. It was difficult to know how much people on the outside would remember. I had been in the thick of it, so I remembered every detail, but people don't tend to remember things if they aren't relevant to them. I wasn't surprised or disappointed that they claimed to be oblivious to it, I didn't have many feelings towards the news at all. For me, interviewing them was a formality, rather than because I was expecting them to have some insight into the whole thing. I knew Neil had managed to groom a lot of the friends around us at the time, so I don't believe that they played oblivious maliciously. They probably were very naïve to the dark world I had been in.

The one person that did come as a surprise was Kelsey. She was interviewed after I gave her name as the yard manager at the time. I had always admired Kelsey as a teenager, she wasn't a people pleaser, and she said things how she saw them. She'd been one of the gossipers during the time of the events, so I knew that she'd have something to offer Joseph during a statement, even if it was to say that she had heard the rumours around the farm. I thought she'd say that she had heard some gossip and had seen Neil and I sneaking around the place, but she didn't say anything at the time because she felt she couldn't prove it. Kelsey had never been the sort of person to stand back and witness a wrongdoing, without acting on it, so I thought she hadn't acted at the time, because she was waiting to catch us before stirring up the hornet's nest. I remember a story that Geraldine had told us shortly after our arrival at the farm, where Kelsey had gone barmy at a visiting vet, and thrown them off the farm, for being too forceful with an unwell horse. She had banned the vet from ever visiting the farm again because she was furious for the way the vet treated one of the horses. As far as I was concerned, that meant that Kelsey had scruples and that made her worthy of admiration. How wrong I was.

Instead, Kelsey told Joseph that she'd witnessed me flirting with Neil, but that it wasn't reciprocated at all on his part. She had Joseph put that in her statement. She basically slut shamed me. That was the second time I experienced a burning rage during the police process. I seethed an uncontrollable rage that took all the energy I could muster to stop me outing her to the world for being a paedophile enabler. Not only had she chosen to ignore the behaviours that she had witnessed at the time- that I'd forgiven up to that point, but she had then denied that Neil had ever reciprocated the flirting. As far as I saw, her denial was a complete betrayal given that I knew that she had borne witness to the gossip. It's not even as though she wanted to stay out of the investigation by saying *'I don't know'* when Joseph asked her what she knew. She didn't deny any knowledge; she flat out defended Neil by saying that he didn't reciprocate any flirting I offered. I knew at the time that she had known. I had forgiven her for not acting at the time, because none of the farm people acted to stop it, but I could not forgive her a second time when she was asked to set the record straight by Joseph. She had been given a second opportunity, years later, to do the right thing and speak up, but she didn't.

The impact of Kelsey's statement hit me harder than the realisation that I had been a victim of grooming and sexual abuse. For years, I had admired Kelsey. She was the woman I looked up to as a teenager. We had remained social media friends long after I had left the farm, and we regularly commented on each other's posts. She was the person I had wanted to be when I was growing up; a powerful and brilliant businesswoman. She didn't take nonsense from anyone. She was incredibly talented, firm and fair, and I thought of her as the perfect role model. She was comfortable in her skin, hardworking and the epitome of 'girl power', competing in a world largely dominated by rich white men. She had fought and earned her place at the top, as an amateur competing against professionals at the time. But her statement to Joseph completely obliterated my opinion of her. It called into question my own judgement of people. *Have I been wrong about all these people, all these years? Who else have I been wrong about? What else have I been wrong about?*

It had turned my own history upside down. *This was the woman that I looked up to and respected.* It set a chain of events running through my mind that caused me to doubt myself. *If I have been wrong about Kelsey, in addition to Neil, then were any of the things I experienced as a teenager real? Had I lost my teenage years to rose tinted glasses. Had I missed the signs with Kelsey as I had missed them with Neil?* I felt as though I had lived a lie for those pivotal years. The years that help to shape who you became as an adult. It had a knock-on effect for a few months. It made me question everything- made me doubt every thought I had experienced throughout my life. It had me scrutinising every friendship I had ever formed, every person I had ever crossed paths with, I didn't trust myself to make sound judgement calls. If I had been so wrong about the people that I had let into my life, what about the people that were in my life before Neil and since? My memories were no longer filled with thoughts, but were systematically scoured to look for inconsistencies, ulterior motives and second guessing. I felt betrayed by those people, and I felt betrayed by my own judgement.

*

Joseph also attempted to interview Geraldine, but she was too unwell after the health setbacks she had experienced in recent years. It couldn't be helped. If she was unwell, she was an unreliable witness, so it didn't matter whether she spoke the truth or denied it like Kelsey, so I didn't dwell on it too much. It was frustrating, but given how her daughter, Kelsey's, interview panned out, at least I could be grateful that she didn't slut shame me as well.

Joseph also attempted to interview Peter, who was friends with Neil. Peter confirmed to Joseph that he was aware that Neil and I had been in a 'relationship' and that Neil had confided in him at the time, but he couldn't *remember* meeting me, nor could he *remember* exchanging any texts with me. Once again though, another spanner was thrown into the works when Peter refused to offer this information in a formal statement that could be used in court. Instead, his information was given informally as a chat between Joseph and Peter. Joseph gave Peter a week to decide whether he would offer a statement, but after a week passed by, Peter refused to provide a statement as evidence.

Joseph had tried to find out if Peter could be forced to provide a statement given to his occupation as a social worker. Several occupations such as social workers, medics, police, etc. are obliged to offer a statement if questioned by the police, but as Peter was *a* social worker, and not *my* social worker, it meant that he was not obligated to give one. The result was less than ideal for me, and I was starting to feel despondent at the amount of people that were refusing to admit the truth. At least Peter would have been someone *from the other side* and had confirmed that *something* took place between Neil and me, even if he couldn't say when.

I found it annoying that those loopholes existed in the judicial system. As far as I was concerned, if someone chose a career within a protective service, be it police, social work, or the healthcare system, it should have been compulsory that they reported or responded to the needs of a vulnerable person, whether they were in their care or not. What sort of person acts to protect children from Monday to Friday but then turns a blind eye to child abuse at the weekend?

I began to question everything I knew. I began to question my sanity. *What kind of a world am I living in that allows people to turn a blind eye to events they know to be wrong?* The more I found myself going around and around in circles, at the unfairness of it all, the more my mood began to spiral out of control. If I wasn't shaking with adrenalin in fight or flight mode when I had to nip to the shop or down to pick the children up from school, I was completely numb and detached from my surroundings. It was a perpetual state of exhaustion. Some weeks I didn't sleep for more than two hours a night, other times I'd sleep for twenty-three hours straight. I didn't know what was up or what was down. My whole world had been turned on its head, and I was so close to throwing the towel in and giving up on ever being vindicated from the years of self-hatred and shame.

Over the Christmas period, the investigation continued. I'd put it to the back of my mind over Christmas. My anxiety levels were decreasing. I would no longer become a quivering wreck whenever the thoughts of Neil or the investigation came into my head. It no longer consumed my every thought. I was kept busy with my final year of my degree, and the children were getting excited for Christmas.

Marilyn was interviewed by Joseph over the New Year. She was able to recall quite a bit of information that I had forgotten during my interview. She told Joseph about how she had spoken to Geraldine a few times, telling her she had suspected something was going on between Neil and I. She recalled Neil hovering around me all the time, and the rumours that were circulating at the farm during my teenage years. She recalled Geraldine stopping Neil from being on the farm unless Anne was there (which lasted all of a couple of weeks), but at least it was enough to acknowledge that suspicions were rife at the time, adding more credibility to my version of events over that of Kelsey's. Obviously, Neil had made no comment to these allegations during interview, so he hadn't offered any explanation or excuse for these events.

Life carried on as expected for the next couple of months. I was busy with my studies and the kids were in their routine with school and nursery. Like for most people, 2020 didn't quite pan out as expected, and by March time, chaos descended on us all as Covid-19 forced us into isolation. The pandemic had pushed the police investigation to the back of my mind. Like with the rest of the world, I assumed that the process had been put on pause, with police work under restriction to comply with social distancing. Our life as a family had changed dramatically, as we focussed on keeping safe and healthy. We needed to shield as a family as Trevor was extremely clinically vulnerable, so the four of us remained at home in our little bubble, not stepping foot out of the front door for 6 months. It was nice. The outside world felt like another world away, but we had so much to keep us occupied in the house that we didn't think much of it.

We home-schooled the kids, and I studied my degree remotely, so we always had plenty of things that needed doing without making us miss the outside world. I hadn't thought about the investigation for a couple of months when Joseph called me out of the blue. I knew it was him immediately as my phone rang. I couldn't explain the gut feeling, but it was confirmed when I looked at my phone and saw the *"Private Number"* flashing on the screen. As always when Joseph rang, I felt my stomach churn and my heartbeat accelerate. He told me his sergeant was satisfied that the investigation had crossed the minimum threshold of evidence, which meant that my case could go to the CPS. I was equally thrilled and apprehensive. I knew that we had jumped over one hurdle of the case, now that Joseph's superior had approved it, but I also knew that the criteria for the CPS would be far more stringent.

The CPS had a higher threshold of minimum evidence that they would need to meet before it was considered a prosecutable case. Additionally, they would only take cases to court if they thought there was a reasonable likelihood of achieving a conviction. It's not the CPS's job to judge whether innocent or guilty. Their job is to look at the quality of evidence provided and decide whether they think a jury or magistrate would be able to convict the accused based on the evidence. They also needed to determine whether it was in the public interest to get a conviction. That included whether the accused can re-offend and his health. It also included whether the accused was mentally sound at the time of the offence to understand what they were doing was against the law. There are hundreds of things that must be satisfied for the CPS to charge the accused with an offence. I understand why things are like that, but it's a hard pill to swallow from a victim's perspective when you *know* the accused is guilty.

Joseph rang me back about six weeks later to inform me that the CPS required a bit more information. He called it the crossing of 't's and the dotting of 'i's, but I had mixed emotions about it. Part of me was relieved; at least it meant the CPS hadn't thrown it out straight away. At least they didn't say it was weak and nonsense, and no amount of further evidence could be beneficial to the case in terms of pursuing it. It also had a bit of the opposite effect, though; I thought that it meant the case was weak and more evidence was necessary to take the case further.

Joseph had a list of about 18 or so *"further lines of enquiry"* that he had to undertake. Four of those things were things I could help him with. He started by asking me if I had any phone records from the relevant period. I didn't and told him as such.

It's 15 years later, I thought.

I said I had the same number, but nothing in my possession. My old phones had long been recycled or binned. At the time, I had no reason to think that I would ever need to keep them *'as evidence'*. He also asked me if it was likely Neil had any records still.

How the hell would I know? I've long given up trying to understand how Neil thinks!

I understood that he needed to clear that up, but given that I hadn't spoken to Neil in 7 years and virtually all the years previously I had been manipulated by him, it was unlikely that I'd have any idea what he saved or hadn't. Joseph also asked me if I could provide him with pictures of me and the lorry interior. The CPS didn't fully understand the layout of the lorry, and that there was a separate living area and cab. I told him I'd do what I could. He also asked me for information regarding CJ's admission to the hospital and whether there would be any paper trail. I told him there was a huge insurance claim, and that I'd see if I could get them to forward the paperwork from the vets regarding the admission and discharge dates.

Thankfully, I was able to find plenty of pictures of me at the time of those ongoings. My mum had been an eager photographer of my show years with the horses. As a result, I had 5 or 6 dated albums of me with the horses, which allowed me to accurately document my appearance at each age. Thanks to Facebook, there were also many pictures taken of me at school, scattered around various friends' profiles. As luck would have it, my school had a different uniform for sixth form and lower school, making it easier to identify me in pre and post 16 years. The only exception to this was that my birthday falls at the beginning of the academic year, so identifying my age in year 11 would have been hard. Was I 15 or 16? Thankfully, we could quickly determine the rest of the years because of the uniform. Joseph had wanted the pictures of me at 14 so that Neil wouldn't be able to deny knowing my age at the time of the offences. Joseph wanted to prove that I didn't look 20 years old when I was 14, so Neil couldn't claim that was his defence.

I also spent a couple of hours searching for information from the vets, confirming the exact dates that CJ had been a patient at the veterinary hospital. I also had pictured from my friend's wedding, where CJ had his accident. It was used to add credibility to the events as it provided exact dates in which CJ was injured and then discharged as an inpatient from the hospital. I forwarded the paperwork from the vets to Joseph with the pictures. Joseph asked my dad and Trevor to provide a statement. They were conducted over the telephone given the Covid-19 predicament but signed and emailed back promptly.

Joseph was also going to try and get a statement from Anne.

*

As I had predicted, Anne refused to speak to Joseph.

The Coronavirus Pandemic of 2020 threw a few spanners into the works. I finished my degree in June and received my 1st Class Honours in Biology. I had started looking around for a Master's course in the March before and had applied to undertake a Master's, and news of my undergraduate degree classification, meant that I was accepted on the course. I was beyond elated. I had thought that doing a Master's degree, would be like undergoing a gap year, before moving on to graduate entry medicine the following year. *It will be less intense than medicine, and will give me a bit of breathing space whilst all of this is happening with Joseph and Neil.* How very wrong I was! I was enjoying every minute of the programme, but I suffered from a serious case of imposter syndrome the entire time I was there. I constantly felt overwhelmed by the intensity of the workload, and I felt a little foolish for thinking that a Master's would be an easy ride.

I hadn't struggled academically for the entire time of my undergraduate programme. It was like being back at school. I didn't have to work particularly hard, and my brain never felt taxed. As long as I remained disciplined and kept to my deadlines, I never experienced any difficulties. My Master's was a whole different kettle of fish. From the get-go, I was surrounded by the most intelligent people I had ever met. My peers were smarter than me, the technical staff were infinitely smarter than me and the Professors were so unbelievably intelligent, that I felt overwhelmed just being in the same room as them! It is the first time in a long time that I thought I had bitten off far more than I could chew. Homelife was chaotic as we were shielding, there were long periods of home schooling the children and trying to keep them entertained for the solitary days. In addition to this, I had the battle of undertaking a very intensive full time Master's degree, teaching Undergraduate students alongside that degree, and dealing with all the fallout from the Neil saga, that was still going on in the background.

Despite my struggle, and inferiority complex, my time during my Master's was one of the most rewarding things I had ever done. I was fortunate to have been given a coveted place on the programme, and even more fortunate to be working alongside some of the smartest people in the country. The doctors and professors were very supportive throughout the programme, and I regularly found myself using them as a soundboard for my stresses. They were empathetic and approachable from day one, and when I shared the news of the overlapping police investigation, they stepped up to the mark and put additional support in place for me.

I also developed good relationships with my peers on the course, and I learnt so much from them. They taught me the value of teamwork, and collaboration. Over the course of my undergraduate years, I had been a lone ranger- determined to do everything on my own, because I couldn't trust that other people would have my back. My constant need to control my environment meant that the only people I chose to depend on were those closest to me; Trevor and my immediate family. I was a giver, I'd offer help to anybody, but I very rarely accepted help from anyone outside my immediate circle. *If I'm in debt to them, then they have me over a barrel.* The friends I met on my Master's course helped me to understand that I don't have to believe that everyone is out for themselves all the time. They helped me to realise that people can be trusted.

Joseph kept in touch via phone and email during the next few months to assure me that things were still happening behind closed doors, even if he couldn't give me any more updates. He seemed to understand that I was the sort of person that needed continual updates. I have never been the sort of person that is happy to receive the bare minimum information, *ignorance is not bliss, and whoever said that needs a harsh dose of reality.* I needed to feel in control; no news, is worse than bad news. It's not that I've ever been pessimistic, but if I had all the information available, I felt as though I could process it and remain in control.

My need for control came up during one of my counselling sessions with Katriona. I described to her about my need to feel like I could control my environment.

"Do you mean that you don't like taking direction?" She probed.

"No, not at all. I don't know if I'm using the word 'control' properly. Sometimes, I really revel in other people telling me what to do. I like that someone else is taking the decisions away from me, I find it helpful. When I say control, I think what I mean, is that I don't want other people to be accountable for what happens to me. I feel in their debt if they have to do something on my behalf. Perhaps, I'm misrepresenting the word 'control' for 'accountability.'"

She looked at me, a little confused and waited for me to regather my train of thought.

"I don't like it when my safety or reputation is left in the hands of others. So, for instance, with this whole investigation. There have been so many points where I have wanted to throw in the towel, because I'm so certain that someone higher up the food chain is going to pull the plug on it. That means, that I have no control in that; they are then accountable for my mental stability, because if they pull the plug, and I have no say, then their decision is going to affect my health. Whereas, if I have all the information, if Joseph keeps me completely informed, I can brace myself for impact, or even pull the plug, before someone else gets the chance.

Also, even the little things, like driving. I hate it when someone else is driving, and I have to be the passenger. Even if I trust the other person implicitly, there is an element of accountability for my physical safety, and I hate that. I hate that I have handed over the reins to someone else. I enjoy driving, so, it's not that I don't want to drive, it's because I don't want to be a passenger more.

It's not that I hate instruction. Sometimes it would be really good for someone else to make the decision for me. I find it so difficult to make decisions sometimes, it's almost like I freeze, and a completely innocuous decision like dinner plans, can make my head spin. However, someone else making the decision about what we eat, doesn't affect me from a safety or reputation point of view. That being said, if Trevor makes the decision about dinner, I have to be the one who goes to Tesco to buy the ingredients because then I am the one who controls the environment. My mental health will be affected if I forget something and get stressed because I have to go and do a second shop to get the missing food. I know it's stupid, I know my need for control is irrational… but its not really about the control, it's about making sure that I will be OK at the end of the scenario."

"It's interesting that you use the words 'safety' and 'reputation' a lot when talking about control. Why do you think that is?" Katriona asked.

"Dunno… ummm… Perhaps because I never felt safe around Neil? Or because I was so drilled into thinking that my reputation would be ruined if it all came out about us?"

*

There was a lot of to-ing and fro-ing between Joseph and the authoritative bodies regarding Joseph accessing the relevant paperwork. He was trying to chase up the DVLA to get a history of the car I had identified as Neil's during the time of the offences- the number plate I had given to the 101 service. Additionally, Joseph was still trying to get my school nurse record to see whether there was any information about the possibility of a safeguarding issue. Months passed, and Joseph could only tell me that he was still working on it, but as many people were working at home, it created difficulties in obtaining paperwork from the archives.

Eventually, in the middle of October, as I sat in an online lecture as part of my Master's course, I got a call from *"Private Number"*. I answered the phone, expecting it to be another phone call to explain that he was still working on the case, but something was different when Joseph spoke.

"Hi Tanya," he said, and I made sure my mute button and web camera were turned off. "So, I haven't been able to get the paperwork back from your school or the school nurse records. I keep getting sent from department to department, trying to locate them in the archives, but I'm going around in circles. Well, I went back to the CPS to see if they were fundamental to the charging decision, and they said the paperwork wasn't fundamental."

I leapt up from my seat and immediately felt the twisting of my guts as I paced backwards and forwards.

"They have decided that I am to charge Neil with 8 counts."

"What?!?" I exclaimed as my feet stopped me dead in my tracks. "You are charging him?!?"

The CPS had decided that Joseph could charge Neil with eight counts! I squealed. *Eight counts! Eight bloody counts!* I could hear Joseph smiling down the phone at my relief. I puffed out my cheeks and let out a massive sigh. My words tumbled out of my mouth, incomprehensible to the average man, but it seemed as though Joseph understood me.

"No, he doesn't know yet, the news has only just come through to me. So, I now have to *bill* them on the system. What we would normally do, is call Neil back into the station, but because of Covid, I'll just inform his solicitor instead and we'll take it from there."

"When will he know?" I asked.

"Sometime today, as soon as I've finished on the phone with you."

We almost came to the end of the call before I realised that I didn't even know what the charges were.

5 counts of engaging in sexual activity with a child age 13-15 without penetration
3 counts of engaging in sexual activity with a child age 13-15 with penetration

I was left completely dumbfounded. I didn't know what to say. I thanked Joseph profusely for everything he had done over the previous 14 months. He was very humble about it, but I was genuinely, so unbelievably grateful that he was *my* DC. I knew that it wouldn't be the end of our contact and his workload for my case, but I was so grateful that he'd been able to get me over that hurdle. It felt like a huge obstacle a few months before, but, as far as I was concerned, the CPS decision to charge was the mental reassurance that I needed. The charges gave me validation. They proved that what happened to me was wrong. That it didn't matter what Neil had told me over the years, letting me think it was my fault. It shouldn't have happened. Relief doesn't cut it.

I spoke with my ISVA a couple of days later. Her name was Anita. Since I first reported Neil to the police, she'd been my point of contact, but we hadn't needed to speak much as things hadn't progressed. We had spoken every couple of months, but it was more to check-in than go over anything to do with the case.

I told her about the eight charges he had against him and what they included. She told me that the three counts with penetration were indictable offences. That meant that the Crown Court would be the one to deal with them. She explained the next few stages of the process. Initially, there would be the First Hearing in a Magistrates Court within a few weeks. All cases started at the Magistrate's Court. Neil would not have the opportunity to plea at the magistrates. If the charges weren't as serious, it would be possible for a Magistrate trial (unless Neil wished for a jury trial), but that wasn't possible with indictable offences.

At that point, I was still battling with my need to regain the control he took from me. I asked Anita whether I would be able to go to the first hearing. She advised against it as it can conjure up legal issues later, as I would be privy to information needed for the courts. I wanted to be able to look him in the eye and stand up to him. *I need him to see that I am not a child anymore, that he can no longer control me.*

We were put back in a National Lockdown, and the date of the First Hearing was in the middle of it. I wanted to go. I wanted to feel it happening, and I felt like I couldn't believe it until I saw it. I needed to see him in front of a magistrate. It felt so surreal. Part of me still couldn't believe I had found the gumption to report him. It had also been strange as I had only met Joseph twice throughout the whole process. For the previous nine months, everyone had worked virtually rather than in person, so all communication had been by telephone and email. It felt like it had all happened behind closed doors. I felt as though I couldn't believe it until I saw it with my own eyes.

Part of me wanted to prove I was a strong independent woman who can't be intimidated. I also felt like that was something I needed to do by myself. It's not that I didn't appreciate the support system that I had in place. My friends and family were an incredible support, and I was so very grateful that they had my back, but it felt like a battle I needed to face head-on. *I need to do this for me.*

Tanya Pursglove

CHAPTER 19

Neil attended Magistrates Court in November 2020. Even though I knew not to expect much from that hearing, I still lost a week of sleep leading up to the date. I felt on tenterhooks. I spent the days fuelling myself on caffeine to counteract the night-time insomnia. I was grateful that I was in the middle of my Master's as that offered some distraction in the day, but the night spent tossing and turning, felt incredibly lonely. I couldn't supress the voices in my head. *What if his legal team find a loophole and the whole case is dropped? What if he gets Covid and dies a martyr? The poor man, they'll say, died awaiting the opportunity to prove his innocence.* Those intrusive thoughts never let up in the night. The darkness only exaggerated the darkness of my mind. I couldn't turn the light off at night anymore. As soon as I nodded off to sleep, the sleep paralysis demons would loom over me. I would lie there as a demon-like figure hid in the corner of my room until I couldn't move, as I flitted between the world of sleep and awake. Once I was silent enough, quiet enough, my dream demon lurked over me and clutched at my throat. I fought and fought to breathe, but I couldn't. Every time I felt as though I was going to die. It happened for months.

On the day of the Hearing, I paced around continuously. I couldn't settle, I couldn't switch off. I marched around staring at the clock, willing the time to pass, so I knew the Witness Care Unit would ring with an update. There was no point in my stressing. The magistrate's court was purely a formality; there would be no opportunity for discussion. *He won't be able to say anything other than confirming his identity,* I told myself repeatedly, but it didn't make a difference. I couldn't calm myself down. Exasperated with myself, I got in the car and went for a drive alone. I needed some space; I needed the icy wind in my face. I was suffocating.

I had adopted a similar principle during the prior summer, seeking out distraction to process my thoughts. I would bake every day- cakes, bread, patisserie goods, macarons. The list was endless. I spent the entire summer in the kitchen. Sometimes I even baked through the night whilst the rest of the house slept. It was just me, my stand mixer and the music. I found it helpful to process thoughts and emotions if I was busy whilst I was doing it. It also felt better by being productive whilst I felt restless. *At least I have something to show for it,* I thought. I was too mentally tired to sit and read, and I couldn't keep focused on the TV. I flicked through social media but I'd be triggered by the tiniest detail. It didn't take much, perhaps a memory that popped up on my timeline where Kelsey or Julie and Liam had commented. Nothing remotely to do with Neil, but just enough to remind me about what was happening.

I received a phone call later in the afternoon from a lady called Rosie. She worked with the police in the witness care unit. She became my primary contact for discussing the court process. It was her job to keep me up to date with the court proceedings and became my go-between for various services available to witnesses. If Neil decided that it would go to trial, she would be the person who liaised with the court to ensure that I was kept away from the public and had measures in place to give evidence comfortably.

Rosie informed me that the morning had gone as expected and that the magistrate had referred Neil's case to Crown Court.

"The Plea and Pre-Trial Prep has been pencilled in for the middle of December. You need to be prepared for it being moved though, so don't get too hung up on the date. These things can be moved around up to the instant that he walks into court, so be prepared for last-minute changes in plans," she said. "You won't be allowed to attend, but I'll be the one who rings you to let you know when they arrange for the trial to take place. Have you got any questions?"

"What happens during the Hearing?" I asked.

"Well, Neil will have the charges read out to him and he'll enter a plea or guilty or not guilty to each count. If he pleads not guilty, the judge will then listen to the arguments made by the CPS and Defence, and then he'll instruct them when the trial will take place. We are currently booking the trials about 12 months in advance, so it's not likely the trial will take place before Christmas next year."

I had expected that this would be the point of the process that would take the most time. I had already waited for 15 months, so it didn't bother me that it could go on for another year. I had lots planned to fill that time and provide me with adequate distractions. *I've made it this far, what's another year?* My anxiety peaked and troughed over the months between each step and levelled out between each milestone. It only intensified as each step of the investigation approached. Medication had helped a little to take the edge off, but the thing I found the most benefit was sitting with Katriona for an hour each week.

For me, the charging decision was the most critical step in the process. I was confident that Joseph had believed my story, even though he had to remain impartial. He never spoke inappropriately about Neil, but he would give me the impression that he knew that Neil was not a good person. For me, the most crucial step was having someone who had never met me -the CPS- believe what had happened. If they believed me, then they would fight for me. Joseph's job was to collect evidence- even the evidence that could jeopardise my case. The CPS's role was to fight for my rights to justice. They would fight for me.

I had been on a jury several years before, so I knew that it was impossible to predict what a jury would do, even if the case seemed cut and dry. I had found it hard to convict someone of a crime when I had been on a jury. The case I had to decide someone's guilt had been a relatively straight forward burglary, but there were too many arguments raised by the defence team for my conscious to say *guilty beyond reasonable doubt*. Ultimately, I couldn't convict as there was too much doubt for me to risk sending someone to prison. I knew how difficult I had found labelling someone a criminal, so I could only imagine the turmoil that a juror might experience by labelling someone a paedophile. It's probably the worst possible thing that someone could be labelled. *I think I'd rather be labelled a murderer than a paedophile, at least there might be some sort of explanation for murdering someone- crime of passion or temporary loss of sanity... but there isn't a justification or explanation for paedophilia. Paedophiles are a universally hated sub-group of criminals.* Given that there was no forensic evidence in my case, 16 years after it started, and only the testimony of 5 witnesses and Neil, I knew a jury trial would be unpredictable.

The magistrate dropped all of Neil's bail conditions during the interim; which, technically meant that nothing stopped him from contacting me if he wanted. I wasn't concerned as he hadn't made any attempts to contact me during the investigation, so I didn't think he'd be foolish enough to try it after being charged. Crown Court was less than a month away, so I wouldn't have to wait for long to see when the trial would occur. *One step closer to being over with; not long now.* I just wanted to survive each step of the process and move onto the next step in one piece.

The time went by quickly, and before I knew it, it was the date of the hearing. I searched for the information online, but the court only produces information 12 hours in advance for the public to view. Neil's name wasn't present on the court information when I checked it the night before, so I spent yet another restless night pacing through the house, unable to sleep. I had a dreadful feeling that something had happened. *What if the CPS have dropped the case and forgotten to tell me? What if he's dead? What if they've decided he's no longer a risk and so there was no point in prosecuting him anymore? What if... what if..?*

My restlessness remained with me all day.

"I just need to get out," I snapped at Trevor. "Let's just go for a ride up the Peaks and get some breathing space."

It was 4pm on the day of the Hearing and I still hadn't heard anything. I'd spent the day refreshing the court pages over and over, hoping to see his name and an update, but there was nothing to see. I finally I got the call I'd been waiting for about 5.30pm.

"Hi Tanya, it's Rosie from the Witness Care Unit. How are you?"

"What's happening?" I blurted, unable to stop and exchange pleasantries.

"The Hearing didn't take place but has been adjourned until the end of January. There weren't enough court rooms to cater for social distancing, so it's had to be postponed."

I did not take the news well. *Why am I the last person to know everything? Neil would have known not to attend the court yesterday! Why couldn't they have let me know too, so I wasn't going nuts all day?* It felt as though he had more rights than I did. I had to pull over. I felt so sick.

I was told that the new date would clash with a huge Master's exam. *Fucking perfect.* The Christmas period was hectic, so I didn't have much time to dwell on the upcoming date, thankfully. I spent the holidays teaching undergrads and battling through my coursework before scheduling a couple of days off to enjoy the time together as a family. Considering we were shielding as a family and that I had never spent a Christmas without my extended family, we had a lovely day. It was lovely to spend the time together, watching the children playing with their new toys.

Throughout January, I had kept busy with work and revision. It wasn't until a week before the court day *and exam* that I began to feel as though things were on top of me. I scheduled a chat with my tutor, Kate, to discuss my worries. She put my mind at rest and told me not to worry about the exam. She put plans in place for me to be assessed later in the year if it all went pear shaped or if I had a colossal meltdown in the middle of it. The weight from the exam decreased but my reluctance to let Neil get the better of me once again infuriated me. Although Kate had made alternative arrangements, my stubbornness refused to let me miss out on another educational opportunity because of Neil.

The day of the Hearing and the exam arrived. It felt as though my brain had been set on fire. My mind constantly jumped between Neil and my exam stress. I sat the exam as I had planned, but it's fair to say that my heart wasn't in it. As soon as I mentally switched off from work, I felt as sick as a dog. I wasn't allowed to leave the exam until the finishing time, so I sat there in a complete trance, wondering what was happening in court. I had to fight the urge to look at my phone as the exam rules didn't allow us to have the phones.

The instant Kate released us from the exam, and I turned my phone back on. There weren't any missed calls, thankfully. I had a short debrief with Trevor about the exam and had just made myself a coffee when my phone rang. I accepted the call and disappeared back upstairs.

"Hello, am I speaking to Tanya," she waited for my response. "Hi Tanya, I'm calling from the witness care unit. Rosie is on annual leave today, so she has left me her case load."

Please let the trial be before Christmas, I thought to myself as Dawn scrolled through the details on the computer. *February 2021 at the latest,* I bartered with a higher power.

"Ok, so they have scheduled a Sentencing Hearing for next month, I'll put the details in a letter for you," she continued.

"I'm sorry, what?" I asked, the confusion etched over my face as I caught a glimpse of my reflection in the wardrobe mirror. "A Sentencing Hearing?"

"Yes, for sentencing… the end of February," she said in a matter-of-fact tone, completely passive to the news she had just given me.

"He pleaded guilty?" I begged for the answer.

"Yes, the sentencing has been scheduled for the end of next month."

I squealed an ear-piercing screech down the phone and shouted at Trevor. *He's pleaded guilty, he's pleaded guilty, he's pleaded guilty!!!*

I asked Dawn to repeat what she had said as I thought she was reading the wrong person's information. I asked her to check Neil's details to make sure she hadn't read the wrong information to me. She said that, according to the system, it looked as though Neil has pleaded guilty. I felt instantly elated, euphoric. *It's over. It's over.* My mind shot through a tunnel at warp speed, I was aware of the distant sound of Dawn's voice down the phone, but I couldn't compute what she was saying. It was like I was half tuned into to a radio station, picking up odd words that I could understand. The sentences were incoherent. *Neil has pleaded guilty!*

Of all the scenarios I had prepared for, Neil had thrown me a curve-ball. After he decided to give a 'no comment' interview, I had expected that he would fight it the whole way. I had prepared myself for the CPS to drop the case. I had prepared myself for his defence finding a legal loophole. I had prepared for Covid getting him before the courts could. I had anticipated a jury trial and, although I hoped that a jury would find him guilty, I had prepared myself for if he was found not guilty. There were a million other scenarios I had mentally planned for, but an admittance of guilt was never one of them.

The revelation had left me with more questions than answers. I stood in the garden and rang my parents and friends and explained what had happened as far as I could tell. My brain fired on all cylinders. I couldn't focus. My whole mind was a whirl of information; questions unanswered, emotions unprocessed. My thoughts were fragmented and made no sense. My joy dissipated and frustration replaced it. The more people I spoke to, the more questions my brain found.

Why did he plead guilty? Why didn't he take his chance on a trial? Was he afraid of being confronted with the whole truth? Had he told the people in his life a different narrative? Did he not want people to hear everything? Was he hoping that he'd just slink off quietly and nobody would know? He's done this to silence me, hasn't he? As soon as I stand in that witness box, he knows his world will come crashing around him. This is him, shutting me down. He's playing the victim here- he'll have told everyone that he hasn't got the energy to fight this. He's told them I'm a liar, but that he knows his innocence will never be proven because I'm so good at it. He's going to turn this around on me. If I'm silenced, all those people will only ever hear his version of events. Or is this him feeling guilty? Has he been waiting years for the truth to come knocking on his door?

Right from the beginning I thought he might admit to this, the same way as he admitted it to Anne when she confronted him. Is it guilt or is this damage limitations? But why go 'no comment' and then plead guilty? It doesn't make sense. Was he hoping it would all go away? Has he been advised he'll walk away with a slap on the wrist if he pleads guilty, but if he's found guilty, he'll be sent to prison? Why has he done this? Why?

My eyes flitted from side to side as I read the questions that exploded across my brain. *Why? Why? What's the end plan here? It can't be this simple.*

My mind was blown. As soon as the kids were in bed, I cracked open a bottle of gin liqueur. I had every intention of getting drunk; I wanted to reach oblivion. I wanted to turn my brain off and silence the thoughts. I wanted to sleep. I hadn't slept in such a long time, not quality sleep. For the previous two years, I had been surviving on about 3 hours of sleep a night. Not solid sleep either, but disturbed sleep. I was waking up in the middle of the night for no reason, other than my brain had forgotten how to shut down.

I reached the bottom of the gin liqueur, and I still felt sober. I wondered if my adrenalin was overriding the alcohol, keeping me sharp and alert instead of letting me relax. I wanted to stop my mind. I wanted my brain to realise that it was over. I opened a bottle of gin- a Christmas gift. I sat knocking them back, one after the other, until half a bottle had gone. It was the middle of the night- pitch black and freezing cold, but I felt nothing. Trevor stayed down with me as I got drunker and drunker. I still couldn't relax. I was so drunk, but it hadn't changed anything. It hadn't shut the noise in my head. I needed an outlet, and the alcohol hadn't helped. As it was the middle of the night, and there was no chance of bumping into anyone, I walked out the front door and paced the street. I walked miles up and down our road over the course of the following few hours. I spent the miles trying to make sense of the day and find the answers to my unanswered questions. I was seething. I was so furious with Neil for silencing me again. He had denied my right to hear his excuses.

As I paced the street, I had an overwhelming urge to walk to his house. The courts had released him on bail. *He'll be awake like me, except he'll be sat there, calm and without any questions. He hasn't just been sideswiped. He'll have known that he was going to plead guilty for months. I bet he'll be relishing at pulling the rug from under me.* I had the urge to knock on his door and demand answers. I knew that I was very drunk, but the alcohol had only given me the determination to seek his explanation. I had got drunk to silence my questions, but all the gin had done was prompt more questions and more thoughts. I was so frustrated, so overwhelmed. I completely broke down.

For the first time in nearly ten years, I had allowed myself to give in to every emotion I had been unable to identify. I sat wailing on the doorstep of my house for about an hour. It was the first release I had experienced in years. I had cried about what he had done a couple of times, but I had never truly just let go. I rang my mum as I needed her no-nonsense advice. My mum had always been blunt but I had reached the point where I needed her to rip the plaster off and just say it how it was. We spoke for an hour as I paced the street and cried down the phone to her. When our conversation came to an end, I walked back into the house and cried for a bit more with Trevor.

Eventually, the alcohol knocked me out. I slept from about 6 am until 11 am, completely out cold. It was the longest, deepest sleep I had experienced in years. I woke up to the sound of my phone.

Private Number. Joseph.

I had emailed him the afternoon before, wondering if it was true that Neil had pleaded guilty. Joseph confirmed that it said the same on his system. He didn't have access to any of the details, so he couldn't confirm what had happened in the court, but he did say that he had a sentencing date for February. I was still drunk, so I couldn't recall all the questions I had for him, but I spent about 30 minutes on the phone, discussing as much as I could remember from the previous night. I told him that I wanted to make a victim personal statement and that I wanted to read it out in court on the day of the sentencing. He told me that he'd get back to me to finalise the details and book a time to go through my VPS.

*

It took a couple of days to recover from the gin. Thankfully, I had already planned to have a few days off, which allowed me to process the information. I rang Anita, my ISVA, and we discussed the practicalities of attending court for the sentencing. She would arrange the Witness Services at the court. Witness Services were the people that put plans in place for vulnerable witnesses; victims. *I hate that term "witnesses". I'm not a witness, I'm a victim. I'm not a "survivor", I'm a victim. Why do people constantly want to give me another name, another title? Brave, survivor, witness? No. I'm none of these, I AM A VICTIM.* I'd had this conversation during counselling with Katriona. I needed to take ownership of victim and not those other terms. I needed to constantly reassure myself that victim was my title, because if victim was my title, it helped to cancel out the other titles that I had given myself over the years: *accomplice, slag, whore.* I needed to be a victim because if I was a victim, it happened *to me,* not *by me.* If I was the victim, I was not the guilty party.

I spoke to Anita about my wish to attend the sentencing. That I felt as though I needed to go and see it with my own eyes because up to that point, everything had seemed so surreal. We discussed my VPS and the types of things I should include and shouldn't include in it. I should not refer to any specific details of the offences, as the court will have already considered my video interview. I needed to focus on how he affected me over the years, both at the time and since they took place. Anita asked me to talk to the Witness Care Unit (Rosie) to establish the sentencing date and time. That was so Anita could liaise with the services to ensure I was cared for on the day.

I rang Rosie straight after I hung up the phone from my conversation with Anita. I hadn't spoken to anyone from the Witness Care Unit since I had screamed in Dawn's ear. I spent 30 minutes explaining that I wanted to attend the sentencing and arrange for how this could happen. I decided that I wanted to go alone. Apart from the Covid concerns, I also felt like I wanted to show that I didn't need someone to hold my hand. I'm not sure if it was stubbornness, defiance, or resilience that I wanted to exhibit, but I wanted to show that I am now a strong independent woman and wouldn't need an entourage to support me. Thankfully, the courts were available to view from home via a video link, so my entourage could still view it without having to attend in person.

I sat down one evening to write my VPS. It was harder than I had thought it would be. I didn't know what to include. I opened up my laptop and stared at a blank document. *Where do I begin?* The question that Anita had put to me had rattled around my brain- *how has your abuse affected you?* I didn't know how to answer it. I tried to revisit the things that Katriona and I had discussed over the past 16 months, but everything seemed fragmented and incoherent. It was then I decided to look through the folder on my laptop and open up a lengthy document that I had started over a year before.

During one of my very many therapy sessions, I had been to Katriona's and stared at the packed bookshelf within the Summerhouse. I told her that I'd been looking for books to help me identify with another person, a character, that I could relate to, but I had struggled. I said that I had read a few books, but all the experiences I had read about were different from mine. A lot of the abuse books had been written from the perspective of a victim who was afraid of their abuser. I had also found books that were written about familial abuse- stories that were obviously so black and white in terms of unacceptability. I had not been able to find anyone with my perspective; I had not been able to find anyone who was in love with their abuser.

"Why don't you write one?" She asked. "Even if you don't do anything with it, it might just help you get all your feelings out on paper. It might help you process it."

That night, I came back home from therapy and began to document everything that happened. I started to write this book. I looked over my early years with Neil and played them out as my brain had seen them at the time. As I progressed over the years of our relationship, I wrote how my experiences changed, and the impact this had on me as a developing human. By the time I reached the present day, I would write what had happened. I wrote about the day I reported him, the day I heard of his arrest, the day I heard the charging decision.

I sat in front of 90,000 words of the way that Neil had affected my life over the years and yet, I still struggled to identify ways that I could show to a courtroom full of people.

I clicked on the new document and the words began to fall onto the page:

I know the convention here is to address the court, but the truth is, there is only one person I need to hear the statement that has taken me 17 years to write.

There was only one thing for it, I would have to address my VPS as an open letter to Neil.

*

I spoke to Joseph over the following few days. He was trying to find the time for me to do my VPS. I had changed my mind about speaking it live in court and chose to make a video recording instead. The change of heart came after I saw Anne in the car during a drive. I thought I'd be fine reading my statement out in front of her, but after seeing her in her car, I wasn't convinced I'd get through it without falling to pieces. I thought that trying to read my VPS aloud would have been a mistake. I didn't want my voice to crack. I wanted to make sure every word was audible to everyone in the room.

I wrote my statement. It took about 15 minutes to read aloud. On Thursday, I made my way to the sexual violence hub to record it for the court. Joseph was there, although his colleague Cheryl was the person, I delivered it to; Joseph still hadn't been video interview trained. We talked for a short while before starting. I was more nervous than I thought I would be. Of all the things that Joseph had heard me say, the VPS was the least graphic. The difference was that my video interview was conducted clinically, whereas the VPS was the emotions surrounding how Neil had impacted my life over the years. It felt more personal than describing the way he had touched me. More humiliating.

CHAPTER 20

The day before the sentencing, I received the notification of my failed exam. I was devastated. At the time, I thought I had been able to keep myself under control, focussed and that I'd been able to box Neil up and push him aside for a few hours, but I was furious with myself for being a failure. I was so angry with myself for letting myself down, for letting Neil win again. I dissected myself, punished myself for being so ordinary, so average. I looked to my past at what a prodigy I had been- how everything had come so easily to me before Neil. I'm nothing anymore. *I'm not excellent at anything.*

To put the icing on the cake, I also found out that I had been in contact with someone Covid positive. *Shit.* I booked an emergency test as soon as I found out and then tried to organise alternative sleeping arrangements for a quarantine period. I couldn't afford to take it home with me and spread it around my shielding family. The day then got even better when I realised that I couldn't attend the sentencing hearing the following day because I had to self-isolate. *Fuck.* I rang my mum on my 90-minute journey home from university. I burst into tears and had to pull off the motorway. That was twice in a month where I had broken down in tears. Previously, I hadn't been able to cry at all. *Is this a sign that I'm through the worst of my depression, or is it a sign that I have reached breaking point?*

My mum offered some practical advice and arranged accommodation to self-isolate until I received a series of negative tests. I was grateful for the isolation if I'm honest. I was so worried about giving my family Covid and so angry with myself for failing my exam that I just wanted to be shut away on my own. I was furious and disheartened from top to toe.

I received a call from Rosie at the Witness Care Unit, which only accelerated my depleting mood. I knew to expect her to call, as the arrangements for court are only finalised 12 hours before, but what I didn't expect her to tell me was that the courts had adjourned the sentencing. I was inconsolable. It was the shittiest way to end a horrible day.

"Why?" I choked back the tears.

"The defence team are still collating the reports from his medical records," she said.

"But they've had 4 weeks to get it. No actually, they've probably had longer, because his guilty plea wouldn't have been a spur of the moment decision, they'd have known that for weeks. Why couldn't they just get it ready then?"

I fell into a circle of self-pity. I rang the GP that night in the pits of despair and asked her for some sleeping tablets. It had been so long since I had a decent sleep, and the news of the court adjournment had extinguished the light at the end of the tunnel. Thankfully, the on-call GP sympathised and agreed to a short course of sleeping tablets to reset my system and buy me some time until I could get in touch with Katriona and talk it out in therapy.

Nothing changed over the next couple of weeks. I'd had contact with Russell, my personal tutor at university, who had also been an enormous support and had put plans in place for me from a university perspective. Additionally, the new date for the sentencing hearing was scheduled for the end of March – *another month away?* In the meantime, I had tested negative for covid multiple times and had moved back home. I was relieved to be back, and it was nice being in my own space with my family again. A few days before the court, I had decided to waive my rights to anonymity. I wanted to use the opportunity to share my story and draw attention to the type of childhood sexual abuse that had plagued my growing years.

Given that I found it therapeutic to talk about my story, I thought it was a chance to discuss my narrative.

These types of stories don't hit mainstream media often, but they seem to happen everywhere. I imagine that most adults today can think back to their teenage years and remember 2 or 3 young people that they went to school with who had older boyfriends. The frequency of these events is astounding. They might not necessarily be as extreme as my scenario, but it certainly wasn't unheard of for a 14-year-old girl to have an 18+-year-old "boyfriend"- I can think of 4 or 5 girls in my year group that fell into this category. This is where the problems lie. Those older "boyfriends", of course, aren't boyfriends but abusers. But these adults/ predators exploit the common occurrence of this type of abuse and normalise it, so the victim thinks that the abuse is a normal part of growing up, a normal relationship. I could use my voice and experience to explain that this isn't normal, that this is, in fact, abuse.

I emailed the Constabulary Press Office and explained that I wanted to waive my rights to anonymity. Within an hour or so, someone rang me back and thanked me for contacting them. They explained that someone would get back in touch with me to describe what the process might involve and offer me some suggestions for telling my story. It felt like a relief. It felt like I had regained my voice after losing it to his guilty plea.

The following day Jon, a press officer from the constabulary, rang to discuss the case against Neil and asked how I wanted to approach the waiving of my rights. I didn't know what it would involve, but I imagined that I could offer a short quote for the police to include on the day of sentencing when they release the report to the media. As I didn't know how to approach this, nor could I think of anything profound to say, Jon asked me to go through my story from beginning to end. So, I described how I met Neil and the years of grooming, sexual activity, sexual violence and ultimately, the ending of the abuse. It took about an hour, giving a short account of the pre- and post- 16 sex and how it changed me as a person. I discussed the things that people would have seen -becoming withdrawn and uninterested- and how I felt at the time -obsessed and infatuated- and with some reflections on what I now realised had happened. Jon asked me if I would consider being recorded and using that as a press release alongside a short statement summarising

Neil's offence and the sentencing outcome. I said yes, but that I would take the weekend to weigh up the pros and cons of waiving my rights in such a public manner.

Over the weekend, I thought about it and releasing a video recording of my experience seemed logical. It would allow me to discuss what happened to me in lieu of a trial. I felt like it would give me my voice back- the voice Neil tried to silence by pleading guilty. Jon asked me to come in the following day; two days before sentencing, and tell my story.

I was excited; it felt like a positive step. Finally, I could reach out to people and explain what happened and how someone could prevent it. It felt like I was using my voice and experience as a platform for the public's education to draw attention to the way abusers take over their victims and programme their every thought. The video was 2 hours long and included most of the details discussed in my police interview. I also explained what happened in the post 16 years; I hadn't spoken about these during my interview, as they weren't relevant to the prosecution but offered insight into why I kept active with Neil. I explained how initially, he made me feel like the most important person in the world, but then how this changed once I was under the thumb and sexual experiences became more brutal.

When I had finished, Jon explained how they might consider editing the video. He acknowledged that it was long, but he also said it contained so much helpful information. We decided that they'd start the editing process and release the video as a series over a few days. He also asked me if I would be interested in the Constabulary's Youth Engagement Programme. I was eager to take part in something like that; I had said to my husband a few days before that it was something that I would love to do. He said he would put me in touch with their Youth Engagement Officer to discuss the possibility of taking part in a school outreach programme. I left the Police HQ feeling optimistic.

My optimism disappeared the following day when Rosie called and told me that sentencing had been adjourned again for three weeks.

*

Finally, my day in court arrived. Rosie rang me the day before to confirm the court had listed the case for noon on Wednesday. She explained that a lady called Katelyn would be my witness services liaison and take care of my every need. I felt so relieved that it would finally be happening that all my anxiety had diminished. I felt excited that this chapter of my life would finally have a line drawn under it.

I spent the evening twitching like a toddler coming down from too many E-numbers. I put out all the things that I would need to get ready in the morning. My ironed clothes were hanging up on the wardrobe door, and my handbag filled with the necessities for the day. Covid restrictions meant that the cafes within the court were closed, so I had been advised to take food and a drink with me. I decided against taking food as I knew there would be many anxiety-induced toilet trips and food would only exacerbate the problem, so instead I only packed a water bottle alongside the shoes I had chosen to wear. I spent the evening in the bath and tried to unwind before eventually crawling into bed and sinking into a deep sleep at about 2 a.m.

I awoke with a jolt at 7 a.m. and sprang out of bed like I had many years before when the sleep paralysis demon had startled me, but this time, I was filled with euphoric adrenalin rather than fear. I used the morning as an opportunity for a bit of self-care and applied a hair and face mask, that forced me to slow down. *Just breathe Tanya, just breathe.* I took great care whilst getting ready, applying my makeup, and straightening my hair. *He always loved my curly hair; He's never going to see it that way again.* I didn't want to look like a woman barely holding herself together, I wanted to look like a force to be reckoned with. *Urgh, roots,* I thought as I held a hand over my centre parting. But the hairdressers had been closed for a few months, so little could be done to correct the dark regrowth on my now blonde hair.

I had picked out a navy-blue ensemble to wear; *black is too draining, brown too dated, and grey too likely to show any hints of perspiration.* I dressed in navy suit trousers and a navy-blue buttoned blouse and teamed it with a pair of navy-blue stilettos; *professional.* I had the foresight to appreciate the long walk from the car to the courthouse, so I put the stilettos in my handbag and donned a pair of black ballet pumps to drive in. *At least I'll be able to make a quick getaway if necessary.* I set off for court, having gone through a mental checklist of the essentials I wanted to take with me.

The drive was uneventful, and I spent the thirty minutes playing Elton John's "I'm Still Standing" at full volume, trying to manifest self-empowerment and belief. I arrived at the shopping centre car park in good time, parked up and started the walk to the court. The anxiety started to set in, but I was determined to walk with my head held high and at least try to look confident, even if I could feel my guts gurgling beneath my blouse. As I approached the courthouse, I saw Anne and Neil's car drive past me towards the car park. *Thank God. I'll get in there and disappear into the witness room before they get to the court.*

I walked up the steps to the main entrance and into the courthouse building. An old man with oxygen equipment was being searched by security when I got through the main doors, so I struck up a conversation with the other security guards.

"It's quiet in here, I expected it to be really busy," I started as I waited anxiously watching the doorway for Them.

"Yeah, Covid," said the huge, bearded bloke from behind the counter, whilst using the desk to swing side to side on the swivel chair. "Can't have anyone in here anymore, only those necessary to the court- no public viewing."

"I see," I said as I took my eyes off the door beside me to answer him.

I twisted around to see the security guard indicate for the old man to turn around so he could scan his back with the magnetic wand.

Oh fuck! Nope, nope, nope. I quickly turned my head back to the door as the realisation of the old man in front of me was Neil. *Nope, nope, nope, surely it can't be?*

Although surprised by his presence, I felt nothing. I had been worried about our first encounter after all those years. I had worried about feeling intimidated. I had worried that I would feel sorry for him or a pang of guilt, but there was absolutely nothing. No feeling of hate, disgust, sadness, betrayal, or sorrow; I felt nothing towards him. It was as though we were strangers brought together by chance. Security waved Neil through and I felt relieved that the space had increased between us.

"Can I wait here?" I whispered over the desk. "That's the man in the Sentencing Hearing that I'm here for and I'd rather not be shut on that side with him."

"Ummm... yeah, of course, I'll ring upstairs and get Katelyn to come down and meet you now, what's your name?"

"Tanya." I paused and looked back towards the door. *Any minute now, Anne will walk through that door.* "Actually, do you mind if I just make my way up to find Katelyn? His wife will be in here at any minute and I don't want to be here when she comes."

A security guard, who I learnt was called Charles offered to walk me up the stairs. Katelyn greeted me cheerfully, as she thanked Charles for taking me up once she knew that Neil had been waiting in the lobby. Katelyn showed me into the room where I would remain for the day.

"Do you mind if I take my mask off? I think the adrenalin has made me out of puff," I asked.

"Of course, do you mind if I take mine off too?" She said, "I can leave it on if you're not comfortable."

"Please take it off, it will be nice to see a face for once."

I had relied on body language and facial expressions for so long. It was one of the survival mechanisms I had developed over the years of abuse and carried long into adulthood. It was not until Covid had forced everyone to hide their faces, that I realised how dependent on this skill I had become to recognise an imminent threat. Once people were hiding behind their mask, I lost the ability to interpret danger or safety, and spent large proportions of my day in fight or flight mode, trying to gauge whether I was at risk or not. Of course, I was never at risk, but my brain couldn't compute that information without the reassurance of my hyper intuitive skill.

We discussed the plan for the day, and Katelyn told me it was unlikely that we would deviate much from the proposed time. We spoke about the case and the years of abuse that I had experienced-ironically, recalling the events and storyline of my sordid past, helped to settle my anxiety. I don't know if she was humouring my need to divulge this information, or if she was genuinely interested, but she came across as keen to hear what I had to say.

I had often found that people sat in one of two camps when the conversation of child abuse came up; either people try to shut the conversation down and bury their heads, or people want to pry for information, whilst trying to avoid appearing rude. I didn't mind people asking me what happened, as long as they didn't mind my candidness about it. I didn't like nuances or insinuations because meaning was lost when people are allowed to interpret events. Since having "come clean" about what I went through, the truth had become the most important thing in my life- there wasn't room for interpretation or speculation, *the truth shall set me free.*

Time seemed to move so slowly, whilst we waited to be called to court. My whole body felt as though it had been electrified- every nerve was exposed and live, constantly feeding messages back to my brain about the environment. The fabric on the bench where I sat was itchy through my trousers; the fluorescent light burnt my retinas as I teetered on the knife edge of a developing migraine. My guts churned and gurgled beneath my blouse, and I began to worry that Katelyn could hear it.

"Sorry, I just need another wee," I apologised as I squeezed past her for the fourth time in an hour to get to the toilet in the adjoining room. "I don't normally go this often; I think it's just the nerves kicking in."

As I dried my hands on the paper towels in the bathroom, they called us into court. The Hearing before ours had overrun, and the court needed cleaning between parties, so it was a little behind schedule. I grabbed for my shoes and shuffled my feet into them before Katelyn and I made our way up another flight of stairs to the courtroom. He was already in the dock when we got in there, and the Usher guided me to my seat. The reduced capacity in the courtroom meant that Katelyn and I were the only people on the public benches. What once would have been a full ensemble of public spectators and journalists was now only made up of the judge, the barristers, a couple of court officials, Katelyn and I, and of course Neil and a Bailiff behind the Perspex dock. As I sat down, I looked across the courtroom at a screen mounted on the wall, adorned with "Press" and the names of my friends and family who had been allowed to watch the streamed proceedings. *Breathe Tanya.*

We hadn't been seated for a minute before Neil's defence barrister began to ask for an adjournment, as they were still waiting for *another* medical record to arrive. *Anything to stall for more time,* I thought.

"This is going to happen today, it has been rearranged twice already! The Complainant is here, we are all here, this *will* be happening today," the Judge erupted.

"Your Honour," she said, "We are waiting for a report on the Defendant's mental status from a psychiatrist. I firmly believe that it is crucial to the outcome of the Hearing."

My brain switched off from the goings on around me and curiosity took over me. I turned my eyes to look at Neil and the sounds of the legal jargon disappeared from my periphery. He must have felt my eyes on him because he looked back and held my stare. *Look at him, he looks so small, so frail. Why don't I remember him this way? He was such a mountain of a man; so tall. Now he looks so little, so inconspicuous. I'd walk right past him if I saw him in Tesco. For the last two years I have walked around there on edge, because I had imaginary visions of him, but it was never him. I had been picturing him completely differently. The last two years have not been kind to him. He looks pathetic. What is he thinking right now? Does he still see me as a child? Why is he looking back? Is he curious too, or is he trying to make me feel guilty? Is he trying to intimidate me? It's not working, I don't feel intimidated, I feel pity. Don't break eye contact Tanya, make him look away first. Show him that he has no control over you anymore, do not back down. Take ownership of your space.*

Neil broke eye contact to look back at the Judge and the noise re-entered my consciousness.

"I will adjourn this case until the 2.30 p.m. During the interim, the court appointed practitioner will make a complete assessment of the defendant's current mental health, and then we will move forward with the Hearing," the Judge concluded as he gestured at the lady with the laptop sat across the entrance from me.

The court bailiff opened the Perspex dock where Neil sat and waved him through the transparent door. As he came out of the dock and made his way towards the exit past my seat, he stopped and looked down at me as I sat there, as exposed, and vulnerable as I had been as *that* girl. I held my breath and looked down at his old, tired hand as he steadied himself on the bench in front of me. *Don't. Don't do it. Don't you dare say a word.* He paused for a second before opening his mouth.

His defence barrister caught sight of it and ushered him out of the door. *What the fuck? What was he going to say? Surely, he wasn't about to talk to me. Surely, he's not that stupid to try and communicate with me in front of the judge and two barristers?* To say I was astounded was an understatement. I had to ask Katelyn if she had seen it. *Am I going mad?* Thankfully she confirmed that she had seen it, also, or I might have questioned my own sanity. She explained that he would have got into so much trouble had he said anything to me. Part of me was disappointed that he didn't get any words out.

Katelyn and I made our way back to my hidey-hole. She asked if I wanted to go and fetch some lunch, but I declined. I didn't want to risk eating and upset my very temperamental digestive tract. She went for her lunch as I rang everyone to fill them in on the proceedings. I sat and flicked through my phone for half an hour until Katelyn came back, and we continued our discussion from the morning. She was so easy to talk to and kept my mind off the sentencing. At 2.30 pm sharp, the tannoy announced the case details, so I donned my stilettos, and we made our way up.

As we got up the flight of stairs to the courtroom, there was a bit of commotion by the courtroom entrance. Katelyn said that she would investigate, so I sat down on one of the chairs, 15 feet away from the door. I started to rhythmically tap my teeth with my index finger, the *tap, tap, tap,* calming my anxiety.

1... 2... 3... 4... 5...6... 7... 8... 9... 10...

1... 2... 3... 4... 5...

When she returned, she explained that Neil had fainted in the short space between the two entrances of the court; she fought back the urge to roll her eyes. There was a bit of fussing about by the court officials, and I could hear them say that Neil had diabetes and hadn't eaten anything that day. One staff member went to fetch some sugary foods and returned with a mini roll and a satsuma. There was a discussion about calling for an ambulance, and I let out an audible groan. I had tried my best to keep my mouth shut, but I had reached the end of my tether. I was impressed that I had made it *that* far before voicing my displeasure, but alas, everyone has a threshold.

After 15 or 20 minutes, they coax Neil off the floor and sit him on the chair opposite me. Katelyn suggested that we walk around the corner; I think she felt my frustration. As I turned the corner, I burst out laughing. I'm not sure if it was a laugh of genuine amusement or whether it was my hysteria prevailing, but I couldn't contain it. I was sure that I was out of earshot of all of them, but I was beyond caring. I felt nothing towards them; they were less than strangers to me.

Someone came over and asked if I would accompany them to the courtroom as the judge had expressed his wish to speak to me. It felt a little odd that the Judge had requested it, so I was intrigued. I was guided into the room and asked to sit where I had sat before. Once sat, the Judge apologised to me for the day's events and explained that he would have to adjourn the sentencing once again.

"I'm very sorry but the hearing cannot continue today. Aside from the faint by the defendant," he rolled his eyes so loudly, I felt sure the court reporter would have had to document it. "The defendant has failed to notify the court at any point during the last 11 weeks, that he is unable to mobilise on the stairs."

What does that matter, he's already on the floor of the court room? He's already up here, so we don't need to be worried about his inability to climb the stairs! I refrained from vocalising it out loud because the judge was spitting feathers at the incompetence of the defence team or Neil. *Don't make an enemy of the judge Tanya.* The Judge then explained that the sentencing would take place at another centre, one adapted to the needs of a disabled defendant.

"Will I be allowed to go?" I asked.

"Yes," he said.

"Thank you, Sir,…. Umm.. Your Honour"

Katelyn and I stood and exited the court. I asked her to wait in the small space between the two doors before walking out to where Neil and Anne were sitting. I was fuming and wanted to compose myself before showing my face. I clenched my fists and hopped on the spot like a boxer preparing for a fight. I took a deep breath, swung open the external doors and walked out with my head held high. I had become an expert at displaying a poker face and used the moment to shine. The CPS barrister came rushing behind me and asked if we could go back to the hidey-hole for a chat, so we made our way down the stairs and back into the witness services room.

Once inside the room, I took off my mask, both literally and metaphorically, and allowed my face of exasperation to show. I felt so frustrated that the process still hadn't ended. The CPS had explained that it was just an unfortunate set of circumstances. Despite her professional demeanour and detachment, it was clear that she was experiencing a similar set of emotions to me. She explained that it was potentially good news, as it meant that the Judge hadn't ruled out a custodial sentence. I must have looked confused because she explained that giving Neil a custodial sentence would mean he would need to walk down the four flights of stairs to the court's custodial suite, rather than the two flights of stairs up to the court. The fact that the Judge hadn't gone ahead with the sentencing suggested that he still thought a custodial sentence could be an option. I was surprised, as I had resided myself to the fact that a custodial sentence was entirely off the cards.

The CPS barrister thanked me for attending the court and supporting the prosecution in the case against Neil. She said that it encouraged more people to come forward when they successfully prosecute a case. It felt weird and uncomfortable to receive thanks- a bit like another title I had acquired, but I tried to be gracious despite squirming like a bag of eels inside. She mentioned that she would like to keep the case until sentencing as she wanted to see it through to the end. I liked her, she came across as detached, but I appreciated that in that scenario. I found it easier to keep myself detached from the court process as I knew my emotional investment in the process could easily destroy what was left of my sanity.

＊

Eighteen weeks after Neil's first crown appearance, we made our way to a disabled-friendly court where sentencing took place. I had every intention of arriving at court as early as possible. I wanted to make sure I was there well before he arrived; I didn't want a repeat performance of the last hearing. I got there 2 hours before the 11 am hearing and was escorted up to the witness room. It was a large bleak room, much bigger than the previous one I had been in the first courthouse. Draughty old windows that failed to offer any view lined its bare beige walls. Around the edge of the room, black chairs pressed against each other whilst a TV with a built-in VHS player sat unused in the corner.

It wasn't long before my witness service volunteer joined me. She seemed nice, but we didn't quite have the same click as Katelyn and I had during the previous hearing attempt. Either way, she was sweet and kind but a bit too attentive for my personal preference. I understood that I was perhaps a bit different to other victims in a similar position; most I imagined would likely be fearful or anxious, but I had been waiting for that day for 18 weeks; my emotions had left. I felt awkward when she asked me if I was alright. *I'm fine. I just want to get this over and done with.* We sat around for what felt like ages. She hadn't been involved with a witness during a sentencing hearing before, so she was keen to get my perspective on it. I explained how we had reached this point and the journey since his first appearance in Magistrate's Court, months before. I found it helpful to talk about the offences and the process to where I found myself on the day. It helped the time move quicker, and I was too distracted to try and make small talk or discuss other life events, away from Neil or the court.

About half an hour before we were due in court, the Prosecutor came in and introduced himself. He had replaced the previous Prosecutor as she had been unable to attend the hearing at the new venue. He seemed lovely, warm and kind. I asked him what his ballpark figure was for the sentencing outcome, and he didn't mince his words when he said that Neil would likely be going to prison. That was the first time anyone told me what I wanted to hear in plain and simple terms. I felt elated at the prospect, but all the time that he spoke, I reminded myself not to get carried away as the crushing defeat of a suspended sentence would have been devastating. I explained that I had been told to expect a suspended sentence and asked him why he thought so strongly that it would be a custodial one instead.

"Well," his RP accent echoed in the empty room, "the pre-sentence report does not display any kind of remorse or accountability for his actions. Quite frankly, if I was defending this case, I would have advised him that it would have been better not submitting one at all, than to submit this one."

"Can you tell me what's in it, or am I not allowed to know?" I asked shyly, not knowing whether my question was stupid, or not.

"Essentially, although he admits the events took place, he has stated that it was entirely consensual, and you are now only reporting it because you are after financial reward."

I burst out laughing at the absurdity. A deep belly rolling laugh, that I had not been able to produce in the previous 2 years.

"He has entirely missed the point of the whole situation he finds himself in," Keith continued, "that the law does not accept a 14-year-old child to consent to sexual activity."

"Could someone please show me the money? Because the last thing I heard, I could potentially get a couple of thousand from Criminal Injuries Compensation- that's less than I earn in a month!"

We all laughed. *Neil's swan song could be his best joke yet.*

I didn't have to wait much longer before the Usher called me into court. I made my way with the Witness Services lady through the empty court halls and the two sets of doors into court. They had started the process by the time I had got there. I imagined that they had gone through the formalities of identifying the people in the room before my arrival. As I arrived, the Usher guided me to the almost deserted public gallery. It was previously only occupied by Neil's friend, Peter. Anne hadn't attended.

Behind a Perspex Covid shield, the Barristers sat in their gown and wigs. Neil sat with his head held low behind his defence barrister and at the side of a Court Bailiff. It was difficult for me to see through the Perspex because my face kept reflecting back at me. However, when I squinted and unfocused my eyes, I could just about make out his face. He didn't look in my direction but kept his head held low. The Judge wasn't in the room but appeared on a TV link above the courtroom entrance.

Keith stood and began reading the highlights of my story. It was weird to hear a well-spoken man talking about another man putting things in my vagina. He periodically paused to discuss how this related to each point of law for the benefit of the judge. I sat through it and listened to what events aligned with which charges. It was the first time I had heard what points of my story were the *'illegal bits'* and what weren't. Kevin indicated at the end of his speech that the starting point was five years in custody. He then played my recorded VPS for the court to hear.

"I appreciate that the convention here is to address the court, but the truth is, I need only one person to hear the statement that has taken me 17 years to write.

It doesn't matter how many words I have learned over these years, the right ones won't come to me when I need them the most. So, I sit here, typing this, trying to find a way to convey to you and the court how you invaded my life, but the right words will not appear. The more I think about it, the harder it gets and the only conclusion I can come to, is that those words don't exist.

The difficulty comes because you came into my life when I wasn't quite a child anymore, but I was on the fragile bridge that spans the gap between childhood and becoming an adult. It feels uncomfortable to admit that I am the victim of childhood sexual abuse, but that is what it is. In the eyes of the law, I was considered a child, and that is the only reason we are in this position now. Yet, the words 'sexual abuse' depreciate the impact that this has had on me. 'Sexual abuse', I used to believe, only implied that you invaded my body, that you physically penetrated me. What these words fail to describe is how you came to do that. They fail to describe the manipulation, the mind games and the predatory behaviours that resulted in the loss of my autonomy.

I thought what I was experiencing was a normal part of growing up. I thought that was how life was supposed to be; how relationships were supposed to be. I got the excitement and the secrecy, initially. It was our secret. You smothered me with attention, but what I didn't realise at the time, was that you saw the vulnerability in me. You saw an easy target; a young girl, smart and open, susceptible to the attention you poured on her.

Before you, I considered myself a confident girl. I had the world at my feet. I was a promising student, diligent, courteous, and academically advantaged, but your interference in my life turned that upside down. I began to fail at school and I lost sight of my future. Over the years of your grooming, you moulded me into a person that only you could control. My friendships and relationships began to break down, in some cases, irreparably. My education, hobbies, and friends no longer fuelled me; you were the only one who could control me.

My social circle had never been large, but we had always been tight until you came along. You would dominate every aspect of my thoughts and plans until I could no longer think for myself. It was always "how will he react to this?". Eventually, I didn't even need to ask this as it became so deeply ingrained that there was no division between our opinions. I stopped going out, I stopped meeting with friends, and I stopped attending school. My small circle imploded, and all that left me with was you.

By that point, you took great pleasure in the power you had over me. You would build me up with constant flattery and then watch me as I came tumbling down. I never knew where I stood most of the time. But let's not forget that this wasn't a simple case of being in a destructive relationship; it was predatory behaviour on your part.

At 56, you undoubtedly had the upper hand. You had years of experience behind you. You knew exactly how to get what you wanted, whilst I was a young teenager, naïve and blind. I couldn't see what was happening. I couldn't see my self-destruction. I couldn't see that my mind didn't belong to me anymore, but every thought conceived was from the thoughts that you had placed there.

I had always been part of a close family. We were open with each other; we talked, we told each other about our day, and our plans for the future, but you ruined that for me. Instead, you filled my teenage years with secrecy and lies. You consumed my every thought, and it makes me sick with fury that you put me in that position. I carried all the shame and guilt for lying to the people that raised me. But I also believed that I was to blame for this. You allowed me to believe I was to blame for this. That the gravitas of the situation was because I hadn't stopped it and that I was irresistible. You made me believe that I had encouraged you. Even now, I battle with my thoughts over this. The gnarly guilt that sits in the pit of my stomach is down to you, making me believe that what happened between us was my choice. I tell myself repeatedly that I didn't have a choice. My mind was under the control of somebody four times my age, yet some days, I still cannot escape the dark cloud that follows me around.

This is where my age becomes relevant because I wasn't equipped with the foresight to know what was happening. I couldn't see that you had governed my every thought and every aspect of my life. I thought it was normal for someone to smother you in attention. I thought it was normal that we seemed to have the exact same thoughts. I didn't have the experience to determine that the thoughts I had were there because you had put them there.

I lost my teenage years to you. I lost the transition between child and adult. I lost the ability to develop into the person I would have become. Those pivotal years that determine how a person will react to the world and fit in the world, belong to you. It's not just years of growth and development that I have lost, but also any dignity that I had managed to salvage from those years too. After all of these years, I must lay bare all of those secrets.

My family ask me to explain about the years that I was left shattered by your betrayal. They trusted you around me. You sought out those closest to me and earned their trust. Then you used that trust to violate me, leaving me broken, distrustful and without an education. You left me without any sense of self after the years of your indoctrination.

I cannot overstate how much power you exerted on me. Your constant presence, interference and command of my time resulted in my teenage years being spent at your beck and call, giving in to your every command and making myself available at a moment's notice. If we weren't physically together or talking on the phone, the control you had already exerted on me meant that you were always on my mind. Every decision I made, every thought I had revolved around you and the seeds you had previously planted. It's 17 years later and I still lie awake at night wondering if my thoughts are my own or are a result of you. I question my sense of self. Am I the person I was supposed to be?

Our life experiences shape who we become and those dynamic interactions between our daily influences and our continually developing personality decide who we are as people. Likewise, those ordinarily fleeting situations that we experience dictate our personality and individuality. But for over nine years, your relentlessness meant that you had more influence over my life than any other experience I had encountered. Not just the two years of charges you admit to, but for the many years following that don't fall under the court's jurisdiction. Through the ages 14 to 23, you invaded my every being.

Even after I met my now-husband, you tried to engage with me for months. Were you afraid that I was no longer under your influence, or were you fearful that I'd finally see the light? You may not have crossed the legal boundaries during this time, but you certainly failed in your moral obligations to let me go.

The secrecy, lies, shame and guilt brought their friend for company. For years I have been battling with my mental health as a direct result of you. I hadn't realised that I had been walking around in a constant fog of depression until it came to a peak years later, by a chance encounter. For years, I had lived two separate lives; the one where you existed and the one that I allowed the rest of the world to see. It wasn't until these two worlds collided that I was able to identify that you were the sole cause of my mental health deterioration; that you had been the one to subject me to years of mental torture. Breaking down on that day was one of the most painful yet clarifying moments of my life. Finally, I could see what you had done to me.

Up to that point, I had felt undeserving of any good that came my way. I kept people at arm's length. Even the relationships I had formed with my husband and children and the relationships that survived your grasp were subject to scrutiny. I struggled to connect emotionally with any of them. I was always worried that something would happen to those relationships because I had been a terrible person in my other world. The shame of you never left me.

You quashed my ability to trust people. I felt as though people were out to use me in the way that you had. I doubted whether people were genuine or if they were all out to take advantage of me. I doubted that people would ever believe me because you were such a master manipulator. The dirty secrets and the shame that have followed me around for 17 years -over half my life- could no longer be kept private; they ate at me.

I cannot sing highly enough of how the police have treated me throughout this process, but the process itself has left me with scars. To heal from the damage you have caused, I sat in a room and discussed every aspect of you to 2 male detectives I had only just met. I had to explain the way you touched me, the way you invaded my body in graphic detail. I couldn't skirt around any of the information. I had to recall every single touch and explain every term I had used, for the sake of clarity.

The depth of that information was beyond anything I have ever been able to discuss, even with my closest confidante. Yet there I sat, being recorded by two male police officers that I had met 5 minutes before. They asked me to explain how I felt at the time, so I had the added shame of telling them, not only how you abused me but that you had made me want it. To add insult to injury, I later found out that you chose to remain silent during your police interview. That wasn't a right given to me. If I wanted to heal, I had to explain everything.

This process has been tortuous and is now ending abruptly. Whilst it's probable that the courts will look at your guilty plea with favour, you and I both know that you haven't done this for any other reason than self-preservation. There is no remorse, only fear. You are fearful of the things that I could say under oath. You are fearful of explaining yourself, answering questions, and justifying what you did to me for so many years. So, although I get to avoid the prospects of being dragged through a trial, your guilty plea has helped nobody but yourself- my questions remain unanswered.

I sit in turmoil, wondering how you have been able to manipulate so many people into believing that you are the victim here. How, even though you have admitted to what you have done, you are still trying to maintain control of the situation and silence my voice by not allowing me the right to explain everything in a trial.

People tell me to be grateful that I won't have to live through one, but that was my opportunity to hear your reasons for abusing me.

Through pure stubbornness and resilience, I refuse to be silenced, and this is the only reason I have been able to find a few words to describe a small percentage of the ways that you have impacted my life.

I have been incredibly fortunate to have survived your grip to be where I am now. To be able to say that I finally have an education and a career, but it is only through having such a fantastic support network that I have made it this far because I'm confident without them, I'd be dead. I am lucky to be blessed with my loving family and the friends who stood by to catch me the minute you let me fall. Those same relationships that you had tried so very hard to destroy.

I have now got my life back after losing the best part of 17 years to you. You won't get that same sentence, nor will you outlive the sentence you gave me because I will carry that burden for life. You chose that for me."

It was strange and uncomfortable to hear and watch myself on camera. It also went on for much longer than I thought it had at the time of recording. Listening to myself for 15 minutes was not easy, *they are all judging the quality of my words*, I thought, as I looked around to try and read their expressions. As my VPS came to an end, Neil's defence Barrister stood and began to recount the mitigating circumstances around the offences.

She began by acknowledging the seriousness of the offences, but then she dived straight in with how difficult prison would be for a man with a list of ailments as long as Neil's. She discussed his history of heart attacks, his bipolar, his COPD and kidney damage from diabetes. She described how he was under hospital care for these illnesses and how leading up to the sentencing, he had been prescribed two courses of antibiotics for a chest infection. She told the Judge that his psychiatric assessment revealed he would likely kill himself if he received a custodial sentence.

The Defence Barrister started to request that the Judge consider the possibility of a suspended sentence in light of Neil's medical issues.

The Judge interrupted her.

"I will continue to listen to your submissions, but I think it would be more appropriate to address the length of the sentence rather than the type of sentence."

What?! I clenched my fists in uncertainty. I was sure it meant that she had decided that Neil's offences had met the custodial threshold, but I didn't trust my ability to understand what was happening.

As the Defence Barrister rounded up her argument, she looked in my direction. She said that despite the seriousness of the offences, the defendant pleaded guilty at the earliest convenience and spared the complainant the ordeal of a trial. I wondered if she had even listened to my VPS, given how I had described my struggle with no trial and that I felt as though he had silenced me.

I thought the Judge would take a few minutes to consider the sentencing guidelines and the offences that had taken place, but she immediately started summing up her thoughts. She directed Neil to remain seated during the process.

"You fall to be sentenced for 8 counts of sexual activity with a child. I'm satisfied that you were 55 years old at the beginning of these offences whilst the Complainant was 14. The law is there to protect young children, because that is what she was, a child. The presentence report appears to suggest that you still believe that because she was a willing participant that somehow you have no culpability for it. I reiterate, she was a child." the Judge began. "Certainly, if the contents of the presentence report are right you have very little victim empathy and you fail to recognise that over a number of years you went on to groom her and became somebody who was manipulating her and dominating her. I make it plain I sentence only for what is on the indictment, although it is right to say that in 2006 you proceeded to have sexual intercourse with her when she was 16 and purported to have a relationship with her.

I hope you have been listening carefully to her victim impact statement that she made because as a child involving her in sexual activity at the age of 14 onwards has had a devastating consequence on her life. In the years that followed from meeting you what happened between you and her has had a profound impact upon her. You fail, it seems, to appreciate that on the contents of the report.

You are now 72 years of old and I have read the medical letter from your doctor setting out that you now have a complex array of physical health conditions and I acknowledge that any custodial sentence will present a serious challenge because of those conditions.

Nonetheless, in relation to counts 5, 7 and 8 this is behaviour that falls into category 1A. In saying that I am referring it to the sentencing guideline. They fall into culpability A because of your grooming behaviour and because of the very significant disparity in your ages; you were, as I have said, 56 and she was 14. The starting point for activity that involves penetration is five years, but this is not one occasion of sexual penetration, this is more than one occasion and, as I have said, counts 5, 7 and 8 all reflect further occasions, count 8 two further occasions. In addition to that what I am going to do is in respect of those counts pass a sentence that reflects the totality of what you did. In other words, it subsumes the sentence of counts 1, 2, 3 and 4 because I will pass concurrent sentences in respect of those. I will deal with those in a moment.

The five years, therefore, increases to eight years. The question then is whether it should come downwards for your health and age and the particular impact that a custodial sentence will have upon you and I am satisfied that it should and I reduce that sentence to one of five years. Giving you credit for a plea the sentence of the court in respect of counts 5, 7 and 8 is one of three years and nine months. It would have been significantly longer were it not for your age and health.

In relation to count 1 and count 6, those are counts of touching that did not involve any aggravating features in the sense that it falls into category 3A. That has a starting point of four months reduced to three months for a plea. That takes into account all the aggravating factors I have referred to already.

In relation to counts 2, 3 and 4, they are category 2A offences with a starting point of three years. On mitigation I reduce those to two years and, giving you a discount for your plea, 18 months' sentence in respect of counts 2, 3 and 4.

All of those sentences that I have set are concurrent to each other and concurrent to the three years and nine months. That is the least sentence I can pass on you," she concluded.

I was elated, dumbfounded. I genuinely thought he would be going home that day, but instead, I turned to see the Court Bailiff handcuff him and escort him out of the back of the room. He never looked up. I heard nothing but the sound of metal clinking and jingling as the cuffs were locked. He was utterly expressionless.

I left the courtroom with Keith following just behind me. We went back into the witness room, where I let out a sigh of relief, ripped off my Covid mask and flopped into the hard black chair. I was so relieved it was over, so pleased that he received a custodial sentence, but most of all, just so glad that I had kept myself together for the whole process and had remained as expressionless as Neil. Keith congratulated me on my VPS. He said that he'd never seen a judge respond to a VPS in the way she had. He said that I got the whole thing 'just right'. I was so pleased. At the time of writing it, I had struggled to find a way of conveying how Neil had made me feel.

I sat in the witness room for another hour as I rang my nearest and dearest to tell them what had happened. They were overjoyed too. They were pleased that it was over and that he had been sentenced to prison. But, like me, they had expected him to receive a suspended sentence and had prepared themselves for having to console me. As I tried to pull myself back down to earth in preparation for the journey home, I made one final trip to the toilet to part with another nervous wee and left out of the front door of the courthouse, with my head held high. I was euphoric.

CHAPTER 21

Several days passed, and I felt as though it had all been a dream. I visualised Neil's journey in the back of the *'sweat box'*. I thought about Neil's induction into prison and the questions and intimate searches he would be subjected to on his arrival. I googled relentlessly at the induction process, at other prisoners' accounts of those first few nights in prison. Naturally though, I didn't find anything that was specific to vulnerable prisoners. *That's what Neil is now, a vulnerable prisoner. Vulnerable.*

I felt guilty. Pangs of guilt would stop me in my tracks as I tried to continue my day. I'd flit between smug and guilt. I felt guilty for feeling smug. I felt smug because he'd fallen on his own sword and he was paying the price. Then my mind would wander to how he'd be feeling, but that was my mistake, because I was placing my emotions on him; I was imagining how I would feel if I was inside. I had forgotten to take into account that Neil and I didn't think, didn't feel the same things. That's why I was feeling guilty, because I imagined Neil inside feeling scared and confused, but the reality of that, is he probably wasn't. When I reminded myself that Neil and I do not feel the same things, I forced myself to try and look at it from his perspective.

Neil would be angry and resentful. Some of that anger would be at me, he'd be angry that I had *betrayed* him. That I had been bitter and vengeful. That much had been made clear in his pre-sentence report; *consensual and in it for the money.* But I imagined that a lot of his anger would be directed at himself; that he had got me so wrong and massively underestimated my strength and resilience. Neil had relied on the notion that he had made me *need* him for so many years. He had reprogrammed my brain, he had sculpted me into the perfect receptacle. I was willing, I was malleable like a piece of clay on a potter's wheel. I was the perfect girl, because from the outside I was loud and bubbly, oozing with confidence; nobody would have guessed at the thousand emotions that had run through my brain over the years of his grooming. Nobody suspected hesitancy at his advances. Nobody thought that I was not a willing conspirator too. I flirted obnoxiously, relentlessly, *she must have wanted it.*

Neil had seen all those traits in me. He saw me as the perfect target for his advances. He saw the people pleaser in me, he saw the actress, he saw how I adapted quickly to each situation. *She'll keep quiet, because she needs me.* What Neil failed to recognise, is that I would eventually grow into a woman. He failed to see that I would rise like a phoenix from the ashes of my charred childhood. He had not considered that life, in the interim, would make me strong; teach me resilience. He foolishly thought that he was strong enough to contain my spirit. That's why Neil would be angry. Neil would be angry with himself for misjudging me; for forgetting that the spark inside me that originally attracted him, would come to the surface once again.

I imagined Neil sat in his cell. I wiped the image of him being scared and lonely away from my mind and replaced those images with Neil making *friends* with the other vulnerable prisoners. Those prisoners that were kept separate from the general population because they were at risk from retribution from other inmates. Neil would see himself as superior to those other VPs because they were rapists, child molesters, abusers. Neil didn't see himself as any of those things, *what we did was consensual.* Neil would have erased his memory of the coercion, the brutality, the degradation of a little girl. *Tanya wanted it, she gave herself to me.* I hoped that altering the narrative would help me to feel less guilt, I had hoped that making him the villain would make me feel less shame and self-blame, but it didn't.

For weeks, my brain cycled through a range of emotions; guilt, euphoria, smugness, sorrow, denial, jubilation. I couldn't have been more confused. My emotions would change in a second's notice. I didn't know where they would go, and living with all those feelings was exhausting. I still couldn't sleep, I still spent the nights wide awake, reliving the years of lost innocence. My innermost thoughts would come to the surface in the dead of night, when I was away from my 'audience', and I didn't have to put a show on. I would lie there and think about Neil and how he made me feel as a young teenager. *Why did it feel so real? Was any of it real? What if it was real and I've just sent someone to prison? That makes me the bad guy.*

I had spent so many hours, trying to look on each individual situation I had experienced with an 'adult' set of eyes. I'd apply the knowledge of how I know grooming to work; the psychology behind it, but it didn't seem to matter how much logic I applied, my emotions wouldn't align with it. It was frustrating because I knew all the right things to say to myself, to try and convince myself that he was the bad person in this scenario, but I could never feel it. *It was my fault. It was my fault for tempting him, for luring him in, for needing him so badly, that he couldn't resist any longer. It was my fault that we had an affair, my fault that he's in prison.* I could tell that the people around me were exasperated by my constant questioning, constant cycling of emotions, but I needed answers. I needed to know why it happened.

A few weeks after the sentencing hearing, I received a letter from the Witness Care Unit to finalise all the details of the court process and tell me what happens after. I was informed that the Witness Care Service would be handing my case over to the Victim Probation Service and that they would ring me in a few weeks to introduce themselves. The Victim Probation Service worked alongside the *normal* Probation Service that deals with the offenders and its role is to keep victims informed of some of what happens behind the scenes. *Some.*

I received a phone call from the probation service some weeks later and after exchanging a few pleasantries, the conversation moved on.

"I think part of me just really feels out of the loop. I have so many questions and I thought that court would answer those, but it hasn't," I said to Delilah. "Like, I don't even know which prison he's in. I don't want to know so I can visit or anything like that, but I just feel more in control if I know. I can't explain it, I suppose it's a security thing. I don't suppose you can tell me where he is?"

"I'm afraid not," she said, "he's a vulnerable prisoner, so it's his right that we are able to keep him safe during his time in custody."

"No, I understand," I began, "and I don't mean to rant at you, because I know you are just doing your job, and the rules mean I'm not allowed to know, but this whole thing is just infuriating. It still feels as though he has more rights than me in this. It can't even be argued that it's because there is a small chance that he's not guilty, because there wasn't even a trial... he ADMITTED guilt, so they can't even say that it was a biased jury, or unfair trial, because he told everyone that he did it... but he is still entitled to know more about me, than I am about him. Take this for instance... during the process of collecting evidence, his team had access to my entire medical records from 2003 to present date. In that file will be information about every conversation I had with my doctor, my STI screening after I was raped, my C-sections, my mental health. He could know all of that, and it's such an invasion. Yet, the best part about it all, was that I wasn't even supposed to know that we were waiting on a medical record for 18 weeks before sentencing. I wasn't even allowed to know that he would use one conversation with a psychiatrist to try and help attain a lesser sentence."

"I know, Tanya, it does seem unfair, but these are just the rules we have to abide by," Delilah spoke softly, trying to stop me raging.

"I just have so many questions that he could answer; that the system could answer, but I have to live with the acceptance that I'll never know. It's so frustrating because I thought sentencing, a guilty plea, would offer me answers to everything. I thought that a big black line would be drawn under it all and I could just move on like a whole, new, reborn person. I thought I would feel so different after it was done, but the reality is that it hasn't changed anything. I don't feel any different, I don't feel any less at fault here, nothing has changed. I'm no better off now, than I was 2 years ago." I ended my ranting and paused for air.

Silence.

"Have you thought about Restorative Justice? I'm not sure it will be possible in this case, but I can put you on to the team, if you think that will help?" Delilah asked.

"Is that where you bring offenders and victims together to talk about what happened?" I asked.

"Yes, I'll email them and ask them to get in touch with you and talk through what it involves, and you can decide whether it's something you'd like to pursue."

"Yes, ok. I think that might help get some of the answers I need."

I thought about it for a few days, and I didn't know how I felt about it. Part of me wanted to see how I'd feel if I spoke to him with an adult brain, I wanted to see if he would try and twist things, and if I would be able to see it as an adult. I wanted to see if I had grown, or whether I'd still believe the lies he was able to tell me. I wanted to see if a child would believe the lies, to confirm that I was not the same child anymore. But there was an element of me that didn't want to make myself vulnerable to him again, because I wasn't sure if my mental health would stand up to a second round of Neil.

When the restorative justice representative rang me a few days later, I put those feelings forward. I asked her what the process would be because I didn't want Neil to know it was something I had considered. I didn't want to put control right back in his hands. I explained, that one of the reasons I had reported Neil in the first place, was because I wanted to take back the control that I had lost. That giving him the small amount of control I had reclaimed, would completely undo all the progress I had made.

"No, he won't know, until risk assessments have been made," Ava said.

"So, what happens in a risk assessment?" I asked.

"Well, we approach the prison and the Probation Service, and discuss the likelihood of a positive experience. So that includes whether Neil is showing any remorse, whether he's actively engaging with the rehabilitation programmes within the prison, whether he's trying to manipulate the system or whether he is actually taking accountability for his actions. After that, we risk assess the situation. So, if he is showing positive signs of rehabilitation and remorse, we'll sit as part of a large multidisciplinary team and discuss whether it is safe for you to be in contact with him, via a mediator. So, this could be through a face-to-face meeting, via letter, or a telephone conversation. If at any point, we doubt this is having a positive impact on you, we will decide that it can't happen."

"But he won't know any of this is happening?" I asked.

"No, all of this is done without his knowledge, he doesn't know anything unless we deem it suitable for a conversation to happen. If he is taking positive steps, we get back to you and then you have to consent before we can approach him," Ava continued. "It's quite a lengthy process, it will take many months to get this moving, and get him assessed. We can do it once he's left prison, but more often than not, these conversations happen during the custodial time, as most offenders just want to get on with their life once out on licence."

"The thing is, I'm not sure I do want to have any communication, but I don't want to regret missing the opportunity, particularly if it takes a really long time to sort out."

"Well, we can move forward with getting the teams together, if you want, and then if you decide you don't want to do it, we can stop it before Neil even has to know about it, but at least it will give you 6 months or so to decide."

"Yeah, ok. At least that gives me time to work out if I need anything answering that far away. I mean, it's only been a few weeks since he was sentenced, so everything is still new and raw."

Over the course of the following months, I periodically revisited the idea of getting answers from Neil, but as more time passed, the less and less I wanted anything to do with him. It didn't stop the crazy cycle of emotions, but it did cement the idea that I was finished being manipulated by him, I deserved more. Six months after the conversation with restorative justice, I got another phone call from them to fill me in on what had been happening in the interim.

The long and short of it was that he hadn't changed. Ava couldn't give me specifics *Neil's right to confidentiality and all,* but when I asked what had happened at the MDT meeting, she was able to confirm that Neil was not taking accountability or responsibility for his offences. He still maintained that it was something *we* did and not what *he* did. I was told that he wasn't engaging with the mandatory rehabilitation programmes effectively, and that it would not be safe for me to have any kind of restorative justice intervention with him.

Interestingly, the MDT feedback had answered most of the questions I had; Neil does not feel guilt, he does not hold himself responsible to what his actions had on a little girl. I laughed when Ava explained that Neil hadn't engaged with the programmes, not because I found it particularly funny, but because it had reinforced the thoughts I'd had in the interim. Neil still could not appreciate the damage he had inflicted on me. He didn't think himself as a paedophile or a predator, Neil viewed himself as superior to those kinds of people. As far as Neil was concerned, that 14-year-old child had willingly and eagerly given herself to a man 4 times her age, and it had nothing to do with the power dynamics at play.

I started to forgive myself for my actions as a child. I started to appreciate that those things happened to me, not with me. Neil's lack of remorse or guilt wiped the feelings of guilt that my actions had landed him in prison. The guilt never truly went away, but I came to accept that there would always be an element of guilt, because that was what I had been conditioned to feel for a long time, from an early age. The guilt, self-blame and shame would likely stay with me forever, so I just had to learn to live with the baggage that I continued to carry around. Once I had accepted that it was a part of me, it held less weight and I no longer dwelled on it.

Periodically, I'd have flashes of nausea, but instead of those flashes becoming waves, I was able to control them and within a couple of seconds, my body was able to propel it away. I no longer dwelled on those thoughts, on those feelings, but I could acknowledge their existence and carry on with my day. My nights were still disturbed, and my darkest thoughts would still return throughout the twilight hours, but, I had learnt to live with it. It became a new way of life and just something I had to deal with as they happened.

*

Several months down the line, I had given up chasing the constabulary press office for the release of the videos that I had done with them. After a few huge events causing delays: a number of high-profile murder cases, the death of Prince Philip and the obligatory mourning period the police had to show, I came to the realisation that there would never be a right time for the videos to be released. I still needed my story to be told, I still needed people to hear what happened, I still needed to reach out to people who had been going through the things I had experienced.

I decided that I would create my own and put them on social media for the world to understand how the grooming process happened and how people can help victims of this behaviour. I recorded an interview to discuss the things I had been through and how I felt at the time, and how this opinion changed as the years passed. The videos went online and were circulated many times, being viewed by thousands of people. On the whole, I received many positive comments, but once again, I was labelled brave, courageous, strong, and once again I found myself cringing. It's not that I wasn't appreciative of the support, of course, I appreciated the support, but I worried that the message I was trying to get across was being lost.

It wasn't about my journey into adulthood, it wasn't about standing up to monsters, I was trying to highlight how these things can happen to anyone. How, even the people you don't consider vulnerable, or the people who *'ask for it'* can still become victims. I was a child, but I wasn't vulnerable; I didn't tick those boxes that would have made me more susceptible to abuse, I was normal. I was just a confident girl, who enjoyed attention.

Over the course of a few days, those videos were shared into vigilante paedophile hunters on social media, and the message was being lost. Of course, there was still an outpouring of support: *well done for being so brave, you are an inspiration, you are so strong!*

but these words of support were being lost between the hatred for Neil.

People like this should be hung.

I hope he gets shafted in the showers.

Taxpayers' money is keeping these people safe.

He'll be having his 3 meals a day and 24-hour sky tv, there is no justice.

With a bit of luck, he'll get his comeuppance inside, they don't like nonces in there.

Those phrases made my stomach turn. I didn't feel that way towards Neil. I didn't want any harm to come to him during his time inside. The only thing I wanted for him was loneliness. I wanted him to experience the length of loneliness and isolation that I had felt during my own time in a cell. I wanted him to feel as though he'd lost his freedom, lost his right to a voice. I didn't want revenge, or to see him hurt. I didn't want him to be fearful for his life. That wasn't my aim, I didn't want any of that for him. I wanted him to spend time in my shoes. Seeing such vitriol and hatred towards the man I once loved made me feel sick.

Although I stopped loving him many years before, watching him suffer didn't bring me satisfaction. As mentioned, I cycled through smugness in the early days after his sentencing, but it wasn't smugness at his loss, it was smugness that I had taken back the control that he'd had over the entirety of my adult life. I wasn't smug because his demise was satisfactory, I was smug because I had overcome the hold he had on me.

Once the hatred and vitriol towards Neil dominated the comments under the videos, I turned the viewing to Private, so that they'd disappear from the pages of the many people that shared them. My message of hope towards those other victims of sexual abuse had been diluted in the sea of venom. My opportunity for education had been adulterated with nastiness and anger. Whilst people were angry on my behalf, I didn't ask for their anger, their frustration; I had enough of my own that I battled with daily without carrying everyone else's too.

It's easy to be angry at Neil but being angry at him doesn't change anything about the problems we find ourselves in today. It doesn't stop what happened. What we should be doing is looking for the chance to make a difference. We need to sit back with an open mind and analyse every situation. There were so many opportunities during my time of abuse that people could have stopped to ask questions, but they didn't, and we need to ask why.

One of the problems I have encountered is people's unwillingness to listen to the victim. Most people have the overwhelming urge to want to 'fix' things; they want to right a wrong, but this wrong cannot be 'righted'. No amount of pain or suffering that Neil experiences will ever undo the years of damage I have received. His long and suffering death will not bring me comfort, nor will it provide some divine retribution, or balance out the good versus evil. What we do need to do, is to sit up and take notice. We need to look at the people around us and watch for injustices.

We need to stop silencing victims. We don't even realise that we are doing it, but we are all guilty of wincing or flinching when victims are open and candid about their experiences. What we don't realise, is that the victims see every micro gesture of shock and disgust- even when it's not aimed at the victim, and the reaction causes them to censor their experience. We are unwittingly silencing our victims, and what is happening when we do this, is that we don't learn.

We don't get the insight, we don't get the reveal of the magic trick that perpetrators use to lull their victims. We are unintentionally becoming enablers of this crime. By denying a victim to speak their truth, their whole truth, without judgement, without anger on their behalf, we are allowing the cycle of abuse to continue and opening the doors for many more people to fall victim to grooming and sexual abuse.

*

Something that a lot of people still fail to realise is the length of the shadow that is cast on the victim's life. For years I have carried around the shame of my abuse. I carry it with me, because there is still the element of feeling as though I should be accountable for my actions as a child. The shockwaves from abuse permeate every area of my life and they do not just disappear, even after my apparent vindication from a guilty plea and prison sentence.

This is not a woe is me moment, I don't need pity or sympathy, but what I do need is understanding. I need people to understand what the effects are of abuse, because for years, I was in complete denial about the things I experienced as a child. I was in denial about how Neil's actions impacted my life. This is my opportunity to lift the veil, to give you a peek of life after abuse.

I get triggered by everything. A waft of a cigarette will cross my nose and I feel a sickness, so deep in my stomach. It's not a nausea of fear, it's not a nausea of anticipated trouble, it's a constant reminder of the bad decisions I thought I was making. Have you ever had a moment when you have a flash of being a horrid person- maybe it was an argument where you called a friend something awful and instantly regretted it after? That deep twisted guilt that sits in the pit of your stomach, that you can turn off most of the time, but occasionally it will pop to the front of your mind. That regret hasn't gone away, you still feel awful. That's what my trigger does for me. Except, the tape that roles through my head isn't an instant moment, but plays out 9 years of bad decisions, one after the other. The intrusive memories of people calling me a slag, a whore, a homewrecker. The guilt and regret are like shackles, holding my brain suspended in time when I hated myself for so long.

I try to control my environment wherever I can. I can't listen to the radio because I can't control the music that will be played. The first few bars of a song can set me off for the rest of the day. My brain will connect webs between the memories, and I get stuck in a vortex of fear, disgust, self-loathing, and shame. I circle between the thoughts that made me hate myself so much and flashes of trauma that I experienced at Neil's hand. My playlists are my safe space. I keep them on loop because I can't risk the music apps using the algorithm to find similar music in case it plays the wrong song. If it's playing over the sound system in a shop, I'll turn around and walk out, spending the next few months avoiding that shop, just in case.

If I'm out on the roads and see a Toyota Landcruiser, my mind is transported to the back seat, where I feel the pain, the degradation, the humiliation I felt in that car. I see the leather seats, Neil knocking the car through the gearbox, the way he twiddled the CD player to get the perfect bass for the music. I smell the air, the sex, the tobacco. My brain becomes 14 again and I feel as overwhelmed as I did all those years ago.

I am triggered by ten pence pieces. I know it's absurd, I know it's bizarre, and I know its irrational, but that's what triggers are; absurd, bizarre, irrational. I hate coin change, I hate the feel of money, I hate recoiling when the cashier drops coins in my hand because it makes me look ridiculous. The weight and the feel of a ten pence piece takes me back to the overwhelming panic of Neil forcing his tongue into my mouth, taking away my body autonomy as he pushed against me in the car. It makes the hair on the back of my neck stand to attention, and my immediate reaction is to flee.

It's impossible to name all the triggers. That's the nature of triggers, you don't see them until they turn up, randomly, without warning. These triggers have been here since my early twenties, but I never really understood why until more recent years. I didn't know why I flinched if someone looked me a certain way, I didn't know why I had an eversion to certain songs, certain smells, certain phrases. The dust cloud created by Neil will never truly settle, I can only hope that I learn to see through the haze.

Some of the triggers aren't even external, some of them are a result of years of conditioning behaviour, years of training to be the perfect receptacle. I find myself repeating phrases that Neil used to say, then I shudder at the realisation that I would never have said that unless I had met Neil. Some of them are completely harmless, in that they aren't said to hurt people (including myself). One of these came out of my mouth a few weeks ago. As Trevor and I were sat four or five cars back at a set of traffic lights, the lights turned to green. The car at the front of the queue was clearly a little distracted and late pulling away.

"Wrong shade a green for you?" I grunted at the car ahead.

I immediately had to check myself, for those words were not mine, but something that Neil would say if we were out in the car. Cue my intrusive thoughts went into overdrive and I realised that I had parroted his words. *How many other things have I said over the years that were straight from him vocabulary?* I wracked my own brain for hours, wondering how many things Neil had scratched into my hard drive, that were just waiting to come back out.

Neil ruined my innocence, I no longer see an older man and a younger girl and assume they are father and daughter, or grandfather and granddaughter when I walk through my town. I stare suspiciously as I look for cues in their body language that tell me he is abusing her. I fight the urge to go up to them and pry for information. I can't spot a car parked out on the country roads and assume it's ramblers or dog walkers. To me, those people in the car are having an ilicit affair and somebody is going to get very hurt.

I can't raise my children without fear that someone is going to abuse them. My youngest was recently invited to a birthday party at the home of one of his classmates. He's six. It's the first party that either of my children have been invited to, that didn't take place in a soft play centre, and I didn't know what the etiquette was for parents. *Do I leave him or do I stay?* My fears weren't that of other parents. I wasn't worried that I'd look strange by staying in the house when I was expected to come back to fetch him. My fears were that my son would be in the care of someone I didn't know well, regardless of a dozen school friends attending and I was worried my child would be sexually abused.

I've made consent a huge deal in the lives of my children. From a young age, my children were taught the anatomical terminology for their genitals. They understand the term penis and testicles. That's not because they have also taken an interest in anatomy, it's because it was important for me to ensure that they understood the importance of identifying private areas. I have drilled into them that nobody is to touch or look at their genitals, that nobody is to ask them to touch or look at someone else's genitals. I really didn't want to be that parent that forces intimate body areas to be secretive or private, but I don't know how else to protect my children from being exploited whilst they are so young. As they get older, I will obviously have to adapt to new situations, and explain why my views when they were young were so strict.

They have obviously witnessed the happenings around the police investigation and the court process. They've seen mummy cry and lose her temper. They've seen mummy shut herself away for days on end as she recovers from the trauma. They've seen the strain and the pressure that mummy has felt, and they've felt it too. They've asked me why we've sat in the carpark because mummy can't risk bumping into someone in Tesco, they've asked me why my police friend keeps ringing me. They've asked me why I have CCTV cameras outside the house. They've been through this too. Whilst I've tried to protect them from the depth of the trauma, they know that a 'bad man hurt mummy when she was little'. They are too young to soil their innocence; they are too young to understand abuse, but that hasn't stopped the shockwaves of my abuse affecting them. They have never met Neil and yet, Neil has an impact on their lives every day.

CHAPTER 22

The book is now coming to an end. Although it's not the end of my story, it is the end of Neil's. He is now approaching 74 years old and has been convicted of 8 counts of sexual activity with a child. That will be his legacy. People will not remember him for any of the good he may have done throughout his life. People won't remember him for his dry sense of humour or the stories he would share. He does not have enough time left on earth to undo the damage he has done to himself. He will forever be remembered as the grown man who chose to have sex with a child. He'll forever be remembered as a paedophile, and I honestly don't know how I feel about that.

I continue to grieve for the childhood that I lost at his hand. I am saddened by the realisation that I am a completely different person to the one I would have become had he not walked into my life. I am not unhappy, but I cannot look back on my teenage years without recognising that all those memories are tainted with impurities. It feels like a part of me died during those years, and I look back and I see a parallel pathway between the life that was, and the life that is. Teenage Tanya is gone. She went up in flames and no longer exists. She died the minute I realised that the love story ceased to exist. I mourn her, I grieve for the life that was lost, but I do not regret her existence, because she paved the way for the woman I have become.

My relationship with my parents has become stronger than ever in recent years, but there are still friendships and relationships that have never recovered from the Neil era. My relationship with Marilyn has never fully repaired. We remain close now, and we can ring each other up in a moment's panic and be there for one another when the chips are down, but there is always an underlying current of contaminated water that prevents the closeness we once had, reforming. We had once been so close, that we could read each other's thoughts, but the wedge that Neil had driven between us had produced such a crack, that no amount of repairing had been able to hide. We love each other dearly, but we've both come to accept that the closeness we once had will never be the same. I hate him for that. I hate that, even long after he exited my life, the shockwave he produced continues to ripple.

I am often asked whether I hold my parents accountable for what happened between Neil and I. I'm asked whether I am angry that my parents didn't try to stop it, and I'm always left surprised that this question would ever come up. No, I don't hold my parents responsible for it happening, nor for the length of time that it did happen. My parents did the best that they could under those circumstances, and around their commitment to work kept a roof over our heads. They had thought that I had been left in a safe place at the farm and their main concern was that I was going to injure myself around the horses, not be groomed by a paedophile. In reality, I spent very little time with my parents over my teenage years. Both held multiple jobs, not for career progression, but so that we could continue living. My dad would be out at work before I even got up for school, and he didn't get home until the early evening- by which time I was already at the farm. My mum's routine was very similar. They thought I was at the farm all weekends doing the hobby I loved. They thought they were doing the best thing for me, by providing me the opportunity to develop independence in a safe environment. They were trying to hold the finances together on minimum wage jobs and had put the trust in the people of the farm to keep me safe in the meantime. Why wouldn't they?

Even when Neil came to our house, and inserted himself in our family so seamlessly, that my parents had very little reason to be concerned. It's only now, when they look back, that they can form connections between events that took place, and my changing attitudes. I had inadvertently groomed my parents as subtly as Neil had groomed me. My change in personality wasn't abrupt but happened over the course of years. I didn't just wake up one morning and suddenly turn into a socially reclusive depressive; those things happened gradually and could easily have been attributed to hormonal teenage development. Hindsight provides 20:20 vision.

The one thing I have learned throughout this whole process is that nothing is ever black and white. The law might have a definitive stance on what is acceptable and what is not, but what I have realised is that society or personal emotions don't necessarily align in the same manner. Some people have chosen to stand by Neil, apportioning the blame on me, whilst others are gunning for his head. I wonder how many of those who sympathise with him have their own moral compass about where sex with a child is no longer acceptable. Would I have more of their empathy had I been 13 or 12, or would that have been acceptable as well? Would they have aligned their allegiances with me if I'd been a shy retiring child rather than the confident, outgoing girl I was? If I was a boy, would Neil's behaviour still have been excused, or if I had demonstrated fear, would they have stepped in to stop it? I'll never know the answers to these questions, but that doesn't stop them from cycling through my head.

Whilst I try to view my experience with an open mind, and look back on it with a reflective approach, I will never truly understand or believe what happened. I cannot fathom how so many people who witnessed inappropriate behaviour between a 56-year-old and 14-year-old, chose to do nothing. Unlike my parents, those people saw it with their own eyes; even gossiping about it between themselves. Not only did their silence actively enable the abuse to continue, but their denial when questioned by the police at a later date, also perpetuated the protection of a paedophile above that of his victim.

"I always used to see Tanya flirt with Neil, but he never reciprocated."

Seriously, when did we start slut-shaming 14-year-olds?

At the time of the offences happening, someone made a comment to Marilyn. I later find out that the following comment was the one that sparked the concern in her in the first place.

"Oh, don't worry about Tanya, she'll be outside flashing her fanny at all the men."

In all the years, with all the suspicions and gossip that circulated on the farm, not once was Neil warned to stay away from me. Geraldine had once asked Neil not to attend the farm until Anne had arrived, but he was never given the reason why. Only one insinuation was ever made. I on the other hand was approached no less than half a dozen times.

"Oh, you and Neil sneaking off around the back, in the dark."

"You two are spending a lot of time together."

"Are you two at it, or what?"

"Oh, you'll be off too busy with Neee-ulll."

"You should stay away from him."

"It feels like there are three people in my marriage."

All the above comments were made by adults; adults that had been trusted by my parents to look after me. I was the one that was approached, that was warned to back off. They put that responsibility on the child.

How can a 14-year-old be held accountable for her actions by society, when the law itself says that she is not of legal age to consent to sexual activity? In light of the #metoo movement, shouldn't women be supporting women. The alarming part is that two of the above statements came from women who have daughters. Kelsey's comment to the police was given at a time when her daughter was just a couple of years younger than me when Neil first touched me. Would they have the same attitude to their daughters experiencing the same situations as I did? Probably not.

My life over the last 36 months has completely turned on its head. Thirty-six months ago, I hadn't realised I had been the victim of childhood sexual abuse. I felt so much guilt and shame and carried so much of the blame for having an *'affair'* with my *'friend's husband'*. It hadn't once occurred to me that I had been the target of a sexual predator, but rather I had been in an unconventional and destructive relationship. I hadn't realised that Neil was the trigger of my destructive tendencies, poor mental health or terrible coping strategies. I thought those characteristics were innate, which led to a long period of self-loathing and constantly feeling ashamed of my behaviour.

One of the arguments that always had me wincing was surrounding the conversations around the #metoo movement or when discussing dead and disgraced celebrities like Jimmy Saville or Michael Jackson. They always start along the lines of *it only takes one person to come forward and then they all start coming out of the woodwork,* or *why do these people wait until these so-called perpetrators are dead, before coming forwards; they don't give them the opportunity to prove their innocence.* I may have even thrown similar statements out in the past, when I was young, and still fighting Neil's corner. When I was long down the road of recovery, a person close to me once made one of these comments.

"You hear of these women going alone to the hotels of these men, what did they expect was going to happen? They should have had more sense than that. They should have expected that there would be some sort of sexual advance. You can't tell me that the bloke should be held accountable for that when it was willingly accepted by the woman."

"Well, that proves my point," I responded, mid argument. "People underestimate the power dynamics within the pair. I didn't push Neil away, I didn't say 'no' at any point. It was an expectation of me, and it was something I knew would happen when I put myself in those situations. Does that mean that it was my fault because I allowed it?"

"No, that's not what I said, you are misunderstanding the point I was trying to make."

"But that's the exact thing that circulated around in my brain, that kept me silent for so many years. I held on to the notion that I consented because I never told him 'no'. But I didn't appreciate the power dynamics between us, I didn't realise that I was able to say 'no'. I thought because I hadn't said 'no' that I had given consent. That's the difference between giving consent, and not saying 'no'."

I had made my point, but I knew that I wasn't fully understood. For so many years, the absence of 'no' has meant that consent is granted. It's almost like the default setting for sexual activity has been 'yes' unless 'no' has been clearly stated, but that is not the way it should be. The absence of 'no' does not mean 'yes'. It's the reason why I stopped giving evidence once I had reached the age of 16 in my chronological evidential statement with the police. I thought, because I never told Neil 'no' that he had been granted permission to do those things. I had assumed because I hadn't said 'no' to Neil when he forced his penis into my bum, or when he got me so drunk that I didn't have the capacity to say 'no', or the countless other times that I just lay there and let him get on with it; that I hadn't been raped. I didn't fight him off me, I didn't say 'no', I just flopped and waited for it to end. That is not consent, but I didn't recognise this until many years later. That is why I could not see Neil as a sexual predator, because as far as I was concerned, my lack of 'no' had given him consent for him to do those things to me.

My counsellor, Katriona, describes how predators are like Teflon- nothing ever sticks to them, but their victim is like Velcro- stuck fast to every feeling of blame and guilt that the predator throws at them. I can very much relate to this now. For years I have been emotionally drained by the baggage I was forced to carry around by the man who loaded me up like a mule. The man who was trusted around me, who not only groomed me but groomed those closest to me. The man who tried to drive a wedge between me and anyone in my life.

Whilst I have reached a point in my life where he can no longer control me, the scars left behind him will never go. They may fade over time, or I may get better at covering them, but they will always be there waiting for me to show weakness before they burst right back open. They are something I will carry with me forever, but they will not define me. I am more than my scars, and I am more than the abuse I received at the hands of that man.

I have been named many things on this journey. The farm labelled me as a flirt, a temptress, for drawing the attention of a happily married, but weak-willed man. My friends called me Jolene as they gently mocked me as the 'other woman'. Anne called me a third wheel, and later a fish-eyed cow when the shit hit the fan. My family called me a depressive and later called me resilient. Neil called me his lover, his fuck-buddy, then he called me vengeful. My children call me mum, and my husband calls me wife. Society calls me many things; brave, inspirational, a survivor, naïve; whilst the court calls me a witness, or complainant. I spent 15 years calling myself a slag and a whore and then 3 years convincing myself that I am a victim. But the truth is, I am all these things. I am not *just* a victim.

EPILOGUE

I wanted my book to end with a bang, on a note of empowerment and self-discovery, but alas, there are always forces at play that we cannot fully understand. Instead, I sit here, Amaretto and Coke at hand, stewing over the day.

I received a phone call midday from the Victim Liaison Officer. Neil is dead. He died months ago, but I slipped through the cracks, and they had forgotten to notify me. The lady was very apologetic, but I sat there having completely detached from reality. Neil is dead.

The words she used washed over me as though I had a waterproof guard completely encasing my body, my mind. I had the sense to ask whether it was self-inflicted, and she hypothesised not, but what did it matter? Dead is dead.

He'd been admitted to hospital from prison in the beginning of April and died on the 10th. My mind flashes back over the last 3 months to think about how many times I have thought of him, how many times I have said his name. At the end of May, I thought about the anniversary of his incarceration. I was satisfied that he'd seen a whole rotation of the earth around the sun inside prison. I felt pleased that all the anniversaries had been spent inside. I pondered at whether he would recognise each anniversary, like I did. The anniversary of when he told me he loved me, the anniversary of the first time he touched me, the anniversary of CJ's accident, the birthdays, the Christmases, the anniversaries of the times he raped me. I doubted he would remember those as clearly as I had done. I doubted that we saw the same reel of memories, but I was satisfied that at least he had been inside for each one. Except he hadn't. He hadn't seen 12 months, dying in custody at 316 days.

I had wondered how I would feel at the notice of his death. I had expected that I would eventually be told of his demise, but try as I might, I could not foresee how I would feel at the time, and even now, as I stare at the empty drink, I still fail to identify my feelings. The relationship between the abuser and the victim is a complex array of emotions, and even the 130,000 words I have written in the book cannot convey the complexity, nor even touch on the feelings that are trapped inside. Society and those close to me try to tell me how I should feel. I should be glad, it's *one less strain on the taxpayer; one less paedophile to walk the streets*, but those statements couldn't be further from what I feel right now.

I feel sorry for Neil. I feel sorry that he lost the opportunity to right a wrong. I feel sorry that he died with a blackened mark across his name. My conscience is clear. I know I did the right thing, and I have no regrets about reporting him, but I wished he'd had the opportunity to understand the true impact he had on my life. I wished he'd have had the opportunity to read this book and see how his actions have led me down a path of self-destruction and self-loathing. But I'm also sad for me. I wish my memories of him were untarnished, so at least I could get some peace from the finality of death.

It's not just me that craves the peace though and Neil's death just reminds me of the distance the ripples of abuse travel. Naturally, as soon as I found out about his death, I googled to see if there was a funeral notice. It's been 3 months since his death, so I searched for historical references to the funeral or any kind of obituary, but of course, there aren't any. One simply does not advertise the death of a convicted paedophile for fear that the funeral, should turn into a circus of celebration.

I imagine that he has been cremated and either sits in an urn within Anne's house or was immediately scattered on the grounds of the crematorium after cremation. Again, I can't imagine that he was buried because of the risk of vandalism once people had identified a headstone. I don't imagine his funeral was a large affair, but its lack of mourners only enhances the sadness of it all. I imagine Anne and her sister attended, maybe Peter, the social worker, and perhaps a few people that had been at the farm. I can't imagine any songs were sung, but I'd be lying if I didn't say that I was curious as to what music played as his body entered the service, or as the curtain drew around his coffin. I wonder if it was something we had listened to years ago.

I think to all the people that have been affected by his actions, by his conviction; how confused they must also feel right now. Aside from the public, who would rejoice at his death, he is survived by Anne, by Peter, by his surviving children, but the grieving process must be complicated. There's a tremendous sense of confusion about how to grieve for someone who committed such monstrosities, but when all said and done, this was not all he was before he died. The system had reduced him to a number, but beyond that he had been a husband, a neighbour, a friend, a father. All those people will now be struggling to understand how they feel, juggling with the emotional strain of grieving for a paedophile.

Their grief will be silent. They can't voice how sad they are, how they have a profound sense of loss, because nobody wants to hear it. Nobody outside their inner circle will understand how torn by their emotions they feel. Neil's actions, all those years ago not only isolated me, but have now isolated all the people who loved him throughout. Once more, the shockwaves of abuse continue to rip into the lives of many.

I don't expect many people will understand the complicated mess that has been left by the news of his death. I spoke to a relative of mine shortly after I had heard the news and her response, yet unsurprising, was still nothing short of what I expect many people to think.

"Well, are we going to draw a line under it all now? You've got what you wanted; he served a life sentence."

It's this kind of attitude that emphasises just how much work needs to happen throughout society of the impact of sexual abuse. It's not what I wanted, it's not justice to know he died. It hasn't evened the score. I'm no better off than I was 10 years ago, nor when he was convicted, nor how I felt yesterday before I knew he was dead. I suppose, part of me is temporarily worse; not because I have a guilty conscience, because I haven't, but because now there are a whole new array of emotions that I must wade through.

Am I supposed to grieve for the man who sexually abused me? Am I supposed to grieve for the man who repeatedly raped me, who subjected me to a series of degrading and humiliating acts? Society seems to think that I shouldn't, that I should cheer and party on his grave, but I am not. Right now, less than 24 hours after I heard of his death, I feel numb, detached and on the cusp of grief. My family will be there to catch me as I fall through a torrent of confusion, sadness, grief, and the shockwaves of abuse continue to cycle, even after his death. The power he had over me will make me grieve, will make me sad that he has gone. Part of me feels as though I've lost an old friend, part of me feels as though I've lost an adversary. There is a part of me that died along with him, the part that he took a long time ago. I had hoped that I would get it back before he left the earth, but instead, it died along with his body. His death hasn't brought about any sense of comfort, but instead a sadness for all the lives affected and I am reminded of the scars of his actions and how deeply they are embedded into my skin.

Printed in Great Britain
by Amazon

29193785R10195